HUMAN DIGNITY

In Memoriam

Kosmas Psychopedis

Kosmas Psychopedis died on 13 December 2004. Words cannot express the sadness felt and the loss encountered. Kosmas, our friend, showed us what it means to be *ein guter Mensch.*

Farewell, Kosmas

Human Dignity

Social Autonomy and the Critique of Capitalism

Edited by

WERNER BONEFELD
University of York

KOSMAS PSYCHOPEDIS
University of Athens

Routledge
Taylor & Francis Group
LONDON AND NEW YORK

First published 2005 by Ashgate Publishing

Published 2017 by Routledge
2 Park Square, Milton Park, Abingdon, Oxfordshire OX14 4RN
711 Third Avenue, New York, NY 10017, USA

First issued in paperback 2017

Routledge is an imprint of the Taylor & Francis Group, an informa business

British Library Cataloguing in Publication Data
Bonefeld, Werner, 1960 -
Human dignity : social autonomy and the critique of capitalism
1. Marx, Karl, 1818-1883 2. Autonomy (Psychology) - Social aspects 3. Capitalism - Social aspects 4. Dignity
I. Title II. Psychopedis, Kosmas
306.3'42

Library of Congress Control Number: 2005922594

ISBN 13: 978-1-138-26682-7 (pbk)
ISBN 13: 978-0-7546-4468-2 (hbk)

Contents

List of Contributors

Hans-Georg Backhaus is a private scholar and teaches at the Johan Wolfgang Goethe University of Frankfurt

Werner Bonefeld is a Reader in the Department of Politics at the University of York

Joseph Fracchia is an Associate Professor in History at the Clark Honors College of the University of Oregon

John Holloway is a Research Professor in the Institute of Social Sciences and Humanities at the Autonomous University of Puebla

Michael A. Lebowitz is an Emeritus Professor, Department of Economics, Simon Fraser University

The late **Kosmas Psychopedis** was a Professor in the Department of Economics at the University of Athens

Helmut Reichelt is an Emeritus Professor, Department of Social Sciences, University of Bremen

Sergio Tischler is a Professor in the Institute of Social Sciences and Humanities at the Autonomous University of Puebla

Chapter 1

Human Dignity: Social Autonomy and the Critique of Capitalism

Werner Bonefeld and Kosmas Psychopedis

I

The world has become a dangerous place. There is not a single news bulletin without a report on the war on terror, accounts of yet more casualties, attacks on populations, security alerts, and further restrictions of civil liberties. Critical judgement appears abandoned in a thoughtless world. The citizen has become a security risk. War is defined as peace-making; liberty and freedom are restricted ostensibly in order to protect liberty and freedom; deception and propaganda have entered the stage of a theatrical politics that, under the guise of choice and democratic values, pronounces the age old wisdom of tyranny – those who are not with us, are against us – as a means of defending choice and democracy. Torture and the disappearance of people into prisons whose existence, paraphrasing Donald Rumsfeld, is an unknown known, have become accepted means in the defence of those same values and norms that protect against torture and incarceration without cause, due process, access to lawyer, etc. Then there is the calculated murder of people by suicide bombers, abductions and beheadings, and assassinations, etc.

The events of September 11 demonstrated with brutal force the impotence of sense, significance, and thus reason and truth. The denial of human quality and difference was absolute – not even their corpses survived. And the response? It confirmed that state terrorism and terrorism are two sides of the same coin. They feed on each other, depend on each other, encourage each other, and recognize each other in their totalitarian world views: them and us. Between them, nothing is allowed to survive. Doubt in the veracity of the action is eliminated by the authoritarian decision to bomb and maim, to search and destroy.

Largely unreported but no less disturbing is the increase in poverty across the world. According to Martin Wolf, an ardent advocate of globalization, the gap in the average living standards between the richest an poorest countries has increased from a ratio of about 10 to one a century ago to 75 to one and under existing conditions of globalization 'it could easily be 150 to one' in half a century (Wolf, 2004). However, the widening of the gap between the poor and the rich is not simply a matter of a world divided into rich countries and poor countries. Whole populations 'exist' below subsistence levels, not only in the so-called Third World but, also, in the rich capitalist countries. Recent estimates suggest that about 33 million people live below the poverty line in the USA – the richest country in the world (Vulliamy, 2003).

In the context of poverty and increasing social strife, Martin Wolf has argued that the success of globalization requires stronger states. As he put it in relation to the so-called Third World, 'what is needed is not pious aspirations but an honest and organized coercive force' (Wolf, 2001). And the developed world? The dynamic of the new economy was sustained by three elements: the enormous increase in consumer debt, especially in the USA, a huge transfer of resources in the form of interest payments from debtor countries to Western banks, especially to US banks, and military Keynesianism – increased war spending – that subsidized the military-industrial complex and sustained the credit-based boom of the 1990s on a global scale (cf. Veltmeyer, 2004). On the other side, then, of Wolf's neo-imperialist demand for action is a world economy that is dependent upon, and overshadowed by, a mountain of debt. Debt entails a politics of debt, and Wolf's insistence that the free economy and the strong state belong together is therefore to the point. Terrorism, as Soros (2003) reports, provided not only the ideal legitimation but, also, the ideal enemy for the unfettered coercive protection of a debt-ridden free market 'because it is invisible and never disappears'. The premise of the politics of debt is the ongoing accumulation of 'human machines' on the pyramids of accumulation. Its blind eagerness for plunder also requires organized coercive force to sustain the huge mortgage on future income in the present.

The dynamic of the constituted irrationality of an economic system that produces poverty in a world of plenty, of an economic system that for its profitable functioning requires the lengthening of the working day in the face of mass unemployment, was well focused by Karl Marx and Friedrich Engels when they argued:

> society suddenly finds itself put back into a state of momentary barbarism; it appears as if famine, a universal war of devastation had cut off the supply of every means of subsistence; industry and commerce seem to be destroyed; and why? Because there is too much civilization, too much means of subsistence; too much industry, too much commerce. The productive forces at the disposal of society no longer tend to further the development of the conditions of bourgeois property; on the contrary, they have become too powerful for these conditions, by which they are fettered, and so soon as they overcome these fetters, they bring disorder into the whole of bourgeois society, endanger the existence of bourgeois property. The conditions of bourgeois society are too narrow to comprise the wealth created by them. And how does bourgeois society get over these crises? On the one hand by enforced destruction of a mass of productive forces; on the other, by the conquest of new markets, and by the more thorough exploitation of the old ones (Marx and Engels, 1996, pp.18-19).

How, then, might it be possible to organize economic relations that satisfy human wants, that recognize the equality of individual human needs, and that therefore allow humanity to walk upright in dignity, and that thus guarantee human autonomy?

II

From within the logics of economic rationality and of political power, human values such as dignity and integrity are a scandal. They are rightly seen to resist the full utilization of technical efficacy of social labour power and its transformation into an effective and compliant resource that feeds the well-oiled systems of economic production and political domination. Indeed, human dignity is a subversive value. It demands social relations in which Man recognizes himself as a purpose and where, therefore, Man exists as the subject of his own social world.[1] The demand for social relations based on human dignity entails thus the intransigence of a critical theory of society against all relations where Man exists as a mere resource or means.

A social theory that does not put humanity at the centre and which therefore is premised on the so-called autonomy of social systems over and above the social individual, has to view humanity as a mere agent of objective forces. Dignity here appears in the perverted form of worth that is conferred on individuals according to their effectiveness as market agents, that is, the worth of an individual is governed by the 'price mechanism'. For example, Giddens (1998) argues that the welfare state imprisons the creative potential of individuals, and he therefore demands the 'release' of labour from the 'welfare state prison'. The empowerment of labour as a self-reliant and self-responsible agent does, however, require greater educational efforts on the part of labour so that it acquires those transferable skills that enhance its capacity to respond flexibly to changing labour market conditions. Against the background of millions and millions of people living in poverty, does it really make sense to attribute their lack of conditions to the individual shortcomings of a whole class? Would the world's poor and hungry be happily employed if they were to have those transferable skills that the theoreticians the new modernity say they must have to succeed?

Instead of social solidarity, the new modernity is said to require the worker to become his own 'employer', or, as Beck (1998) put it, a 'labour-force-employer'. Beck, however, appears to understand that the empowerment of the worker as a self-responsible and self-reliant employer of his or her own labour-power is in itself not sufficient. He suggests, like Giddens, that the new 'modernity' depends on the creativity, self-responsibility and self-reliance of individuals. However, he also argues that the new modernity is socially 'self-reflective'. It is thus said to possess some degree of social responsibility that transcends its fragmentation into self-responsible actors. He creates the idea of a new Man who combines entrepreneurial qualities with communitarian commitments. This is his figure of what he terms the 'communal-welfare employer' who combines two elements: 'it is the combination between Mother Teresa and Bill Gates' (Beck, 1998, p.332). It seems thus that Mother Teresa is to make capitalism humane within a socially extended cloister, and Bill Gates is to invest it with entrepreneurial energy. This,

---

[1] Man with a capital 'M' is used here and throughout in the sense of *Mensch*.

then, is the conventional idea of flexible Man whose endeavour to accumulate on the pyramids of accumulation does not lack its charitable attributes. Others have argued, and rightly so, that the reality of flexible Man corrodes the character (Sennet, 2000). The new adaptable worker is thus seen as a 'just-in-time' worker – ever ready to be called upon, every ready to be made redundant, and ever mobile to go where required and to do what is told in the shortest possible time. In other words, the flexible worker is a worker without time – a worker that can be switched on and off like a machine and who can operate a multitude of functions as a self-responsible object of the world of things. Time is money, and money confers worth upon individuals. 'The economy of time: to this all economy ultimately reduces itself' (Marx, 1973, p.173).

The novel characteristics of the new modern conditions are, however, rather stale. The theoretician of the autonomy of the state argued that human dignity is not an inviolable characteristic of each individual person. Rather, '[t]he *value*, or WORTH of a man, is as of all other things, his price; that is to say, so much as would be given for the use of his power: and therefore is not absolute; but a thing dependent on the need and judgement of another' (Hobbes, 1996, p.59). The buyer, Hobbes argues, 'determines the price', and thus determines the 'value' of each individual human being. Individual worth is thus contingent upon market success. Hobbes also argued that human dignity is different from 'human worth'. Dignity is a public value. As he put it,

> [t]he public worth of a man, which is the value set on him by the commonwealth [that is, the state], is that which men commonly call DIGNITY. And this value of him by the commonwealth, is understood, by offices of command, judicature, public employment; or by names and titles, introduced for distinction of such value (ibid.).

Lastly, there is honour. Honour is a recognition of a person's 'power' to provide help: '[t]o pray to another, for aid of any kind, is *to* HONOUR; because a sign we have an opinion he has power to help; and the more difficult the aid is, the more is the honour' (ibid., pp.59-60). The theory of the new modernity revitalizes these notions of worth, dignity and honour as values of the 'self-determining' 'new worker' who, set free from the prison of the welfare state, is empowered to act as a 'self-reliant' 'economic agent', and who might, when in need, honour the powerful by asking them for aid.

Roughly one hundred years after Hobbes, Diderot's motto 'have courage and liberate yourself from the yoke of religion' summoned reason as human critical self-activity. At about the same time, Kant destroyed the idea that the value of the human being is relative and contingent upon the market, and that dignity is conferred upon individuals by the state. 'In the realm of purposes, everything has either a price or a dignity' (Kant, 1974, p.87). Dignity cannot be sold, quantified, or conferred. Dignity is a general human value that belongs to each concrete individual. It is an indivisible human value. As a general human value that subsists and is recognized in each individual, human dignity entails human equality, not as an abstract equality, but as the equality of individual human needs. As such a concrete value, human dignity subsists through the mutual recognition of individual human needs. It thus is the polar opposite to commodity exchange relations where every human being has its price, and where the individual carries his social power, as well as his bond with society, in his wallet. Human dignity entails the idea of a humanity that walks upright, of Man as an autonomous social being who organizes his own social conditions self-consciously and who is thus in possession of himself as the subject (cf. Bloch, 1986). For Man to live in dignity it is precisely necessary that society never again obtains as an abstraction over and above the social individual. In short, '*every* emancipation is a *restoration* of the human world and of human relationships to *man* [*Mensch*] *himself*' (Marx, 1964, p.370).

Within the critical tradition of social theory, the focus on the human being, her conditions and possibilities, is often belittled as some sort of romantic invocation of a subject that does not exist. Louis Althusser (1996) argued that one can recognize Man only on the condition that the philosophical myth of Man is reduced to ash. Nicos Poulantzas (1968, p.65) radicalized this view when he argued that Marx's theory amounts to a radical break from the 'historical problematic of the subject'. These authors thus seek to dissolve Man as a social subject into the 'substance' of its inversion: the relations between things where Man obtains as a mere personification of structural properties (cf. Bonefeld, 2004). Just like the religious idea of God, social objectivity is affirmed as an extra-mundane 'being'. The critical idea that society is nothing else but 'the human being itself in its social relations' (Marx, 1973, p.712) is thus turned upside down: Capital is the subject (Jessop, 1991). However, objective things can have no dignity. Dignity belongs to subjects. Does capital bestow dignity on the human object? This perspective, then, affirms what Marx negated. He negated the idea of capital as a self-constituted subjective-thing and argued, instead, that its appearance as an autonomous thing is an objective delusion that needs to be deciphered on a human basis. He therefore argued, that the human subject subsists in inverted form, that is, in the form of capital. The human subject vanishes in the world of things that it itself created and continuous to create. In distinction to the affirmation of capital as a subjective thing, the purpose of a critical theory of society is to reveal the human content of abstract forms, and thus to decipher their social constitution (cf. Bonefeld, 2001).

Here one is again reminded of Kant's critical Enlightenment. He demanded from scholarly work that it reveals the true character of the constitution of social existence and argued that the failure to do so amounted to a deceitful publicity (Kant, 1979). Furthermore, he decapitated the value-neutrality of scientific work when he argued that only that 'science is true which helps the common Man to his dignity' (Kant, 1868, p.625). What therefore makes a critical theory of society 'critical' is not dependent on the answers it gives. Rather, its critical dimension is entailed in the question that it asks. Why does this content, that is human social relations, exist in the form of capital? How is it that human beings produce through their own labour a social reality that increasingly enslaves them? The suppression of the human subject in favour of objective structures is uncritical (cf. Psychopedis, 2004). Instead of enquiring about the social constitution of these structures, it presupposes them as always already existing extra-mundane things, analyses their functional requirements of reproduction, argues that human social practice unfolds within a framework established by objective laws, and instead of asking how the human condition might be improved, it honors these structures either in theological terms (the deist conception of social reproduction as something achieved by the invisible hand of the price mechanism) or positivist terms (the endowment of social structures as self-positing subjective-objective things). At issue is thus the standard of critique.

The critical tradition of social theory teaches us not only to think without fear. It also teaches us that Man is the highest being for Man. The focus on the human being is an essential element of the subversive character of a critical theory of society.

> It is Man, who, as a single individual, as a group, or as a mass, understands himself as subject and who defends himself against a merely objective existence – in politics, in religion, in philosophy. One can say that subversion is a truly human phenomenon. Man objects to be a mere football of the almighty. Here he is mere object. Similarly, as a servant of the master he is mere object, regardless of whether we conceive this in social or religious terms. Man is never at the centre of politics (as the political parties say), but he is a means of politics...And an object he remains most of all when he is kept in a state of ignorance...Subversion operates against systems of thought, against political and economic systems, that threaten nature and therewith always also Man (Agnoli, 1996, p.29).

The negation of negative human conditions is the categorical imperative of reason. Is it not reasonable to demand that all relations 'in which man is a debased, enslaved, forsaken, despicable being have to be overthrown' (Marx, 1975, p.182)? The standard of critique is the human being, her dignity and possibilities. The struggle for human dignity is a revolutionary right.

III

Globalization has become the popular term to describe contemporary developments. Its rise to prominence disguises the fact that it remains a rather vague and spongy term. Its lack of precision is symptomatic for a world in flux, and its spongy character reveals, by default, the uncertainty, social insecurity and misery that characterizes our contemporary world. Similarly, the anti-globalization movements. These movements have, on the whole, to be welcomed. Yet, there is no room for complacency. What does anti-globalization means, what does it wish to achieve, and what are its means of resistance? These questions are particularly relevant in a context where the historical alternative to capitalism has fallen into discredit as a consequence of tyrannical regimes that legitimized themselves as socialist. If socialism is, however, not endorsed as the alternative to capitalism, what other alternatives exist and can be hoped for? Resistance against capitalism that does not, in its purpose, aims, and means, pose an alternative to capitalism is a contradiction in terms and thus disarms itself. There is thus the risk of anti-globalization to succumb to an anti-capitalist capitalism that purports to eradicate social injustice while it in reality contributes – be it consciously or unconsciously –

to the realization of its barbaric potentials. There should be no 'understanding' of nationalist forms of anti-globalization, of violent and indeed terrorist means of anti-globalization struggle, of forms of resistance that do not respect human life, and that therefore mimic, in their means and aims, capitalism's indifference to human values, and that, as a consequence, base their calculations on that same constituted instrumental rationality which recognizes humanity only as a means, never as a purpose.

Anti-globalization values such as global justice, global fairness, and global solidarity are most important. These are the values of a humane world, of a world that recognizes Man as a purpose. How can these values be realized? What is their existing meaning, and what does the achievement of a truly just, free, equal, and democratic world entail? What is the 'reality' of human misery and how might it be transcended? Is this reality of human misery and suffering just a consequence of unfortunate circumstances that can be rectified by well-meaning individuals? Is it really possible to argue that contemporary conditions can be improved by the good will of politicians and a benevolent politics that secures general well-being in the name of humanity? Or is our existing misery in fact a necessary reality, however specific its concrete circumstances? The demand for a world based on the values of justice, equality, freedom, solidarity, and democracy has thus to be grounded in a critical theory of society that deciphers the reality of the human condition in the light of its positive transformation. Paraphrasing Kant, what do we have to know to prevent misery?; what can we do to achieve conditions of human dignity?; what must we hope for? These questions are at the centre of this volume.

IV

Hans-Georg Backhaus and *Helmut Reichelt* elaborate Marx's concept of social reality.[2] Oriented on Hegel's dialectics, and developing the insights of especially Adorno's negative dialectics, they show that the structural reality of capitalism has no separate existence from human social practice. At issue is thus the critique of the fetishism of economic categories. Their chapters reconstruct Marx's concept of reality, not as a reality of extra-mundane structural entities, but as a reality of human social practice, however perverted this practice might be in form of abstract economic categories. Backhaus analyses the origins of Marx's labour theory of value and argues that economic theory is unable to define its own subject matter. He therefore argues that the critique of political economy amounts to a theory social constitution. Reichelt argues against the conventional separation between social structures and social life-world and shows that capitalist social structures are inverted forms of human relations. Their critical reconstruction has huge implications for the theory and practice of revolution: if, as they argue, there is no externality to capitalist social forms, how might one conceive of social autonomy

[2] We are grateful to an anonymous reviewer who provided chapter summaries of immense clarity and insight. This section draws on these summaries.

as the means and ends of revolution? It is against this background that *Kosmas Psychopedis* examines the theory of revolution, including the contributions of Kant, Hegel, Marx, Benjamin and Arendt. The categorical imperative of revolution can easily be ascertained. It is the imperative of realising human values, of establishing relations of human dignity, and of securing solidarity as the substance of the democratic self-determination of a society of the free and equal. However, the simple question of human emancipation is most difficult to conceive in practice: Can one, as Rousseau had it, 'force people to be free'? Can revolutionary violence be justified? And how can one coordinate the ends of revolution with the means of resistance? Thus the difficult question of revolution: how can one secure the human content of revolution without compromising this same content in the organizational means of revolution?

The following three chapters examine conceptions of revolutionary transformation through the lenses of Marx, Luxemburg, and Benjamin. *Mike Lebowitz* develops the movement towards human emancipation as a movement of the political economy of labour. Within bourgeois society the concept of labour has a double meaning. It means exploitation, subordination, and indignity; and it means the precise opposite: human self-realization and thus a means of emancipation. Lebowitz explains how Marx's central insight into the collective power of labour is both simple (the collective power of labour appears as the power of capital) and yet very difficult to grasp, given the way in which it is disguised by the social forms of capitalism. On the theoretical level, a political economy of the working class is required to break the illusion of capital's 'contribution'. On the practical level, the divisions separating the diverse members of the 'collective worker' must be replaced by solidarity based upon recognition of their differences and of their complementarities. This recognition cannot be decreed from above – it can only develop through the practical activity of resisting subjects. This is the topic of *Joe Fracchia's* contribution. His thesis that the emancipation of the exploited must take the form of self-emancipation is developed through an assessment of the legacy and contemporary timeliness of Rosa Luxemburg. He places her writings on party/class relations in their historical context, develops her contribution to the dialectics of movement and organization, and examines her alternative account of socialism. Fracchia shows that Luxemburg's position on the crucial issue of the subjectivity of the working class is vastly superior to that of far better known 'Western Marxists' whose significant work on social objectivity leaves aside Luxemburg's important insight into the historical force of experience. *Sergio Tischler* also focuses on experience and examines its material force by contrasting the time of insurrection to the time of capital. He argues that the time of insurrection follows a different rhythm from that of the capitalist form of time as homogenous, abstract, repetitive, monotonous time. The time of insurrection is the time of solidarity, human purpose and democracy. History, he argues does not repeat itself. However, where resistance to oppression did not make history and where history was thus not made, history does indeed repeat itself in the struggles of today. In contrast to the mythologization of the past as a past that legitimizes existing relations of power, the past struggles of the oppressed achieve a new historical form in contemporary struggles, reconciling the time of history as a time of struggle for human emancipation. Examining Benjamin's conception of time, he argues that the time of human solidarity is the time of the democratic organization of necessity through the realm of freedom.

The final part contains chapters by *Werner Bonefeld* and *John Holloway*. Bonefeld argues that struggles against globalization that appeal to a national community in lieu of a critical analysis of the social relations of capitalism are inadequate from a theoretical standpoint. From a practical standpoint, the more popular discontent with capitalism is channelled into nationalism, the greater the danger of an anti-capitalist capitalism that glorifies the national state as a force of a homogeneous national community, including both racist violence and anti-Semitism as means of rendering national homogeneity effective. Nationalism offers a barbaric response to globalization. This then poses socialism as the alternative to barbarism, and Bonefeld concludes that the key that unlocks socialism's door is the struggle for social autonomy. This is the focus of John Holloway's contribution. He argues that one cannot live with dignity in capitalism and that a dignified life begins with the struggle against capitalism. He explains that human dignity entails 'humanity in action' (cf. Bloch, 1986) against all forms of oppression and exploitation. Dignity is the upright walk of humanity.

References

Agnoli, J. (1996), *Subversive Theorie. 'Die Sache selbst' und ihre Geschichte*, Ça ira, Freiburg.

Althusser, L. (1996), *For Marx*, trans. B. Brewster, Verso, London.

Beck, U. (1998), 'Die Seele der Demokratie. Wie wir Bürgerarbeit statt Arbeitslosigkeit finanzieren können', in *Gewerkschaftliche Monatshefte*, no. 6/7, pp. 330-34.

Bloch, E. (1986), *The Principle of Hope*, trans. N. Plaice, S. Plaice and P. Knight, Basil Blackwell, Oxford.

Bonefeld, W. (2001), 'Social Form, Critique and Human Dignity', *Zeitschrift für kritische Theorie*, no. 13, pp. 97-112.

Bonefeld, W. (2004), 'Bemerkungen zur Kritk der Voraussetzungen', in C. Kirchoff et al. (eds.).

Giddens, A. (1998), *The Third Way*, Polity, Cambridge.

Hobbes, T. (1996), *Leviathan*, Oxford University Press, Oxford.

Jessop, B. (1991), 'Polar Bears and Class Struggle', in W. Bonefeld and J. Holloway (eds.) *Post-Fordism and Social Form*, Palgrave, London.

Kant, I. (1868), *Nachlass*, in *Sämmtliche Werke*, G. Hartenstein edition, Vol. 8, Leopold Voss, Leipzig.

Kant, I. (1974), *Grundlegung der Metaphysik der Sitten*, Reclam, Stuttgard.

Kant, I. (1979), *The Conflicts of the Faculty*, trans. and introd. M. J. Gregor, Abaris, New York.

Kirchoff, C., L. Meyer, H. Pahl, J. Heckel and C. Engemann (eds.), *Gesellschaft als Verkehrung*, Ça ira, Freiburg.

Marx, K. (1964), *Zur Judenfrage*, MEW, Vol. 1, Dietz, Berlin.

Marx, K. (1973), *Grundrisse*, Penguin, London.

Marx, K. (1975), *Contribution to the Critique of Hegel's 'Philosophy of Right'. Introduction*, in *Collected Works*, Vol. 3, Lawrence & Wishart, London.

Marx, K. and F. Engels (1996), *The Communist Manifesto*, Pluto, London.
Poulantzas, N. (1968) 'Theorie und Geschichte. Kurze Bemerkung über den Gegenstand des "Kapitals"', in W. Euchner and A. Schmidt (eds.) *Kritik der politischen Ökonomie. 100 Jahre Kapital*, EVA, Frankfurt.
Psychopedis, K. (2004), 'Materialistische Werttheorie und materialistische Wertethik', in C. Kirchoff et al. (eds.).
Sennet, R. (2000), *The Corrosion of Character*, Norton, New York.
Soros, G. (2003), 'Burst the Bubble of U.S. Supremacy', *The Miami Herald, International Edition*, March 13 2003.
Veltmeyer, H. (ed.), *Globalization and Antiglobalization*, Ashgate, Aldershot.
Vuliamy, E. (2003), 'US in denial as poverty rises', *The Observer*, March 11 2003.
Wolf, M. (2001), 'The need for a new imperialism', *Financial Times*, October 10 2001.
Wolf, M. (2004), 'We need more globalisation', *Financial Times*, May 10 2004.

Part I
Critique of Capitalism and the Question of Revolution

Chapter 2

Some Aspects of Marx's Concept of Critique in the Context of his Economic-Philosophical Theory*

Hans-Georg Backhaus

The possibility of a science of value, money and capital appears quite impossible. This is indeed the conclusion one has to reach when surveying the methodological literature of theoretical economics. Here we are dealing with 'non-empirical theories' where, based on academic criteria of a theory of science, objects are referred to as 'urphenomena' and 'a prioris' that cannot be derived rationally. The object of economics is an irrational one. The consequences of this insight concur with the results of the critical reading of classical economic theory by the two Feuerbachians, Karl Marx and Friederich Engels. They recognized that the categories of economic theory are based on such 'presuppositions'. From within the economic standpoint, these presuppositions cannot be conceptualized. The 'economic standpoint' depends upon these presuppositions but its science cannot thematize them and, thus, takes them for granted. The anthropological standpoint is beyond the comprehension of the economic standpoint. It is, however, the anthropological standpoint that is able to reveal the real economy and the theoretical economy as a 'configuration of self-alienation', as an isomorphic onto-theology.

The anthropological or critical standpoint implies that value, money, capital, etc., have to be 'developed' on a 'human basis'. In short, it implies a programme of a '*critique of economic categories*' (Marx, 1858a, p.270), and of the 'genesis...of value itself' (Marx, 1972, p.156). This insight does indeed show the way towards a possible resolution of the controversies surrounding economic-value. The critical explication of economic categories as 'perversions'[1] or 'inversions' includes the

[1] [Translator's Note: Backhaus uses here the phrase '*verrückte Formen*' and writes it as '*ver-rückte Formen*'. His reference is to Marx's phrase '*verrückte Formen*' (*Das Kapital*, Vol. 1, MEW, Vol. 23, p.90). The English edition of *Capital* translates this phrase as 'absurd form'. This translation fails to express the double meaning of '*verrückt*': mad (*verrückt*) and displaced (*ver-rückt*). I have translated '*verrückt*' as 'perverted' to indicate this double meaning, and 'perverted' is used throughout in this double sense. Thus, the notion of 'perverted forms', 'perverted' and 'perversion' means that these forms are both mad and displaced. The phrase such expresses the idea of a continuing change of form between object and subject, where both, subject and object, are 'inverted' forms of a social

critical understanding (*Begründung*) of a differentiation which destroys, once and for all, the categorical basis of academic economics: that is, its differentiation of the categories value and price as 'rational' and 'irrational'. The critical explication lays the foundation for a qualitative understanding of economics, including especially its priority over quantitative economics. Marx only offered fragments of a theory of value, which he formulated in contrast to traditional value theory not as a theory of exchange but as a theory of the object itself. If one were to follow the supporters of Walras and Straffa, all respectful endeavours of theoretical economics would seem predominantly focused on finding solutions for a system of equilibrium in which its elements, mutually and simultaneously, determine each other – the so-called 'products' of input and output. Without second thoughts, Marx is presumed to have sought to solve Ricardo's unresolved transformation of values into prices, which is the primary concern of every solid economist. Marx's statement that his 'present analysis does not necessitate a closer examination of this point' (Marx, 1966, p.165) is seen as a mere escapism, because the 'modern' economist cannot even consider something other than quantitative investigations. If Marx would have concerned himself with Ricardo's 'corn-corn' model, or if he, at the last minute, had turned to the Walrasian 'revolution', he would have saved himself from the 'failure' of his theory. This is how it resounds loud and clear from the lecterns of academic economics.

It is however embarrassing that economics, as a so-called 'mulit-' or 'poly-paradigmatic' (Streißler and Streißler, 1984, p.48) discipline, offers several, and at least two mutually exclusive, models: the so-called 'neo-Ricardian' model and the neo-classical model which is much attacked by the neo-Ricardians. Since these models cannot be proven empirically, their creation as mere thought-experiments provokes a methodological critique: economics is 'not a real science' [*Realwissenschaft*] (Kambartel, 1977, p.142). If the disjunction real and ideal is understood in comprehensive terms and if the determination of economics as an ideal-science (*Idealwissenschaft*) is excluded, then economics is not a science at all. It is 'not yet a real science' (Weimann, 1982, p.279) and it presents 'in the long run, a still largely unresolved scientific task' (Porstmann, 1986, p.197), or indeed a 'mathematized pseudo-science' (Clauß, 1981, p.6).

Such methodological critique has a long history in Germany. Werner Sombart (1967, p.161) mentioned already in 1930 that 'it is immensely difficult to oversee...the great mass of dissertations and *Habilitationen*' in this field. Since then there has been a renewed flood of methodological treatises. However, even from the economist's point of view there are as yet, after an approximately one hundred year long methodological discussion, 'hardly any beginnings of an independent social science meta-theory' (Weimann, 1982, p.278). Against this background, on might suspect that academic economic thought is not only at a 'dead end', but also that its corresponding methodology still preserves the

---

reality that renders Man in his social relations 'invisible'. Backhaus has provided a succinct interpretation of Marx's use of this phrase in his essay 'Between Philosophy and Science: Marxian Social Theory as Critical Theory', published in W. Bonefeld, R. Gunn and K. Psychopedis (eds.), *Open Marxism. Dialectics and History*, vol. 1, Pluto Press, London, 1992. See also Helmut Reichelt's contribution to this volume.]

methodological approach of its ill-fated development. How else should one understand Weimann's resigned statement that only on the basis of basic convictions, only by way of sympathy, more or less by way of decision, is it possible to achieve at least some orientation in the maze of the methodological literature. Given the fundamental dilemma of 'modern' economics, its so-called 'model-Platonism', one should think that the formulation of this basic problem in the older approaches, especially Alfred Amonn's contribution, would play a central role in contemporary discussions. According to him, the problem posed by the economic object is a problem of a 'reality' that has a 'different meaning in the social sciences than in the natural sciences' (Amonn, 1927, p.327). Yet, the more recent, predominantly scientistic approaches do not take up this early formulation of this fundamental problem, which remained unresolved in the old debates where it was, in any case, discussed only in fragments. Scientism sees only one reality: the reality as posed and addressed by the natural sciences. The 'modern' economist has become a prisoner of his own scientistic prejudice – methodology as a restraint on systematic foundational research. The blindness of 'modern' economists in relation to the basic intention of Marx's critique is founded on that same scientistic, instrumentalist understanding of science according to which quality is to be reduced to quantity, and which regards 'truth' and 'reality' as 'metaphysical' concepts that have to be expelled from science.

The reverse holds for Marx. The fundamental issue for the young Marx, and also the young Engels, is not the quantitative determination of the production prices – it is questionable whether in fact they had been aware of this issue in 1843/44.[2] According to them the fundamental issue pre-exists quantitative economics. Marx and Engels raised the issue of the objective substance of economic matter – its perverted existence and independent laws of motion. Positing this question entails a 'critique of economics'.[3]

The Birth of Marx's Concept of Critique in the Context of Economic Paradoxes

We can only focus here on those few aspects of Marx's early 'critique' that have completely disappeared from the literature. Yet, these aspects should be of interest to the 'modern' economist who confronts the early writings of Marx and Engels on economics like the proverbial ox confronts the gate.[4] The motives that led Marx to the critique of 'the' economy, a whole discipline, including both its Ricardian aspects as well as the subjective aspects of Say, are of special interest. What, then, were the considerations that led Marx to abandon his initial scepticism and

---

[2] See however below for my comment on the relevant passage in Marx (1959, p.83).

[3] For a comprehensive treatment of this thesis, see Brentel (1989).

[4] On this, see Scherf (1986, pp.16-32). The circumstance that philosophers, sociologists and students of politics deal with the *Economic and Philosophical Manuscripts* in a similarly incomprehensive and helpless manner, is demonstrated in Popitz's (1967) often republished and quoted book. See also Friedrich (1960).

neutrality in relationship to these competing schools, and to argue in favour of the labour theory of value?

Some Pre-economic Motives for the Critique of the Economic Discipline

Marx started to familiarize himself with the works of classical economics in Paris in December 1843, at the earliest. Until then, that is, during his time in Cologne and Bad Kreuznach, he was only familiar with the early socialist attacks on economics. Still in 1861, Marx paid homage to Fourier's characterization of this discipline as a 'false science', a pseudo-science (Marx, 1861, p.285), and, without doubt, Proudhon's attacks on economics will have made him listen carefully: 'How might economics be a science? How can two economists look at each other without laughing?...Economics has neither a principle nor a foundation...It knows nothing; it explains nothing' (Proudhon, 1971, pp.106-7). The critique of economics by the early socialists in England might well have inspired Engels in similar ways.

There are in particular two theses from Fourier and Proudhon that find expression in Marx's Bad Kreuznacher critique of knowledge, see his third letter to Arnold Ruge (Marx, 1943, pp.141-45). On the one hand, there is their thesis about the unconsciousness of economics in relation both to itself as a discipline and to its object. According to Charles Fourier, the economists 'do not even know, what they are dealing with' (Fourier, 1980, p.118). Proudhon says the same. In reference to a self-critical statement by Say, he argues that economic 'science can not determine its object'. This led Proudhon to the conclusion that 'he [Say] did not know what he was talking about' (Proudhon, 1971, p.107). The crux of economics, that is, its inability to determine its economic object, is thus a central topic of the early socialist critique of economics, and was later reiterated by Auguste Blanqui. Fourier's second central thesis suggests, similar in contents with Georg Wilhelm Friederich Hegel's *Philosophy of Right* (1991), that 'metaphysics, morality, politics, and economics' belong together and are internally related as the 'four precarious sciences', even the 'four false sciences' (Fourier, 1980, p.31). The academic social-'sciences' and social-philosophy were thus to be mistrusted not only for class political reasons but, also, because of their theoretical impotence.

While the second letter to Arnold Ruge attests directly to the reading of the French early socialists – the denunciation of the 'system of industry...and exploitation' (Marx, 1843, p.141) – this topic does not seem to play any role in the third letter. However, this third letter says for the first time that not merely religion but also 'science, etc., the object of our critique' (ibid., p.143).[5] Without doubt, Marx was thinking here not so much about the natural sciences but, rather, about Fourier's 'four precarious sciences', including economics. What Marx has to say about one of these, that is 'politics', will be applicable *a priori* to economics, too. The proposed programme of a critique also of economics thus seeks to help the

[5] [Translator's Note: The English edition translates the German *Kritik* as 'criticism'. The German for 'criticism' is *Kritizismus*. I have translated *Kritik* as 'critique' as it is closer to the German original and less likely to be confused with the ambiguous connotations of 'criticism' as, for example, a mere philosophical conviction or an expounding of formal contradiction.]

economists 'to clarify their presuppositions for themselves' (ibid., p.142), helping them, as it were, to pose their 'questions are posed in a self-conscious human form' (ibid., p.144).[6] Economics is deemed a form of 'mystical consciousness that is unintelligible to itself'. The primary 'motto' of this programme of the critique of economics is to 'reform' economic 'consciousness not through dogmas', that is, an independently formulated economic theory, 'but by analyzing the mystical consciousness that is unintelligible to itself' (ibid.). This consciousness is at issue not only in Say's school of thought but, also, in its antipode, the Ricardian labour theory of value.

It seems obvious that Marx formulates his critique in contrast to the early socialist critique, especially in opposition to Proudhon. Fourier attacks economics as a 'science of servitude', the economists in their relation to 'tradesmen' as 'sycophants', and both as comprising a 'legion of con-men' (Fourier, 1980, p.180). Similarly Proudhon insists that 'for 25 years now, economics has descended upon France like a thick mist, holding back the progress of thought and suppressing freedom' (Proudhon, 1971, p.107). Since, according to Proudhon, we are dealing with 'sophists', the 'whole of economics has to be destroyed' (ibid., p.93). Compared with Fourier's and Proudhon's choice of words, Marx's programme of critique appears, as it were, moderate. He demands the determinate negation and not the abstract negation of economics. According to Marx, and as he learnt to appreciate in his later work, abstract negation remains mired in the criticized object itself. Marx therefore rebukes Proudhon's work as a 'criticism of *political economy* from the standpoint of economics' (Marx, 1975d, p.31). In distinction to this 'first critique' (ibid.) – a priest-like theory of economics as deception [*Priesterbetrugstheorie der Ökonomie*], represented for example in England by Thomas Hodgskin (Marx, 1972, p.267) – a dialectical critique, while it acknowledges the 'first' critique as a preliminary stage, 'starts out from any form of theoretical...consciousness' (Marx, 1943, p.143), including economic consciousness, so that consciousness achieves enlightenment about itself, and its theoretical practice. Marx, then, posits his critique as a means of revealing the constitution of the object of economic thought, an object that it presupposes unconsciously.

One can see that three months after the second letter to Arnold Ruge, Marx formulated a programme of a critique of economics that goes beyond the naïve and uncritical 'first critique' – Marx later characterized it as vulgar socialist (Marx, 1972, p.467) – and its associated meta-critical developments. Marx's study of economics developed against the background of already formulated methodological dispositions, existing forms of critique and topics of investigation. This led him to refine his critical programme, leading to a new form of critique.

Marx's introduction to the *Paris Manuscripts* gives many clues in this direction. In his view, the 'German positive critique of economy...owes its true foundation to the discoveries of *Feuberbach*' (Marx, 1959, p.14),[7] that is, the discoveries made by the Feuerbachian critique of religion and ontology. This is a statement that will

---

[6] [Translator's Note: Adapted from the German original, MEW, Vol. I, p. 346.]

[7] [Translator's Note: See Note 5.]

make 'modern' economists gasp for breath. Their selective reading of Marx's early writing disallows any such openings for critical enquiry. Instead they ask why the young Marx did not adopt Piero Sraffa's approach or alternatively, the one chosen by Leon Walras.

In fact, not only the 'modern' economist but the economist *sans phrase* will be dumbfounded when somebody should propose that the method of the critique of Religion and Metaphysics is adequate for the analysis of the basic concepts of economic science. Yet, there is no doubting the fact that Marx accepts the universal truth of some of Feuerbach's elementary considerations concerning the constitution of the social world, i.e. the world made by Man.[8] Marx is therefore able to start his critique on the basis of an understanding of the isomorphic structures of the onto-theological, social-metaphysical objects or of the isomorphic structures of the political and economic objects.

The revolutionary consequences of this position are clear. If Marx's thesis is correct, then economics must once and for all give up the idea that it is on the way towards becoming an exact science – clearly separated from philosophy. In this case economics would have to deal with a structured object *sui generis*, and that object would exclude or render relative some approaches in certain areas. Marx's determination of the economic object has thus a number of hard consequences for the philosophy of knowledge: he destroys scientism's claim for universality whatever its distinct forms of application.

Yet, Marx's thesis according to which economic and metaphysical objects are structured isomorphically, is neither original nor has it remained in any way special in modern times. The thesis, as is well known, can be found in Hegel. In relation to money, one finds it already in the work of Johann Georg Harmann and later again in the work of Georg Simmel. The Frankfurt philosopher Bruno Liebrucks expounded its insight at various points in his monumental work *Sprache und Bewußtsein* (Language and Consciousness).

The originality of Marx's determination of the economic object lies, in fact, in its direct connection to Feuerbach's critique of theology and metaphysics, especially its '*genetic-critical*...or speculative-empirical method' (Feuerbach, 1960, p.246). Marx, as is well known, immediately applies this method in his critique of the metaphysical theory of the state. However, its scope of application is immensely expanded. Marx notes that already Hegel 'had understood wealth, state power etc...as alienated essence' (Marx, 1959, p.130),[9] of course only in a spiritual way. In general, Hegel has recognized 'that self-conscious Man, insofar as he has recognized and superseded the spiritual work...as self-alienation', as an 'alienated shape' of Man, as a 'product of self-alienation' (ibid., pp.139-40). When Marx argues that his programme of critique has, after the critique of religion, to 'unmask self-estrangement in its *unholy forms*' (Marx, 1975a, p.176), then he of course had in his mind also the economic forms, even though he did not expressively say so.

---

8 [Translator's Note: Man with a capital 'M' is used here and throughout the text in the sense of *Mensch*. The English translation of Marx's texts often translates *Mensch* as 'man' and quotations have been adapted accordingly.]

9 [Translator's Note: Adapted from the German original: MEW, Vol. 40, p.572.]

The forms of economic wealth or the economic categories are determined as 'forms' or 'products of self-estrangement', indeed as material forms of self-estrangement. This also means that they are seen just as other 'forms of self-estrangement'. As 'unholy' forms of self-estrangement, economic objects are now commensurable with the metaphysical and theological forms of self-estrangement, that is, their 'holy', sacred forms. Marx kept this parallelism of his formulations right up into his late work.

Concerning the application of Feuerbach's 'critical genetic method' to economics, two aspects will be emphasized here – the critical and the anthropological.

The critical aspect leads to that specific concept of critique that Marx had formulated in distinction to what he called 'vulgar critique'. This critique was satisfied with showing contradictions between criticized dogmas and institutions, that is, for example, it demolished 'the dogma of the Holy Trinity, say...by the contradiction between one and three (Marx, 1975b, p.91). The 'first critique' of economics, the one of the 'vulgar socialists', is one example of this 'vulgar critique' in that it is limited to the exposure of formal-logical contradictions. In contrast the 'true critique' is to reveal the 'inner genesis of the Holy Trinity in the human brain', expound the 'act of its birth', and its set task is thus merely to 'describe' the economic object in a direct fashion. The new form of critique, also called 'philosophical critique', 'does not show up contradictions as existing; it *explains* them, it comprehends their genesis, their necessity' (ibid.).[10] The 'true critique', which is here also called, in reference to Hegel, '*comprehension*' (*Begreifen*), is obviously that critique which a few months later led to the 'conceptualization' of contradictory economic dogmas, that is, to their critique. In his later work, Marx refers to it also as the 'genetical presentation' of categories (Marx, 1972, p.500). One sees that Marx uses the concepts 'critique' and 'comprehension', explication of the 'inner genesis', or the 'peculiar logic of a peculiar object' and 'presentation', in a largely identical sense.

Not only Marx but also, and quite independently, the young Engels emphasized the anthropological aspect of Feuerbach's 'critical genetic method'. The importance of this aspect is first of all that critique has to '[demonstrate] *ad hominem*' (Marx, 1975a, p.182), and that it 'proceeds from a purely human...basis' (Engels, 1975, p.421). Critique, then, intends a '*reduction* (*Zurückführung*) of the human world and relationships to *Man himself*' (Marx, 1975c, p.168). Marx endorses Feuerbach's 'materialism', arguing that its great achievement was to make the 'social relationship of "Man to Man" the basic principle of...theory' (Marx, 1959, p.127).

The 'anthropological' aspect of this method, which reaches back to Greek thought, has to be constitutive for Marx's concept of critique if it is to be principally different from the vulgar conception of critique. This differentiation is required because the *common sense* conception of critique, like it is applied for example in 'critical rationalism', is absolutely incapable of rendering whole disciplines in their totality an object of critique. This can be a meaningful

---

[10] [Translator's Note: See Note 5.]

programme of research only if the fundamental concepts of these disciplines can be conceptualized, without exception, as products of human self-estrangement. A critique of, for example, 'the' economy in its past, present and also future features is therefore required and justified when it can be shown that the proponents of economic thought understand economic objectivity not as a product of self-estrangement but, rather, constantly confuse, as typical and professional representatives of 'natural consciousness', *first* and *second* nature.

The 'return' [*Zurückführung*] of second nature to Man, not as an 'abstract individual', but as a member of a 'definite form of society' (Marx, 1975e, p.5), this *reductio ad hominem* is the most important principle of his matured critique or analysis of economic categories. Marx demands the 'return' of 'a *relation of objects to one another*', that is, of economic categories to 'relations between Men' (Marx, 1972, p.147). This is the anthropological core of economic analysis.

The circumstance that Marx's analysis of 1843/44 owes its 'true foundation' not only to Feuerbach, but, also, to Hegel – '*all* (!!) elements of critique' are 'hidden' in Hegel's *Phenomenology of Spirit* (Marx, 1959, p.131)[11] – and the circumstance that Marx conceives of 'German Philosophy as a whole' as the 'point of origin' (ibid., p.15) of 'critique', would hardly demand attention were it not for the fact that, even today, economic thinking about Marx's early writings has held on to the quite deluded idea (*wahnhafte Vorstellung*) that it is in principle possible to differentiate between the 'economic' elements and the 'philosophical' elements in the *Economic-Philosophical Manuscripts*. Marx is full of praise for Hegel's treatment of 'non-philosophical science' whose 'conventional conceptions' he does not repeat but 'contradicts' (!) (ibid., p.142). Clearly, Marx also 'contradicts' these 'conventional concepts' of economics and he does so in a Hegelian sense. What needs to be made clear at this point is this: This most important conception of critique that is used by both the young Engels and Marx – and Marx specifically used it in his fully-developed critique of economics – is directly borrowed from the 'Play' of 'Abstractions' in Hegel's *Phenomenology* (Hegel, 1977, p.77). The young Engels makes excessive use this 'play' in his critique of economics, though not always effectively.

The First Step towards 'Revolutionizing' Economics in the 'Economic-Philosophical Manuscripts'

Marx's conviction that economics is only possible as a 'philosophical discipline', or not at all, and that economic questions necessarily entail 'philosophical' questions, stood not just at the beginning of his 'critical study of economics'. The conception of his study as a critical study entailed the philosophical question. Marx, in fact, saw this conviction confirmed because of and as a consequence of his studies. This is why, after his study of Say, Ricardo, etc., he referred in his Preface to the proposed critique of economics also to his own writings of the *German-French Yearbooks*, and that is, to his own 'philosophical' or 'pre-

---

[11] [Translator's Note: Backhaus frequently uses one or more exclamation marks to emphasize certain phrases and insights. The translation retains his unconventional style.]

economic' writings. For professional economists, his reference to these texts contains a most displeasing thesis: Marx argues that these texts 'indicate the first elements of the present work in most general terms' (Marx, 1959, p.14).[12] What is 'indicated' in these texts has nothing to do with economics, at least not with economics as it is understood in the 'modern' sense as a primarily 'quantitative' discipline. What, then, does Marx mean when he says that 'these first elements' are anticipated 'in general terms' in his philosophical writing? These 'first elements' can only refer to the mere existence (*Dasein*) and continued reproduction of the categories as well as to their general and common features as 'forms of self-alienation'. That is, he can only refer to those general characteristics that the economic and the moral, religious, political and onto-theological categories have in common.

In actual fact, one can easily point out key words which are used by Marx, following Feuerbach, in the analysis of non-economic categories and which then return in the context of his economic analysis: splitting (*Entzweiung*); disunity (*Zerrissentheit*); contradiction (*Widerspruch*) – 'inversion' qua objectively unfolding laws of development (*Eigengesetzlichkeit*) in the sense of the 'domination' of the product over Man – 'unconsciousness' (*Unbewußtsein*), 'oblivion' (*Vergessen*) in the process of production – 'abstraction from and indifference to Man – 'estrangement' (*Entäußerung*) and its reversal (*Zurücknahme*) and 'return' (*Rückkehr*), etc.

On the basis of these key words it should be evident that the *description* of facts, of already existing things, *implies* their *critique*; and such a critique requires no normative 'measures' (*Maßstäbe*). Instead, critique deals with immediate 'reality', a reality *sui generis*. The 'forms of self-alienation' present themselves to Man as 'puzzles', 'mysteries', 'secrets', 'aprioris', 'urphenomena', 'things in themselves', etc. – their 'conceptualisation' develops in and through a process that 'deciphers' and thereby reveals a determinate sense. It is clear, such an analysis stands in sharp contrast to the scientistic method of the social sciences.

The Most Elementary 'Presuppositions' of Economics

In my view, the first and most important difference between Marx's 'economics' and all other non-Marxist economic variants, then as now, consists in this: these variants accept economic forms and categories without thought, that is, in an unreflective manner. Marx, in contrast, seeks to 'derive' these forms and categories as inverted forms of human social relations. His central reproach against economic thought is that it assumes the 'ready made forms' as 'already really existing', that it presupposes the 'existence' (*Dasein*) of these forms; that it takes its concepts from 'everyday experience' (Marx, 1987, p.476), reads them off the 'empirical world' (Marx, 1973, p.249), that they are smuggled into the economic theory as if they 'fall out of the sky' (ibid., p.679), and that these forms are only 'dealt with factually' in concrete circumstances; that economic theory 'presupposes these

---

[12] [Translator's Note: Adapted from the German original, MEW, Vol. 40, p.468.]

forms as given premises'. These charges are especially targeted at Ricardo: he is said to have 'assumed all sorts of categories...in the first chapter on...value' (Marx, 1968, p.69).

Marx's central demand is that 'the' economists should not presuppose 'categories' or 'forms' but that they should, instead, develop them 'genetically'. This is where the origin of Marx's method lies. He calls it the 'dialectic method of exposition (*dialektische Entwicklungsmethode*)' (Marx, 1867, p.390) and contrasts it to the method of 'the' economists who are only able to bring about a 'formal abstraction' (Marx, 1969, p.106) that '[subordinates] the concrete to the abstract' (Marx, 1972, p.87). The origin of this fundamental critique of economic thought can be found in the *Economic-Philosophical Manuscripts*. In this work Marx argues for the first time that economics deals with unreflected presuppositions (cf. Marx, 1959, pp.61-62). Almost all its categories are of such character. Political Economy 'takes for granted what it is supposed to explain' (ibid.) – it presupposes what has to be 'explained and comprehended' (ibid., p.62). For Marx, the most elementary 'presupposition', which is also 'presumed' by economics, is the 'concept exchange-value' (ibid., p.61). Economics does therefore not 'explain' and thus fails to 'comprehend'.

This charge might appear strange at first sight. The economist might well respond that he is in fact dealing with nothing else, be it by means of Ricardo's corn-corn-model or by means of Walras's economics of allocation, than the determinations of exchange ratios or relative exchange values. Exactly. The economist 'presumes' not only, as he often tries to suggest to himself, the exchange *activities*. He also 'presumes' the mere existence of exchange value and passes over it in silence.

How much this problematic is made taboo in established economics can be gleaned from the fact that it has been raised to the best of my knowledge only once, and has since been forgotten again, in the methodological literature. Alfred Amonn recognized that the 'economic problem is the content of price, that is, its determinate measure'. The mere 'form' of price is a 'given'. The form of price, he argues, 'is no problem for economics…it simply presupposes the price form, and in our methodological studies we determine the presuppositions of this price form' (Amonn, 1927, p.420). But this task remained a mere programme, which Amonn worked on with as little success as Simmel and Gottl. They also recognized that price as form or the commodity-money-relationship is always already 'presupposed' in the academic price-theory, and that therefore the price-form cannot be thematized in price-theoretical terms. These authors, therefore, know that this is equally valid for the concepts of money and capital. Thus, the statement can be generalized: There are non-theorized 'presuppositions' in economics, and these presuppositions cannot be thematized in economic-theoretical terms. Georg Simmel (1990) therefore wrote a *Philosophy of Money*, which brought to the fore paradoxes that were quite beyond the dreams of economic school-wisdom. In comparison with the earlier acknowledgment of its problematic, the complete suppression of these 'meta-economic' problems in 'modern' economics, and especially also in the approaches that correlate with it, demonstrates the decay of economic theory's appreciation of its own theoretical problems.

Marx's discovery of the presupposition of economics, presuppositions which are beyond economic analysis, shows itself in some formulations where he stresses the importance to transcend the 'economic standpoint', that is, to suspend it critically. The 'first critique', say the one of Proudhon, can thus be accused to have been 'taken in by those same presuppositions of science to which it officially objects and thus of offering a critique of economics form the standpoint of economics, contesting economic thought with the help of economic presuppositions' (Marx, 1975d, p.31f).

Even in his late work, Marx characterizes the left-Ricardian version of this 'first critique' as follows: we find here an 'opposition' (*Gegensatz*) to the economists that 'takes as its starting point the premises of the economists' (Marx, 1972, p.238). And in as much as 'the' economists and 'economics' have to be characterized in general and especially in methodological terms, Marx always describes, not the individual, but those 'Messieurs les économistés' (Marx, 1858b, p.301), or just the 'standpoint of the economist' in ironic terms. The project of a critique of 'the' economy, as it was, is and will be, can be conceived and developed out only on the condition that 'the' economist or 'the' economy can become object of a critical ideological investigation.

This is not the occasion to expound Marx's determination of the 'economic standpoint' – though this is something that even after more than a century since the publication of the third volume of *Capital* has still not been recognized as a worthwhile task. What should be clear, however, is that the determination of the 'economic standpoint' has, at the same time, to bring to the fore the critical 'standpoint' *beyond* economics. What needs to be noted here, too, is that such a determination has to take account of some of Feuerbach's 'anthropological' concepts. Marx conceives of economics as one of many disciplines that need to be criticized, such as, for example, ethics, as a 'specific estrangement of Man' (Marx, 1959, p.106); as one of the 'distinct forms of estrangement' (Ibid., p.131). Thus he argues, Proudhon 'wishes to abolish the practically estranged relations of Man to his objective essence and the economic expression of his self-estrangement' (Marx, 1975d, p.42). What is indicated here as the 'economic condition', in as much as it characterizes the economist himself, is described by Marx only once in detailed terms as the condition of disunity [*Zerrissenheit*]: 'The economists occasionally stress the semblance of humanity in economic relations, but sometimes, and as a rule, they take these relations precisely in this clearly pronounced *difference* from the human, in their strictly economic sense. (!!) They stagger about within the contradiction' (ibid., p.33).

Marx refers here to considerations that he expounded in detail in his third *Paris Manuscript*. Here the protagonists of economics are no longer the followers of subjective economics or objective economics but rather, just as it was the case with the young Engels, the proponents of mercantilism and classical English thought. This antithesis reappears time and time again in his late work.

Mercantilism represents that moment of the economy or of 'private property', which Marx characterized as a '*condition* external to Man' (Marx, 1959, p.83), as 'wealth outside of Man and independent of him' (ibid., p.84), or more precisely: the '(independent) movement of private property' (ibid., p.83).

For Marx, classical English political economy is posited in a merely apparent (*scheinbaren*) opposition to mercantilism. English political economy develops '*labour*...as the sole *essence of wealth* (ibid., p.84), and it raises up '*labour in general*', rendering its 'abstraction as the *principle*' (ibid., p.86). Marx mentioned here 'apparent contradictions' (ibid., p.84), in which this principle of labour as an abstraction 'becomes involved' (ibid.) – presumably an allusion to the controversy over production prices. Still, these immanent contradictions of classical economics are, for Marx, of lesser importance since his concern here is to put together the categorical context of his critique of economics.

Marx's interest is thus altogether different. He is interested in the internal unity of apparently diametrically opposed positions. Both positions represent in fact the two opposed moments or poles of private property: on the one hand its '*subjective essence*' (ibid., p.83), i.e. labour, and on the other side, its 'objective form' (ibid., p.87), that is, money and capital. These opposed moments belong together and in their togetherness entail the 'essence' of private property or wealth; in precise terms: 'the tension ridden' or 'contradictory essence' of private property, '(industry's) *self-ruptured* principle'. In short, 'their principle is, after all, the principle of the rupture [*Zerrissenheit*]' (ibid., p.85).[13]

The 'objective form', that is, the 'wealth that exists outside Man' dominates Man as an '*inhuman* power' (ibid., p.111). In this sphere Man is only active as 'dehumanized (Man)' (Marx, 1975c, p.212). His operation with things qua money and capital 'becomes the operation of an entity outside Man and above Man' (ibid.). One can easily recognize that Marx is speaking here about money that in 'its' functions operates as an 'inhuman' (*unmenschliches*) subject, namely, it make unequal things equal, 'stores' values, 'transfers', etc. The independent laws of things, of things 'outside Man', present the 'objective' or mercantilist moment of the economy.

In contrast to the mercantilist objectivity of dehumanized Man, the 'subjective essence' of private property or, in other words, labour, implies a mere 'semblance of recognizing Man' (Marx, 1959, p.84). It presents, as it was put in the above definition of economics, the 'subjective' in the sense of the 'semblance of humanity in economic relations' (Marx, 1975d, p.33).

Two things are in my view of interest here. First, one must again point out the Feuerbachian origin of the terminology, and this returns us to the crux of the argument. One might, for example, remember the following formulation in Ludwig Feuerbach's *Preliminary Theses for the Reform of Philosophy* of 1843: 'The essence of theology is the *transcendental* essence of Man, an essence posited external to Man; the essence of Hegel's "logic" is *transcendental* thought, the thought of Man *posited external to Man*' (Feuerbach, 1975, p.238).

The isomorphic relationship between the different 'forms of self-estrangement' is obvious. Foundational economic and onto-theological concepts are exchangeable within the problematic of estrangement. The 'essence of economy' is, thus, 'the *transcendental*', that is, the 'essence' of Man's genus activity, that is labour, 'is posited external to Man'. The 'transcendental' aspect of the real economy, namely

13 [Translator's Note: Adapted from the German original, MEW, Vol. 40, p.531.]

the so-called 'forms' of wealth that are displaced and 'externalized' and thus transposed in a sphere 'outside Man', is represented by the mercantilist aspect of economics, and vice versa. The immanent aspect of theoretical economics or the aspect that is 'put back in Man' (Marx, 1975c, p.215) denotes the principle of labour of classical economic theory. This aspect represents the collective labour or genus activity of the real economy.

Marx's terminology changes in his mature economic studies. 'Transcendental', 'posited' in the sphere 'outside of Man', perverted essence, is replaced by the so-called 'forms' of value; and in the place of 'essence of Man' or 'appearance of humanness' we find 'substance' of value, and labour replaces genus activity.

Total social labour, this 'subjective essence' of private property or the 'substance' of value appears to Man as a 'social relation, existing not between themselves, but between the products of their labour' (Marx, 1983, p.77). Marx defines all economic 'forms' or 'categories' as 'perverted forms (*verrückte Formen*)' (ibid., p.80).[14] Marx employs the phrase '*verrückte*' (perverted) forms in its double sense as, on the one hand, puzzling, mystical essence, and, on the other hand, as a sphere 'outside of Man', displaced or transposed.

The 'objective-subjective' or disunited essence of wealth, its 'sensuous supersensible' double character, draws economics into a 'game' of 'abstractions'. 'The economists stagger about...within this contradiction, completely unaware of it' (Marx, 1975d, p.33), as it was put in the above fundamental critique of economics. Economics does not understand the unity of diverse moments and, instead, hypothesizes these as in themselves existing units of essence. Economics is thus unable to recognize that it is dealing merely with 'abstractions' and because of this, Marx defined the economist as the one with whom the abstractions play ball.

In variation of this thought process, Marx argues in the mature *Critique* of 1859 that what the economists 'have just ponderously described as a thing reappears as a social relation and, a moment later, having been defined as a social relation, teases them once more as a thing' (Marx, 1971, p.35). If one replaces 'social relation' by 'appearance of humanness' and thing qua 'value thing' by the thing in 'difference from humanness' that, as a transcendental thing, is transposed in a sphere 'outside of Man', then the continuity of the fundamental character of Marx's critique of economics from the early writing to *Capital* becomes sufficiently clear.

The Birth of the Labour Value Theory in the *Economic-Philosophical Manuscripts*

Money or the Truth of Mercantilism

In Georg Weber's essay *Money*, which was inspired by Marx and presumably edited by him too, and was published in the Parisian *Vorwärts*, one finds a first concrete formulation of Marx's argument in the third *Paris Manuscript*. 'The (!)

---

14 [Translator's Note: On the double meaning of '*verrückt*', see footnote 1.]

economists would like to convince us that money were a wholly inessential thing, that everything would look the same without money' (Weber, 1982, p.512).

Marx, one presumes, was familiarizing himself at that time with Charles Ganilh's neo-mercantilist views, which he later, in his mature work, contrasts to classical political economy and its conceptions of money as a mere 'veil'. The neo-mercantilists have also been partly responsible for the continuous confusion of 'product', 'good', 'use-value' with 'commodity' – a confusion that is especially characteristic of modern 'neo-Ricardionism'.

This manuscript is of particular significance because it shows that Marx's thematization of the concept value does not have an exchange-theoretical beginning but a money-theoretical origin and, as I have discussed elsewhere, a capital-theoretical origin: 'Essence of money as value *sans phrase*, as abstract value' (ibid., p.513).[15] 'As soon as we accept value as something external to Man (!!), then the satisfaction of needs is made dependent on something different than the existence of needs' (ibid., p.514). One sees, right from the start, that we are dealing with value as 'abstract value' as it manifests itself as something 'external to Man' in the form of independent units of essence, of money and capital. Value theory, for Marx, was from the beginning a theory of the economic object, and not at all an exchange theory qua a theory of exchange *activity*.

The First Problematization of the Concept of Value in a Capital Theoretical Context

Marx poses his fundamental insight that the economists argue on the basis of unresolved 'presuppositions' and that their argument therefore operates with essentially obscure concepts, at the start of his 'critical study of political economy' (Marx, 1959, p.14). One should keep in mind also that at this point in his intellectual development, Marx treated all economic schools and theories from a good distance and with scepticism. He thus claimed for himself absolute neutrality in relation to the controversies between Jean-Baptiste Say, the main proponent of the subjective value theory, and his main opponent, David Ricardo.

The first economist whose work Marx read and excerpted is Jean-Baptiste Say. And one of his first comments focuses on the Achilles' Heel of economics: '*wealth*. Already here we find that the concept of *value*, which is as yet not developed (!!), is presumed (!!); because wealth is defined as the "sum of values"' (Marx, 1981, p.319). Say defines such a sum, advanced for production, as 'capital'. We are dealing here with the idea of 'abstract value', which functions at the same time as 'absolute value' in the circuit of capital. For the economists, its mere existence is *the* mystery per se. Marx demands, that its existence should not be 'presupposed' but that it has to be 'developed' – a task whose solution is impossible not just for the subjective value theoretician Say, but also for the labour-value-theoretician Ricardo, and that is, for every economist. At issue is what Marx later characterized

---

15 [Translator's Note: Backhaus is referring to his 'Zum Problem des Geldes als Konstituens oder Apriori der ökonomischen Gegenständlichkeit', first published in PROKLA, no. 63, 1986; reprinted in H.G. Backhaus, *Dialektik der Wertform. Untersuchungen zur Marxschen Ökonomiekritik*', Ça ira, Freiburg, 1997 and 2004.]

as the investigation of the 'genesis...of value itself' (Marx, 1972, p.156). There it is shown that Ricardo 'presumes' value in as much as he, in his search for the 'unchanging measure', permanently confuses 'immanent' and 'appearing' measure. The problematic issue of the 'constitution' of value and therewith the constitution of the economic object, the 'value thing', is as unknown to Thomas Malthus and Samuel Bailey, whom he criticizes here directly, as it is for Adam Smith and David Ricardo. These two are time and time again reproached for this confusion. Necessarily, then, Ricardo 'falls into the commonplace error of the vulgar economists, who assume the value of one commodity' (Marx, 1983, p.84, fn.1) Contemporary neo-Ricardianism reproduces these common sense errors.

The Birth of the New Labour Value Theory in the Context of a Pre-economic, 'Philosophical' Positing of the Problem

The first reading of the classical economists impressed upon both the young Engels and the young Marx that the fundamental, inner-economic contradictions cannot be resolved from within economics itself. The young Engels puts this most clearly when he says that '[t]he (!) economists cannot decide anything' because the definition of 'the' economist is that he 'lives by antitheses (*Gegensätze*)' (Engels, 1975, p.424), 'roams about in antitheses' (ibid., p.425), and is 'firmly set in his antitheses' (ibid., p.439).

Marx sees the dilemma of economics in a similar way. He notes during his study of the controversy between Say and Ricardo that 'the economists topple their respective gods' (Marx, 1982, p.419). Economic thought is necessarily mixed up in antinomies: 'Ricardo develops...Say shows' (ibid., p.395). Therefore, Ricardo's thesis that '*labour* is the essence of private property' amounts to 'an assertion which the (!) political economist cannot prove'. If the economist as an economist cannot 'prove' this thesis, who would be able to develop its 'explanation [*Begründung*]'? Continuing, Marx writes: 'and...we wish to prove it for him' (Marx, 1959, p.118). The critics of political economy want to do something for the economist that this economist cannot do himself. 'Critique' is thus conceived as explanation – explanation qua critique.

If the antinomies of economic thought cannot be resolved economically, then which pre-economic or 'philosophical' formulation of the problem and which methods may explain the labour value theory? Evidently, the Feuerbachian formulations. It is to them, Marx writes, that we are 'indebted' and it is to them that the 'critique of political economy...owes its true foundation' (Marx, 1959, p.14).[16]

Is there, in the *Manuscripts*, an indication that Marx left behind his early neutrality in relation to the theory of value and began to deliver what he said he would, namely to provide the 'proof' [*Beweiß*] of the labour theory of value 'for' those economists who orient themselves on this theory? Indeed such a passage can be found if one replaces the Hegelian and Sayian concept of 'private property' by the concept of 'value'. The young Marx operates quite often in this fashion, for example: 'value is the bourgeois mode of existence of property' (Marx, 1842,

16 [Translator's Note: Adapted from the German original, MEW, Vol. 40, p.462.]

p.229);[17] 'the mode of existence of private property has...become...*value*' (Marx, 1975c, p.219), or the 'forms of private property...for example...value, price, money' (Marx, 1975d, p.32).

It follows that one can also replace the concept of 'private property' in the subsequent sentence by the concept of 'value', if one wants to decipher its proper meaning. The sentence would then read: '[f]or when one speaks of value, one thinks of dealing with something external to Man (!!). When one speaks of labour, one is directly dealing with Man himself. This new formulation (!!) of the question already contains its solution' (Marx, 1959, pp.73-74).

The 'new formulation' of the old economic question is the anthropological positing of the question. The essence of value is principally recognized in as much as its transcendental '*form*' is focused as a 'thing external to Man'. To put it in Feuerbachian terms: the essence of economics is the *transcendental* essence of labour transposed external to Man. The essence of labour appears as a 'thing external to Man'. As Georg Weber put it, in the form of money exists the paradox of an 'abstract value', a 'value external to Man'.

References

Amonn, A. (1927), *Objekt und Grundbegriffe der theoretischen Nationalökonomie*, 2nd ed., Böhlau, Vienna.

Brentel, H. (1989), *Soziale Form und ökonomisches Objekt*, Westdeutscher Verlag, Opladen.

Clauß, F.-J. (1981), *Wissenschaftslogik und Sozialökonomie*, Duncker und Humblot, Berlin.

Engels, F. (1975), *Outline of a Critique of Political Economy*, in *Collected Works*, Vol. 3, Lawrence & Wishart, London.

Feuerbach, L. (1960), *Das Wesen des Christentums*, Fromann, Stuttgard.

Feuerbach, L. (1975) *Vorläufige Thesen zur Reform der Philosophie*, in H. Reichelt (ed.) *Texte zur materialistischen Geschichtsauffassung*, Ullstein, Berlin.

Fourier, Ch. (1980), *Ökonomisch-philosophische Schriften. Eine Textauswahl*, edited by L. Zahn, Akademie Verlag, Berlin.

Friedrich, M. (1960), *Philosophie und Ökonomie beim jungen Marx*, Duncker and Humblot, Berlin.

Hegel, G. W. F. (1977), *Phenomenology of Spirit*, trans. A V. Miller, Clarendon Press, Oxford.

Hegel, G. W. F. (1991), *Elements of the Philosophy of Right*, trans H. B. Nisbet, ed. A. W. Wood, Cambridge University Press, Cambridge.

Kambartel, F. (1977), 'Zur Überwindung des Szientismus und Modellplatonismus in der Ökonomie', *Zeitschrift allgemeiner Wissenschaftstheorie*, no. 1, pp. 132-43.

Marx, K. (1842), 'Debates on the Law on Thefts of Wood', in *Collected Works*, Vol. 1, Lawrence & Wishart, London.

Marx, K. (1843), 'Letters from the *Deutsch-Französische Jahrbücher*', in *Collected Works*, Vol. 3, Lawrence & Wishart, London.

Marx, K. (1858a), 'Letter to Engels, February 22 1858', in *Collected Works*, Vol. 40, Lawrence & Wishart, London.

[17] [Translator's Note: Adapted from the German original, MEW, Vol. 1, p.114.]

Marx, K. (1858b), 'Letter to Engels, April 2 1858', in *Collected Works*, Vol. 40, Lawrence & Wishart, London.

Marx, K. (1861), 'Letter to Lasalle, May 8 1861', in *Collected Works*, Vol. 41, Lawrence & Wishart, London.

Marx, K. (1967), 'Letter to Engels, June 27 1867', in *Collected Works*, Vol. 42, Lawrence & Wishart, London.

Marx, K. (1868), 'Letter to Kugelmann, July 11 1868', in *Collected Works*, Vol. 43, Lawrence & Wishart, London.

Marx, K. (1959), *Economic and Philosophical Manuscripts*, Lawrence & Wishart, London.

Marx, K. (1966), *Capital*, Vol. III, Lawrence & Wishart, London.

Marx, K. (1969), *Theories of Surplus Value*, Part 2, Lawrence & Wishart, London.

Marx, K. (1971), *A Contribution to the Critique of Political Economy*, Lawrence & Wishart, London.

Marx, K. (1972), *Theories of Surplus Value*, Part 3, Lawrence & Wishart, London.

Marx, K. (1973), *Grundrisse*, Penguin, London.

Marx, K. (1975a), *Contribution to the Critique of Hegel's Philosophy of Law. Introduction*, in *Collected Works*, Vol. 3, Lawrence & Wishart, London.

Marx, K. (1975b), *Contribution to the Critique of Hegel's Philosophy of Law*, in *Collected Works*, Vol. 3, Lawrence & Wishart, London.

Marx, K. (1975c), 'Comments on James Mill, *Élémens d'économie politique*', in *Collected Works*, Vol. 3, Lawrence & Wishart, London.

Marx, K. (1975d), *The Holy Family*, in *Collected Works*, Vol. 4, Lawrence & Wishart, London.

Marx, K. (1975e), 'Thesis on Feuerbach', in *Collected Works*, Vol. 5, Lawrence & Wishart, London.

Marx, K. (1974), *The Jewish Question*, in *Collected Works*, Vol. 3, Lawrence and Wishart, London.

Marx, K. (1981), 'Excerpts: Jean-Baptiste Say - *Traité d'économie politique*', MEGA, Vol. IV.2, Dietz, Berlin.

Marx, K. (1982), 'Excerpts: David Ricardo - *Des principes de l'économie politique et de l'impôt*', MEGA, Vol. IV.2, Dietz, Berlin.

Marx, K. (1987), 'From the Preparatory Materials, Economic Works, 1857-61', in *Collected Works*, Vol. 29, Lawrence & Wishart, London.

Popitz, H. (1967), *Der entfremdete Mensch*, Europäische Verlagsanstalt, Frankfurt.

Porstmann, R. (1986), *Wissenschaftstheoretische Grundfragen*, Vol. I, Duncker und Humblot, Berlin.

Proudhon, P.J. (1971), *Was ist Eigentum*, Monte Verita, Vienna.

Scherf, H. (1986), *Marx und Keynes*, Suhrkamp, Frankfurt.

Simmel G. (1990), *The Philosophy of Money*, second edition, trans. T. Bottomore and D. Frisby, edited by D. Frisky, Routledge, London.

Sombart, W. (1967), *Die drei Nationalökonomien*, Duncker und Humblot, Berlin.

Streißler, E. and M. Streißler (1984), *Grundzüge der Volkswirtschaftslehre*, Manz, Vienna.

Weber, G. (1982), 'Das Geld', MEGA, Vol. I.2, Dietz, Berlin.

Weimann, J. (1982), *Die Funktion der normalen Wissenschaft in den Wirschaftswissenschaften*, Fakultät für Wirtschaftswissenschaften, Universität Bielefeld.

* The chapter is a revised version of my contribution to *Marx-Engels-Forschung heute 1*, Schriften der Marx-Engels-Stiftung, Neuss, 1989, pp.48-64; reprinted in H. G. Backhaus, *Dialektik der Wertform*, Ça ira, Freiburg, 1997 and 2004.

Translated from German by Werner Bonefeld

Chapter 3

Social Reality as Appearance: Some Notes on Marx's Conception of Reality

Helmut Reichelt

Introduction

Marx characterizes the commodity in *Capital* as a 'sensuous supersensible thing'. He rarely uses this formulation and its origin has hardly been investigated.[1] Georg Stamatis's (1999, p.235) contention that Marx refers here exclusively to Goethe's *Faust* does not appear sound. Marx's dissertation on the 'Difference between Democritean and Epikurean Natural Philosophy' offers a further clue, at least for those who know their Hegel. This clue is interesting not only for philological reasons. It also gives insights into the core concerns of Marx's method. In the fourth chapter of his dissertation, Marx discusses different natural philosophy conceptions and he emphasizes that 'Epikurus...grasps appearance as appearance' whereas Democritus, in contrast, argues that 'appearance does not by itself show that it is appearance, something different from essence' (Marx, 1841, p.64). Marx knew not only his Goethe but also his Hegel, including the 'most difficult section' (Liebruck, 1970, p.52) of the *Phenomenology of Spirit*, namely the third chapter 'Force and the Understanding: Appearance and the Supersensible World'.

Unique about Hegel's argument is that it amounts to nothing less than a fundamental renunciation and critique of occidental two-world theories, which go back to Plato. Hegel transcends Plato's supersensible world:

> The supersensible is therefore *appearance quâ appearance*. – We completely misunderstand this if we think that the supersensible world is *therefore* the sensuous world, or the world as it exists for immediate sense-certainty, or the world as it exists for immediate sense-certainty and perception, for the world of appearance is, on the contrary, *not* the world of sense-knowledge and perception as a world that positively *is*, but this world posited as superseded, or as in truth an *inner world* sensuous and the perceived posited as it is in truth. It is often said that the supersensible world is *not*

1 [Translator's Note: Marx uses this formulation twice in *Capital* (Marx, 1979, pp.85, 86); and once in his *Contribution to a Critique of Political Economy* (Marx, 1981, p.29). The English version of *Capital* translates it first as 'transcendent' and then as 'perceptible and imperceptible' (Marx, 1983a, pp.76,77), and the English version of his *Critique* translates it as 'an abstract thing' (Marx, 1971, p.42). I translated '*sinnlich übersinnlich*' in accordance with the English version of Hegel's *Phenomenology*, where '*übersinnlich*' is translated as supersensible.]

appearance; but what is here understood by appearance is not appearance, but rather the *sensuous* world as itself the really actual (Hegel, 1977, p.89).

In Hegel's conception, the complete separation between the sensuous world of appearance and the supersensible world of essence is gradually transcended in favour of a second supersensible world, which in its reality encompasses the sensuous world and contains within itself, while maintaining their difference, both the sensuous and the first supersensible world.

Crucial to Hegel's argumentation is the notion of the inverted world. He offers peculiar contrasting examples to illustrate the central significance of this new concept of appearance. One is reminded here of Adorno's *Three Studies about Hegel*, where he differentiates between the constellation of experience *of* Hegel's philosophy and the contents of experience *in* Hegel's philosophy (Adorno, 1971, p.300). Adorno focuses here on a central theme of materialist theory – the moment of categorical unconsciousness of theoretical endeavour itself. He thus interprets Hegel's philosophy in all its aspects as a reflective constellation of social objectivity. 'Of interest is not how Hegel subjectively arrived at this or that understanding but, and within Hegel's approach, how the coercive character of objective appearance is reflected and contained in his philosophy. What needs to be asked, thus, is what does his philosophy express as a philosophy' (ibid., p.296). 'The Hegelian self-reflection of the subject in philosophical consciousness is in truth the beginning of society's critical consciousness about itself' (ibid., p.313). Social theory must therefore – and this is what, according to Adorno, Marx's theory has achieved – translate Hegelian philosophy back into what Hegel 'had projected into the language of the absolute' (ibid., p.318).[2] Hegel is thus telling us more than he is conscious of. 'Using previous examples', he writes in the third chapter of the *Phenomenology*, 'what tastes sweet, is *really*, or *inwardly* in the thing, sour; or what is north pole in the actual magnet in the world of appearance, would be south pole in the *inner* or *essential being*' (Hegel, 1977, p.97). Even when read critically, these examples distract from the significance of the new conception of appearance. More significant, and indicatively taken from the sphere of sociality, is the example of punishing justice:

The *actual* crime, however, has *its inversion* and *its in-itself* as *possibility*, in the *intention* as such...But the crime, as regards its content, has its reflection-into-self or its inversion, in the *actual* punishment; this is the reconciliation of the law with the actuality opposed to it in the crime. Finally, the *actual* punishment has its *inverted* actuality present in it in such a way that the punishment is an actualization of the law (ibid., p.98).

---

[2] The same idea can be found in Adorno (1972, p.289): 'The idea of an objective system whose being is in-itself, is not such a chimera as it seemed after the fall of idealism and as positivism insists. The concept of a great philosophy...finds its justification not in the seemingly aesthetic qualities of its thought capacities, but in its contents of experience, which because of its transcendence in relation to individual human consciousness is enticed towards the hypothesization of Absolutes. Dialectic legitimizes itself by translating these contents back into the experience, whence it came'.

The revolutionary newness of Hegel's philosophy is that it conceives of reality as appearance, as an inverted world that is in-itself self-contradictory. Theodor Adorno touches on this when he, in the above quotation, posits society as 'objective appearance'. 'The supersensible world, which is the inverted world, has thus transcended the other world and contains it within itself; for itself as an inverted world, that is, inverted in and of itself; it is itself and its opposite in *their* unity' (Adorno, 1971, p.131).

Reality as an inverted world consists of the unity of two contradictory movements. Conceptions that are premised on the idea of being as stasis fail here; reality is a being that can only be grasped as a dynamic process: the essence, as Hegel later argued, must appear – however one must always add – it also hides itself in its appearance.

The Concept of Appearance in the Early Marx

Marx's interpretation of Epikur rests on this conception of appearance. In his view, Epikur was the first who understood 'appearance...as appearance, that is, as alienation of the essence, activating itself in its reality as such an alienation' (Marx, 1941, p.64). Marx inverts Hegel's own concept of appearance against him. Marx only outlined this in his dissertation, but it achieves constitutive significance in his critique of Hegel's theory of the state. Marx argues that rational reality does not amount to a dualism of opposing moments, but that (contemporary) reality is reason presenting itself in inverted form. This specific inversion of the concept of appearance is, however, in-formed by the changed understanding of human social activity in bourgeois society. The individual, he argues, does 'stand...in no sort of *real* relation to his material actions, to his *real standing*' (Marx, 1843, p.80).

> The present-day estate of society already shows...that it does not hold the individual as it formerly did as something communal, as a community, but that it is partly accident, partly the work and so on of the individual which does, or does not, keep him in his estate, an *estate* which is itself only an *external* quality of the individual, being neither inherent in his labour nor standing to him in fixed relationships as an objective community organized according to rigid laws (ibid.).

Although Marx here does not yet focus on classes, he nevertheless detects individualization as the decisive characteristic of class society. The notion 'external' intimates this; the labour of society remains 'external' to the individuals. In his economic writings, he describes this condition as 'personification of economic categories', or with the expression 'character-mask'. Essential here is that this 'externality' of social activity finds a corresponding expression in the political sphere: the general affairs of individuals are 'not *actually general*, and the actual, *empirical* matters of general concern are merely *formal*' (ibid., p.62). The externality of social activity in bourgeois society and its state (the institution that provides unity) amounts to a 'mere form'; they are two sides of the same thing. However, this thing is not conceived as pure facticity but as a Man made 'externality'.[3] It points to its constitutive opposite, and contains it within itself. Marx expresses this insight in the following terms: 'Democracy is the truth of monarchy; monarchy is not the truth of democracy. Monarchy is necessarily democracy inconsistent with itself...Monarchy cannot be understood in its own terms; democracy can' (ibid., p.29). 'Incidentally, it goes without saying that all forms of state have democracy *for* their truth and that they are therefore untrue insofar as they are not democracy' (ibid., p.31).[4] True democracy is synonymous with reason – a reasonable reality, which still has to be created, and in which the 'real individuals' will be in possession of themselves, self-consciously organising the social unity of their social existence. This is a most emphatic conception of democracy – there is *no autonomization* (*Veselbständigung*], that is, there is nothing that abstracts from the individuals, as if it were a thing apart. This is the specific characteristic of Marx's conception of democracy.

In contrast to all other forms of state in which a specific element of social existence has autonomized (*verselbständigt*] itself and, in this inversion, assumes power over individuals, the young Marx conceives of democracy as the return of all forms of autonomization, of all externality and inversion: 'Democracy is the solved *riddle* of all constitutions. Here, not merely *implicitly* and in essence but *existing* in reality, the constitution is constantly brought back to its actual basis, the *actual human being*, the *actual people*, and established as the people's *own* work. The constitution appears as what it is, a free product of Man' (ibid., p.29). Marx understands that the reality of bourgeois society consists in and through this specific movement of opposites, between self-determined activity and its independent appearance in the autonomized form of political power (*Herrschaft*). Reality *is* inversion, *is* appearance, in which reason, in its inverted forms of existence, subsists contradictorily through – estranged – forms of social unity. Marx orients himself on Rousseau when he contrasts democracy with other state-forms (monarchy, constitutional monarchy, republic). For him, radical democracy and political state are irreconcilable. The political state amounts to an autonomization and inversion of human social practice and he contrasts it with a form of society based on reason, which in all its specificity and peculiarity rests on and starts with the 'real people'.

> In monarchy, for example, this particular, the political constitution, has the significance of the *general* that dominates and determines everything particular. In democracy the state as particular is *merely particular*; as general, it is the truly general, i.e., not something determinate in distinction from the other content. The French have recently interpreted this as meaning that in true democracy the *political state is annihilated* (ibid., p.30).

[3] [Translator's Note: 'Man' with a capital 'M' is used here and throughout in the sense of *Mensch*. The English translation of Marx's texts often translates *Mensch* as 'man' and quotations have been adapted accordingly.]

[4] We find here the same critical inversion that can later be found in Adorno (1978, p.50): in opposition to Hegel's notion that the whole is true, he argues that 'the whole is untrue'.

This, then, is the background of Marx's critique of Hegel's theory of the state. Hegel, Marx states,

> is not to be blamed for depicting the nature of the modern state as it is, but for presenting that which is as the *nature of the state*. That the rational is actual is proved precisely in the *contradiction* of *irrational actuality*, which everywhere is the contrary of what it asserts, and asserts the contrary of what it is (ibid., p.63).

The young Marx agrees with Hegel's notion that reason exists. Yet, he questions whether reason is already real. He recognizes that Hegel 'correctly perceived' the state. But he criticizes Hegel for his uncritical positivism and also for 'mystifying' the different form-determinations (today we would say institutions) of the state. Why are mysticism and positivism the two corresponding aspects of Hegel's philosophy? In contrast to Hegel's intention, he does not posit social and political 'forms in relation to themselves', that is, in terms of the social content of their forms. Rather he charged that Hegel imparts his logical development of categories on these forms. For Marx, these forms of social and political reality are the forms of an 'unreasonable reality' (a reality that does not rest on reason). Yet, he does not deny that they are forms of reason; reason exists, but not in 'reasonable form'.

Marx's specific inversion of Hegel's concept of appearance accepts Hegel's critique of the two-world theory of occidental philosophy, that is, its dualist conception of essence and appearance. However, he accepts it only in relation to the inverted form of hitherto history. In the still to be achieved reality of reason, essence exists immediately, that is, there is no autonomization of society in relation to individuals.

> Similarly, democracy is the *essence of all state constitutions* – socialized man as a *particular* state constitution. Democracy stands to the other constitutions as the genus stands to its species, except that here the genus itself appears as an existent, and therefore as one *particular* species over against the others whose existence does not correspond to their essence...Man does not exist for the law but the law for man – it is a *human manifestation*; whereas in the other forms of state man is a *legal manifestation*. That is the fundamental distinction of democracy (ibid., p.30).

But how can this human reality, a reality of human-social reason, be conceived? Marx is only able to offer a 'mirror image' whose central elements are derived from autonomized (*verselbständigte*) social reality, in which social unity exists only in inverted form.

> In this situation the significance of the *legislative* power as a *representative* power completely disappears. The legislative power is representation here in the sense in which *every* function is representative – in the sense in which, e.g., the shoemaker, insofar as he satisfies a social need, is my representative, in which every particular social activity as a species-activity merely represents the species, i.e., an attribute of my own nature, and in which every person is the representative of every other. He is here representative not because of something else which he represents but because of what he *is* and *does* (ibid., p.119).

Despite all the differences between Marx's and Feuerbach's conceptions of materialism, they agree on one thing: their attempts to comprehend reality as an inversion, as an inverted form of human or social relations, rests on the assumption that the essence of that reality, the non-inverted unity, can be conceived independently from its forms of appearance. One can see this already in the structure of Feuerbach's *The Essence of Christianity*. The first chapter, 'The Essential Nature of Man', develops a semblance of 'human essence', which Marx characterizes concisely in his sixth thesis on Feuerbach as an 'internal, dumb generality which naturally unites the many individuals' (Marx, 1845, p.157).

> What, then, *is* the nature of man, of which he is conscious, or what constitutes the specific distinction, the proper humanity of man? Reason, Will, Affection...The divine trinity in man, above the individual man, is the unity of reason, love, will...[These] are not powers which man possesses, for he is nothing without them, he is what he is only by them; they are the constituent elements of his nature, which he neither has nor makes, the animating, determining, governing powers (Feuberbach, 1957, p.3).

This essence expresses itself in inverted form in religious consciousness – as forces of an omnipotent God. Human emancipation, for Feuerbach, is thus synonymous with the emancipation from religious consciousness, from Christian conceptions of God, which offer individualized Men a surrogate community that prevents them from creating their own, immediate social relations.

> Human forces particularize and develop themselves in the state, constituting, through this particularization and reconciliation, an infinite essence; many Men, many forces are one force. The state is the embodiment of all reality...Within the state, one represents the other, one complements the other...The state is only Man – the state that determines itself, relates to itself, the *absolute Man* (Feuberbach, 1975, p.233).

According to the young Marx, Feuerbach's conception is only the first step. The critique of religion has to be followed by the critique of the state (which Marx performs in the above outline of his critique of Hegel), and then the critique of economics. Here too, he elaborates opposite movements within and of the same processes of a social unity. Active doing is dualistic within itself. Social activity develops a countermovement against itself *uno actu* (within the one act).

Marx, thus, criticizes economic science in the same way as he had previously criticized Hegel: it cannot be blamed for describing the essence of modern economics. It can, however, be criticized for positing this economics as the essence of labour. It knows only the one economic side of the matter and posits it, like Hegel posits the modern state, as fact without recognising the social constitution of that facticity.

> Political Economy starts with the fact of private property; it does not explain it to us. It expresses in general, abstract formulas the *material* process through which private property actually passes, and these formulas it then takes for *laws*. It does not *comprehend* these laws, i.e., it does not demonstrate how they arise from the very nature of private property (Marx, 1959, p.61).

As Hegel's absolutized the form of the modern the state, that is, proceeded not from conceptualized forms, but from the assumption that these are absolutes, facts. It thus presumed individual laws of behaviour as given forms of activity of an equally absolute conception of subjectivity – like for example Adam Smith's propensity towards barter.

> Political economy throws no light on the cause of the division between labour and capital, and between capital and land. When, for example, it defines the relationship of wages to profit, it takes the interest of capitalists to be the ultimate cause, i.e., it takes for granted what it is supposed to explain (ibid., pp.61-2).

Like Hegel, the economists presuppose existing forms, treat them as analytical objects, without conceptualising their determinate form. Marx argues against this logic of presupposition and is adamant that understanding entails, emphatically, the conceptualization of the genesis of these forms themselves – forms of estrangements, forms which are external to individuals as individuals; traditional science is unable to conceive the genesis of forms.

However, does Marx meet his own standard of critique? Marx describes an inverted world, whose apex is the mode of existence of the worker, in every aspect of his existence that this inversion entails. Each single characteristic of the existence of the worker points towards this opposite movement and he recounts this in criss-crossing terms:

> The worker becomes all the poorer the more wealth he produces...The worker becomes an ever cheaper commodity the more commodities he creates. The *devaluation* of the world of men is in direct proportion to the *increasing value* of the world of things.

This means in turn nothing else than that the product of labour 'confronts it as *something alien*, as a *power independent* of the producer'. The product of labour is labour which has been objectified in a thing:

> it is the *objectification* of labour. Labour's realization is its objectification. Under these economic conditions this realization of labour appears as *loss of realization* for the worker; objectification as *loss of the object and bondage to it*; appropriation as *estrangement, as alienation* (ibid., pp.62-3).

Like his explicit reference to Feuerbach's critique of religion in his critique of Hegel, so too in the section about 'estranged labour' in the *Paris Manuscripts*.

> It is the same in religion. The more man puts into god, the less he retains in himself. The worker puts his life into the object, but now his life no longer belongs to him but to the object...[T]he greater his activity, the more the worker lacks objects (ibid., p.63).

There is no need here to repeat all the facets of Marx's description of the workers' existence. The pattern of the argument remains the same: we are dealing with an inverted world in which active human practice creates its own opposite world. Active human practice subsists in and through an existing contradiction, which appears in the form of an – autonomized – immediate social unity. We are thus dealing with a world in which essence – social purposeful practice, the unity of species being – exists in inverted forms: as objective appearance.

Like in Feuberbach's *Essence of Christianity* and in Marx's critique of Hegel's *Philosophy of Right*, Marx seeks here, too, to describe essence in abstraction from its inverted form of existence. Yet, here too, Marx is only able to develop a mirror image of what emancipated Man, emancipated from his alienated, inverted world, might mean. Characteristically, this happens in the sections *Private Property and Communism* and *Human Requirements and Division of Labour under the Rule of Private Property* – and also in the 'Excerpts of Mill's *Elements of Political Economy*'. At the end of the *Paris Manuscripts*, Marx refers, like Hegel, explicitly to an inverted world.

> Since money, as the existing and active concept of value, confounds and confuses all things, it is the general confounding and confusion of all things – the world *upside-down*, the confounding and confusion of all natural and human qualities (ibid., p.124).

The human essence, the unity of the individual with its species being, exists in inverted form, which has to be eliminated through revolutionary praxis. Only then will individuals be able to relate to each other as individuals.

> Assume *Man* to be *Man* and his relationship to the world to be a human one: then you can exchange love only for love, trust for trust, etc...Every one of your relations to Man and to nature must be a *specific expression*, corresponding to the object of your will, of your *real individual* life (ibid., p.124).

It is often argued (see for example Althusser) that this philosophical argument of the young Marx fails to meet stringent scientific criteria. It is indeed the case, at least in this open, direct form, that the later works are no longer oriented on Hegel's conception of appearance, in which two opposite movements depend on each other in their duality, where each is 'contained' in the other. However, does this really mean that he abandoned the (earlier) conception? In the *German Ideology*, which is argued in pointedly non-philosophical terms, its basic conception is summarized succinctly in the last section of the chapter on Feuerbach: 'The reality, which communism is creating, is precisely the true basis for rendering it impossible that anything should exist independently of individuals, insofar as reality is only a product of the preceding intercourse of individuals themselves' (Marx and Engels, 1974, p.86). In addition, the basic issue of the materialist conception of history, the so-called dialectics between the forces of production and the relations of production, only repeats in different words those same thoughts of the *Paris Manuscripts*.[5]

[5] An explication of this thesis would go far beyond the remit of this essay.

The Inverted World of Capital

Marx's first account of the materialist conception of history is also raised in the Critique of Political Economy. I have already alluded to Marx's characterization of the commodity as a 'sensuous supersensible thing'. In my view, Marx here deploys Hegel's conceptualizations of the third chapter of the *Phenomenology of Spirit*. Marx introduces the commodity as an immediate unity of use-value and value, as a unity of sensuous-concreteness and of abstractness. The abstract exists objectively in the commodity, as the objectivity of value, as 'coagulate' or 'crystallization' of abstract human labour. This unity between the sensuous and supersensible that itself exists objectively, corresponds with Hegel's conception of a second supersensible world that contains both. What needs to be pointed out here, is that this first introduction of the commodity as an 'in-itself of money', as Engels put in a lucid formulation, amounts to a static observation (at the end of the first chapter of his *Critique* and in the first edition of *Capital* Marx mentions that he treated the commodity analytically. I will return to this later). The dualism of two moments that mutually presuppose each other can neither be defined statically nor in terms of its substance, but only as movement. Only when value is developed as value in movement, can the unity of its forms be conceptualized, as it is the case with Hegel's conception of law: 'The law is what remains in disappearance' (Gadamer, 1976, p.42).

Abstract General Labour and the Commensurability of Commodities

The conception of the second supersensible world offers a new conception of reality as well as a genuine conception of law in the social sciences. However, before we focus on this second supersensible world as the 'actual' reality of the modern world, let us look at the 'supersensible' moment of the commodity, of value. The way in which Marx introduces value in *Capital* has time and time again provoked critique, already during his life.[6] Marx's indignant reaction shows clearly that he was by and large aware that his introduction of the concept of value was methodologically not without problems, and possibly even cast doubt on his conception of value itself. Importantly, the purpose of this first chapter of *Capital* is to thematize value in order to resolve the famous problem of commensurability, and therewith the macro-economic aggregation of all products to a social product. The central significance of this is not very clear from the first pages of *Capital*, where he argues that

> exchange-value, at first sight, presents itself as a quantitative relation, as the proportion in which values in use of one sort are exchanged for those of another sort, a relation constantly changing with time and place. Hence exchange-value appears to be something accidental and purely relative, and consequently an intrinsic value, i.e. an exchange value that is inseparably connected with, inherent in commodities, seems a contradiction in terms (Marx, 1983a, p.44).

---

[6] Cf Marx's letter to Ludwig Kugelmann of July 11 1868 (McLennan, 1977, pp.524-25).

However, if value were to amount only to exchange value, and as such were no more than relative in nature, opposite to use-value, then value would be subsumed (*aufgehoben*) in the aggregate sum of the social product. Marx develops this thought in his critique of Charles Ganilh's work, who in spite of his correct understanding of the nature of value falls back on to

> the crudest conception: that exchange value is the proportion in which commodity A exchanges against commodity B, C, D, etc. A has great exchange-value if much B, C, D is given for it; but then little A is given for B, C, D. Wealth consists of exchange-value. Exchange-value consists of the relative proportion in which products exchange for each other. The total quantity of products has therefore no exchange-value, since it is not exchanged for anything. Hence, society, whose wealth consists of exchange-values, has no wealth. Consequently it follows not only, as Ganilh himself concludes, that the "national wealth, which is composed of exchange-values of labour", can never rise and can never fall in exchange-value (therefore there is *no surplus-value*), but that it has no exchange-value whatever, and so is not wealth, since wealth consists only of exchangeable values (Marx, 1976, p.208).

The philosopher Klaus Hartmann surprisingly made the same discovery in his voluminous book about Marx. As he puts it:

> If exchange value would be the only economic conception of value, then it would be posed only as a relational concept, a mediating category, of acts of exchange. One could then not add exchange values and would thus not be able to come up with a total value. This however is said to be possible in as much as Marx intends to show the accumulation of value, and money and capital, and later goes on to provide macro-economic accounts (Hartmann, 1970, p.269).

Hartmann focuses the problem concisely. The resolution can only be an absolute value and he charges that Marx re-interprets relative exchange value to absolute value, that is, Marx engages in a 'deception' (ibid.).

The wealth of bourgeois society has a double character: a mass of a multitude of use-values that as homogenous abstract quantities can at the same time be aggregated into a social product: the many stand opposed to the one that is both identical and not-identical with them. How can this be conceived? Economic theory has still not solved this issue. It still asks how this 'dimensional equality' comes about, how the 'commensurability' of the many use-values is accomplished. Marx, however, develops a different line of enquiry. The products are commodities and as commodities, they comprise an immediate unity between the specificity, concrete, sensuous, and the abstract, supersensible. Although Marx had early on recognized this unity, it was only in *Capital* that he believed that he found its resolution – the unity is to be traced back to the double character of labour, which he characterized as the 'whole secret of critical understanding'.[7]

---

[7] Cf. Schrader (1980, esp. p.202 ff). Schrader argues that Marx only developed the concept of abstract labour when working on Benjamin Franklin. What is important is not that he traces back (*zurückführen*) the values of commodities to 'labour sans phrase', as it was still the case in the *Grundrisse* but the fact that products of 'qualitatively different real labours'

There is no need here to review the debate about the concept of abstract-human labour as the substance of value. The critique of substantialist conceptions of value is in my view correct and that means, the concept of general labour has to be determined differently (cf. Reichelt, 2002). The whole discussion about value has never raised the question whether Marx's conception of the substance of value might in fact not rest on the specific conception of appearance of his early work. Value, this supersensible moment of the commodity, is said to be the result of 'speaking physiologically, an expenditure of human labour-power', of labour which creates value by virtue of 'its character of identical abstract human labour' (Marx, 1983a, p.53), which – characterized as a 'crystallization' or 'coagulation' – exists in the mode of being denied and thus is 'invisible' (Marx, 1987b, p.820) in commodities, and which then 'appears' in exchange. Might it not be that the early conception of essence is repeated here, and that he therewith pointed the theoretical construction into a direction that had such disastrous consequences for the reception of *Capital*? Marx's characterization of classical political economy reveals an important methodological insight. He accepts that it

> has indeed analysed, however incompletely, value and its magnitude, and has discovered what lies beneath these forms. But it never asked the question why this content assumes that form, why labour is represented by the value of its produced and labour-time by the magnitude of that value (Marx, 1983a, pp.84-5).[8]

This formulation implies that the content, which appears in this form, can also be conceived in separation from its form of appearance. The quoted passage can be found in the famous section on fetishism, where he presents many examples that describe the content of this form. Here he explains the function of value and the magnitude of value in bourgeois society through 'mirror images' where the content appears in inverted forms. Especially two examples – the description of Robinson's 'island bathed in light', and the 'association of free individuals', who work with communal means of production and whose 'labour power...is *consciously* applied as the combined labour-power of *the* community', are helpful. They clearly illustrate his basic conception of the value form: 'all the characteristics of Robinson's labour are here repeated, but with this difference, that they are social, instead of individual' (ibid., pp.81, 83).

Already the choice of words indicates that we are dealing here with those same notions that we know from the early work: self-conscious social unity versus inverted and autonomized forms of social existence. Value takes the place of the absent self-conscious subjects who recognize themselves in and through their collective social labour and organize their needs and the development of their productive forces in distinct areas of production.

---

confront each other in exchange. Their value however is estimated through 'abstract labour' 'The analysis of the Franklin excerpts led Marx to the discovery that the word labour was used in the double sense, and this amounts to nothing less than the discovery of the double character of labour embodied in the commodity' (p.203).

[8] [Translator's Note: The English edition of *Capital* excludes 'why this content assumes that form', see the German edition (Marx, 1979, p.95).]

> We will assume, but merely for the sake of a parallel with the production of commodities, that the share of each individual producer in the means of subsistence is determined by his labour-time. Labour-time would, in that case, play a double part. Its apportionment in accordance with a definite social plan maintains the proper proportion between the different kinds of work to be done and the various wants of community. On the other hand, it also serves as a measure of the portion of the common labour borne by each individual, and of his share in the part of the total product destined for individual consumption. The social relations of the individual producers, with regard both to their labour relations and to its products, are in this case perfectly simple and intelligible, and that with regard not only to production but also to distribution (ibid., p.83).[9]

Marx's Robinson example develops the same insight and argues that all essential determinations of value are there and that 'all the relations between Robinson and the objects that form this wealth of his own creation, are here so simple and clear as to be intelligible without exertion, even to Mr. Sedley Taylor' (ibid., p.81).

Are, however, all 'essential determinations of value' really posed? What about the most essential of these determinations – abstract-human labour? No corresponding utterances can be found, apart from a short note which touches upon the interrelation between abstract labour as the substance of labour and the self-conscious social unity of labour in Robinson or the association of free men: 'In spite of the variety of his work, he knows that his labour, whatever its form, is but the activity of one and the same Robinson, and consequently, that it consists of nothing but different modes of human labour' (ibid.). The social unity of labour, its 'general character', that which is 'common' to all productive functions, is intrinsic to the products of labour. But might Robinson be able to determine this generality more precisely? Would he describe that which is 'common to all' products of labour as 'productive expenditure of human brains, nerves and muscle' (ibid., p.51), a generality which is expressed in the concrete labour process only in and through its immediate unity with specific tasks?

According to Marx, generality exists 'invisibly' in the commodity in the form of an immediate unity between use-value and value. It exists thus as the 'ghostlike objectivity of value', in which 'all sensuous aspects are eliminated' (Marx, 1987b, p.823). This unity is thus, as it were, posited for itself when the products of labour are equalized in the exchange process and when it finally is constituted in the form of money. The entire further exposition in *Capital* rests on this conception of value. In this exposition two forms of thought have to be differentiated: the development of the relationship between value and money in the first chapter, and the further development of all other categories, that is, the different functions of money, then capital and profit, the category of rent, wage-labour, etc. Methodological discussions of Marx's dialectics have almost exclusively focused on the first chapter of *Capital*. There are hardly any attempts to show in detail the dialectical

---

[9] The same thought can be found in the above-mentioned letter to Ludwig Kugelmann, see footnote 6.

development of other categories.[10] Marx himself obscured his dialectical method in *Capital*. After the publication of his *Contribution to a Critique of Political Economy*, he mentioned in a letter to Engels that he intended to hide his method even more[11] in the next edition of his study.[12] One has therefore to assume that his method is 'not hidden' in two of his previous studies, the *Grundrisse* and the *Urtext*. He also notes in the Preface to *Capital* (Marx, 1983a, p.18), that his exposition is much improved in relation especially to the first chapter of *Capital*. This then encouraged many commentators to argue that the study of Marx's materialist dialectics in *Capital* has to be based on this first chapter.

What, however, is the connection between this first chapter and those that follow? Marx expunged a most important reference to his methodology in the second edition of *Capital*. This reference can be found in his *Critique* and in the first edition of *Capital* at the end of the first chapter:

> [t]he commodity is the immediate unity of use-value and exchange-value, that is, of two opposites. It is therefore an immediate contradiction. This contradiction has to develop itself as soon as the commodity is no longer analysed now in the use-value perspective, then in the exchange-value perspective, but when the commodity as a whole is posited to other commodities (Marx, 1983b, p.51).

By deleting this sentence, Marx not only obscured the connection between the chapters, but he also eliminated an important reference, namely that he treats the commodity analytically in the first chapter.

There is thus a dilemma: where the 'exposition [is] improved' (in relation to his *Critique* of 1859), the treatment is characterized as analytical; and where the method is 'hidden', a developed conception of value as the presupposition of the complete exposition of all other categories is missing. In my view, it is because of this dilemma that the discussion of Marx's method, in as much as it was oriented on Engels' differentiation between the logical and the historical, has exclusively been focused on the first chapter. Here too, however and yet again only in the first edition of *Capital*, we find an important methodological statement. At the end of the development of the value form, Marx writes that it was of 'decisive importance...to reveal the internal, necessary connection between the value*form*, value*substance* and value*magnitude*, that is, expressed in ideal terms, to show that the value*form* arises from the *concept* of value' (ibid., p.43). It must be remembered that Marx understood his method as a mode of proof (*Beweisführung*) that reproduces the internal, necessary connection of its subject-matter in

---

[10] As far as I am aware my Ph.D thesis, published in the 1970s (Reichelt, 1970), is the only study that at least attempted a detailed discussion of this 'dialectical development of categories'.

[11] 'My writing is progressing, but slowly. Circumstances being what they are, there was, indeed, little possibility of bringing such theoretical matters to a rapid close. However, the thing is assuming a much more popular form, and the method is much less in evidence than in Part I' (Marx, 1861, p.333). For an assessment on Marx's hidden method, see Reichelt (1995).

[12] At that time Marx was following an alternative development of his work.

theoretical terms. The starting point is thus the concept of value which is the foundation of the further explication. For the form of value results from a theoretical operation, which he characterizes briefly in the appendix 'The Value Form':[13] 'Only on the basis of its general character does the value form correspond with the concept of value' (ibid., p.634). He has thus to find a form that is identical in its generality with the generality of the concept of value. Although he does not emphasize here anymore that the form of value arises from the concept of value, the context of his discussion does make it clear that the form of value presupposes the concept of value. Because this discussion often speaks of 'further development', namely from the simple undeveloped form to the developed form ('the specific equivalent form is now further developed towards a general equivalent form' (ibid., p.644)) and because an 'internal necessary unity' is presupposed, 'derivation' became the accepted model of the dialectical method.

The specific concept of value is always presupposed just as the real value is presupposed as 'objectification', as 'material substance', as 'crystallization' of abstract human labour.

> [T]he value of a commodity represents human labour in the abstract, the expenditure of human labour in general...It is the expenditure of simple labour-power, i.e., of the labour -power which, on average, apart from any special development, exists in the organism of every ordinary individual...Skilled labour counts only as simple labour intensified, or rather, as multiplied simple labour, a given quantity of skilled being considered equal to a greater quantity of simple labour (Marx, 1983a, p.51).

The theoretical construction works only on the basis of this premise.

The Conception of Dialectics in the 'Grundrisse'

In the *Grundrisse*, the concept of value is not yet developed and the method not yet hidden. This work is different from all following published versions of his critique of economics because of its conceptual differentiation between exchange value positing relations and exchange value creating labour. Exchange value positing relations is used synonymous with simple circulation – an expression, which can still be found occasionally in the *Critique* but which then disappears. Further, the expression exchange value creating labour can only be found on a few occasions. Corresponding to these expressions is the differentiation between abstract labour as having become historically 'true in practice' (Marx, 1973, p.105), and a 'theoretical truth of labour', which Marx employs as a counter-concept but which he only mentions briefly once:

> Here it can be seen once again that the particular specificity of the relation of production, of the category – here, capital and labour – becomes *real* only with the development of a particular material mode of production...This point in general to be particularly developed in connection with this relation, later; since it is here already

[13] Marx wrote this appendix following advice from his friend Ludwig Kugelmann. Cf. Afterword to the second edition of *Capital* (Marx, 1983a, p.22).

> posited in relation itself, while, in the case of the abstract concepts, exchange value, circulation, money, it still lies ***more in our subjective reflection*** (ibid., p.297; emphases HR).

The concept of the exchange value positing relations or simple circulation is not again used in his later work. It encapsulates a double meaning or its double meaning is revealed in the context of his hastily developed exposition in the *Grundrisse*: on the one hand, 'exchange value positing relations' is understood in a historical context but not in the crude sense of an historical description that was canonized, following Engels' unfortunate formulation, in the orthodox tradition as the relationship between the logical and the historical. Rather, it should be seen as a concept that interlocks the logic of development and the dynamic of development, though Marx did not develop this explicitly. On the other hand, Marx ties the category of simple accumulation to the 'surface' of the capitalist production process – the sphere of appearance.

The presentation of 'simple circulation' also starts with value, but the connection between labour, labour-time, value and money is not shown.[14] The chapter deals mainly with the development of the first categories of political economy and shows their internal connections. The actual development of categories begins with the form of money. 'To develop the concept of capital it is necessary to begin not with labour but with value, and, precisely, with exchange value in an already developed movement of circulation' (ibid., p.259). In simple circulation, exchange value positing relations constitute the categories as different forms of autonomized value or as different modes of movement of the autonomized and ever more autonomized forms of exchange value – thus the formulation *exchange value positing relations*. Exchange value, as money, expresses itself in simple exchange as a 'transient form' (Marx, 1987a, p.432), and it achieves – in its third determination, which Marx conceives of as the unity of the first two functions, that is, price-form and means of circulation, its first reified independence, as treasure and metallic form of money. Only now does the actual 'movement of value' start – as expansion of the magnitude of value. Its movement constitutes itself through a contradiction: the third determination of money, its absolute form, stands in contradiction to its quantitative limitation. Exchange value seeks to come close to the absolute form of money, the absolute form of wealth, through sheer quantitative expansion – a never-ending process. In this third determination,

> money is also negated in the aspect in which it is merely the *measure* of exchange values. As the general form of wealth and as its material representative, it is no longer the ideal measure of things, of exchange values. For it is itself the adequate reality of exchange value, and this it is in its metallic being. Here the character of measure has to be posited in it. It is its own unity; and the measure of its value, the measure of itself as wealth, as exchange value, is the quantity of itself which it represents (Marx, 1973, p.229).

---

[14] Marx added the heading 'II, The chapter on money' to the existing first chapter. The first chapter was to be written later.

Marx enquires about the potential form through which this bad-infinite process might develop and finds it in the unity of two forms of movement within the circulation process. The eternal process of expanding value develops through the constant change of form between commodity and money, the specific form and the general form of exchange value. 'Its entry into circulation must itself be a moment of its stay-by-itself, and its stay-by-itself, entry into circulation' (Marx, 1987a, p.491). Value – arising from circulation – is maintained only, and so subsists through a constant change of form. 'The intransience for which money strives as it negatively sets itself with respect to circulation (by withdrawing itself from it) is acquired by capital in that it preserves itself precisely by giving itself up to circulation (ibid., p.497). Marx arrives here at the concept of capital, although only at the most abstract concept of capital, developed as the movement of value, that at this point is nothing more than a name: 'If we speak here of capital, this is still only a name' (Marx, 1973, p.262).

These few quotations already show the closeness of Marx's argument to Hegel's philosophy. Marx orients his first great exposition of *Capital* on Hegel's logic. It is also clear that we are dealing here not with an external application of Hegelian thought. Rather, Marx develops a language that corresponds to the specificity of its subject-matter, whose being can be thought no longer in terms of a substance but only as a process: being as movement. This movement persists through a constant change between the general form (the money form) and the specific form (the specific commodity). Both, however, are forms of value. Value is 'self-perpetuating' (*verewigen*) (Marx, 1987a, p. 498) through its constant change of forms. 'It exists in the form of the *objectivity* [*Gegenständlichkeit*], but it is indifferent to whether it is the objectivity of the money or the commodity' (ibid., p.939).[15] The sensuous object is here demoted to something that constantly vanishes. The objectivity of the general, the supersensible, is thus a vanishing objectivity. What Marx seems to establish here is commensurate with Plato's world of ideas, something that is unchangeable, eternal. Marx's argument makes this reference to Plato clear. However, this separation cannot to be presupposed as an absolute as if it were an essence apart. In this regard Marx does indeed adopt Hegel's critique of the occidental two-world theory. Rather than separating the world into a never changing eternal condition, the general, and the concrete, sensuous world, he conceptualizes this separation as a contradictory unity of a 'second supersensible world', in which the sensuous world and the first supersensible world are subsumed (*aufgehoben*). Capital is thus conceived as a constant change of forms, into which use-value is constantly both integrated and expelled. In this process, use-value, too, assumes the form of an eternally vanishing object. But this constantly renewed disappearance of the object is the condition for the perpetuation of value itself – it is through the always reproduced change of forms that the immediate unity between value and use-value is retained. What is thus constituted is an inverted world, in which sensuousness in the widest sense –

15 Cf. also his excerpt of Sismodi's work: 'Value tears itself loose from the commodity which created it; like a metaphysical, insubstantial quality, it always remained in the possession of the same *cultivateurs* (here irrelevant: say *owner*), for whom it cloaked itself in different forms' (Marx, 1973, p.261).

as use-value, labour, exchange with nature – is demoted to a means of the self-perpetuation of an abstract process that underlies the whole objective world of constant change.

> When money becomes a commodity, and commodity as such is necessarily consumed as use-value and must disappear, this disappearance must itself disappear, this annihilation must annihilate itself, so that the consumption of the commodity as use value itself appears as a moment of the process of the self-reproducing value (ibid., p.497).[16]

The most abstract concept of capital is therefore at the same time the first concretization of Hegel's concept of appearance, and appearance is nothing but appearance – 'appearance quâ appearance'. The whole sensuous world of human beings who reproduce themselves through the satisfaction of needs and labour is step-by-step sucked into this process, in which all activities are 'in themselves inverted'. They are all, in their vanishing appearance, immediately their own opposite: the persistence of the general. The most easily remembered formulation is Gadamer's: 'The law is what remains in disappearance'. This formulation also characterizes Marx's concept of capital, whose further conceptual development retains this processual unity through this dynamic.

> The exact development of the concept of capital [is] necessary, since it [is] the fundamental concept of modern economics, just as capital itself, whose abstract, reflected image [is] its concept [*dessen abstraktes Gegenbild sein Begriff*], [is] the foundation of bourgeois society. The sharp formulation of the basic presupposition of the relation must bring out all the contradictions of bourgeois production, as well as the boundary where it drives beyond itself (Marx, 1973, p.331).

Karl Marx, as was argued above, popularized his method and eliminated step-by-step all references to his methodology. Why might this have been so? Was it because his conception of dialectics was unclear, as Adorno (1972, p.306) suggests? In any case, it is noteworthy that Marx developed his dialectical exposition of categories without a precise conception of value. It is also noteworthy that the dialectical exposition of categories – that is, the methodological display of the reality of an inverted world as a second supersensible world which contains the sensuous and the first supersensible world – is not possible without a concept of value. This concept presumes the reality of a sensuous generality, which can also be added up as an abstract quantity. The characterization of the commodity as a sensuous supersensible thing presumes the supersensibility of reality; a universal *in re* (in the thing), as the scholastics would have said. In this context, Theodor Adorno speaks about 'objective conceptuality' – without doubt, this was inspired

[16] This conception has to inform the different determinations of capital. The usual definition of fixed capital as the used up material component of the production process reproduces the two-world theory in economic theory: the ostensibly real economy is contrasted with the symbolic world. Marx, however, develops fixed capital as a specific form of circulation. Capital, which retains itself in the change of forms, that is, a circulating thing, is fixed in the production process and circulates, as it were, in 'portions'. Capital is in itself differentiated into two different forms of circulation.

by Alfred Sohn-Rethel in the 1930s. The differentiation is thus expressly that between a reality of an abstraction, an 'objective conceptuality', and the 'conceptuality' of the subjects themselves, who carry this process out. 'Those who perceive conceptuality as a social reality do not have to be afraid of the allegation of idealism. What is at issue here is both, the constitutive conceptuality of the recognising subjects as a conceptuality that exists in the thing itself' (Adorno, 1971, p.209). Like Sohn-Rethel who first advanced the notion of real abstraction (*Realabstraktion*), Adorno merely offers implied postulates. According to him, this 'objective conceptuality' can be traced back to the abstraction of exchange. Yet, it remains a puzzle as to how subjective activity should generate an objective conceptuality.

Exchange Abstraction and Objective Conceptuality. Marx's Concept of Validity

In *Capital*, Marx had the following to say about the act of exchange abstraction:

> whenever, by an exchange, we equate as values our different products, by that very act, we also equate, as human labour, the different kinds of labour expended upon them. We are not aware of this, nevertheless we do it (Marx, 1983a, pp.78-9).

Many have commented that this sentence is unclear. Indeed, it allows for two equally possible interpretations: does abstract human labour constitute itself only in the act of exchange, when individuals posit their products as values, or does this abstract equality 'appear' in the exchange process as something that has already been posited in the production process? Whatever the answer, Marx's conception of this process of abstraction is significant. The concept of value – the world of commodities as an 'invisible' 'coagulate', as a 'crystallization' of abstract human labour as the substance of value – is the concept of a real abstract quantity. Marx therefore talks about value-abstraction: 'If we say that, as values, commodities are mere coagulates of human labour, we reduce them by our analysis, it is true, to the abstraction, value: but we ascribe to this value no form apart from their bodily form' (ibid., p.57). This abstraction is thus the comprehended (*begriffene*) substance of value. Marx – in his own self-understanding – brings to the fore that process of abstraction which individuals carry out in the exchange process, without being conscious of it. He thus appears to presuppose that individuals carry out this process of reduction that is entailed in the equalization of their products, and that they do so in analogy of that process of abstraction which he himself performs.

Just as in nominalism, Marx can only conceive of this process in conventional terms: positing the abstract by 'abstracting' from all diversity and concreteness.

> The equalization of the most different kinds of labour can be the result only of an abstraction from their inequalities, or of *reducing* them to their common denominator, viz., expenditure of human labour-power or human labour in the abstract. The two-fold social character of the labour of the individual appears to him, when reflected in his brain, only under those forms which are impressed upon that labour in every-day practice by the exchange of products. In this way, the character that his own labour possesses of being socially useful takes the form of the conditions, that the product must be not only useful, but useful for others, and the social character that his particular

> labour has of being the equal of all other *particular kinds of labour*, takes the form that all the physically different articles that are the products of labour, have one common quality, viz., that of having value (ibid., p.78; emphases HR).

Marx uses two formulations: he speaks of a 'reduction' to its common character, and a bit later of 'particular kinds of labour'. It does not seem to occur to him that he is dealing here, in the Hegelian sense, with an 'understandable abstraction' of the kind that nominalism construes as an idealtype. By abstracting from diverse concrete circumstances, 'reduction' brings to the fore that which is 'common to all', the universal. Marx attributes this mode of abstraction to Benjamin Franklin's value theory:

> From the outset Franklin regards labour-time from a restricted economic standpoint as the measure of value. The transformation of actual products into exchange-values is taken for granted, and it is therefore only a question of discovering a measure of their value. To quote Franklin...'Trade in general being nothing else but the exchange of labour for labour, the value of things is...most justly measured by labour'. If in this sentence the term labour is replaced by concrete labour, it is at once obvious that labour in one form is being confused with labour in another form. Because trade may, for example, consist in the exchange of the labour of a shoemaker, miner, spinner, painter and so on, is therefore the labour of the painter the best measure of the value of shoes? Franklin, on the contrary, considers that the value of shows, minerals, yarn, painting etc., is determined by abstract labour which has no particular quality and can thus be measured only in terms of quantity (Marx, 1971, p.56).

In the excerpt that underlies this argument, Marx summarizes Franklin's argument in the following terms: 'Franklin...said earlier that the value of things is assessed by labour time. Through the labour of the decorator?...No. Or the labour of the shoemaker? Neither. Ergo through abstract labour, which is neither the one nor the other' (cited in Schrader, 1980, p.202).[17] The last sentence is decisive. Marx interpreted Franklin's method as a reduction that extracts in one-dimensional terms the universal from the many; the universal as abstraction. Marx's choice of words indicates that he has yet another conception of the universal, namely not only as abstractions but, also, as totality. See for example his introduction to the *Grundrisse*. 'It was an immense step forward for Adam Smith to throw out every limiting specification of wealth-creating activity – not only manufacturing, or commercial or agricultural labour, but one as well as the others, labour in general' (Marx, 1973, p.104). Like Hegel's determination of the universal, this, too, is the characterization of a dialectic universal, as a processual unity of abstraction and

---

[17] Schrader sees this excerpt as the original document on the double character of labour, see footnote 7.

totality.[18] In the *Grundrisse*, Marx characterizes the third determination of money as such a universal.[19]

The understanding of labour as totality and abstraction amounts to a dialectical conception of labour, and the Robinson example of the fetish section of *Capital* would have to be interpreted in this way. The question that was earlier posed, namely how Robinson would determine his labour detached from the many specific concrete activities, would be answered satisfactorily with this 'definition'. It is his own labour as general labour that, to use Hegel's words, is 'neither This nor That, a *not-This*, and is with equal indifference This as well as That.

But how can this general labour be conceived of as a real universal, as supersensibility, which exists in the commodity as its 'invisible' substance? Marx offers no specification. This is because he conceives this universal in naively realist terms as something that exists independently from human thought within the product itself, and that is exclusively created by human labour: an objectivity of abstract human labour. This objectivity can under no circumstances be conceived as a 'thing of thought'.

> As value, the linen consists *only* of labour, creating a transparent crystallization of congealed labour. In reality, this crystal is however very cloudy. In as much as labour can be discovered in it,...it is not undifferentiated human labour, but weaving, spinning etc., which does not create its substance. Rather it is combined with natural materials. In order to determine a linen as a merely reified expression of human labour, one has to leave everything aside that really makes it a thing. *The objectivity of human labour, which itself is abstract, without additional quality and content, is necessarily abstract objectivity, a* ***thing of thought****. In this way, flax transforms into a fantasy. However* ***commodities are things****. What they are they have to show in their own material [sachlich] relations.* In the production process of the linen, a definite quantity of human labour power *is* expended. The *value* of the linen as is a mere *objective reflection* of the thus expended labour, but is not reflected in its body. The value of the linen is *revealed*, attains sensuous expressions in its *value relation* to the skirt. By positing its value equal to itself, although at the same time different from it as a *thing for use*, the skirt becomes the *form of appearance* of the linen-*value*, its value-*form* in contrast to its *natural form* (Marx, 1983b, p.30; bold emphases HR).

Marx can obviously conceive of labour as the substance of value only by means of a direct separation between human reflective power and the objectivity of abstract human labour. Contrary to Adorno's view, Marx seems to exclude, right from the start, any attempt at combining the constitutive conceptuality of the subject with that universality which 'resides in things'. Yet, Marx offers many suggestions as to how that might be done.

---

18 'A simple thing of this kind which *is* through negation, which is neither This nor That, a *not-This*, and is with equal indifference This as well as That - such a thing we call a *universal* (Hegel, 1977, p.60).

19 'With money, general wealth is not only a form, but at the same time the content itself. The *concept* of wealth, so to speak, is realized, *individualized* in a particular object...In money...the price is realized; and its substance is wealth itself considered in its totality in abstraction from its particular modes of existence' (Marx, 1973, pp.218-21).

Money as Unity of Objective Positing and General Acceptance

If one reads Marx's work from this specific perspective, then one discovers, in *Capital*, a specific concept of validity, which in the whole literature on Marx has not been recognized, let alone interpreted in explicit terms. For example, in the appendix 'The Value Form', Marx uses 'validity' and 'to be valid' more than 30 times. His conception of validity is completely integrated into his argument and so too is its suggested significance in the context of the genesis of the value form. And this is still the case in the revised second edition where Marx had extensively reworked this 'schoolmasterly appendix' into the first chapter. Marx held on to his substantialist conception, although there are some changes that can be characterized as desubstantialization, to some extent as a transition from, in Hegelian terms, 'substance to subject' or, as Ernst Cassirer put it, from 'substance to function' (cf. Cassirer, 1953). Illuminating in this context is Barbara Lietz's carefully edited *Ergänzungen und Veränderungen zum ersten Band des 'Kapitals'* (Marx, 1987b). Here we find thoughts about the category of value that, though implicit, are not explicitly argued in the second edition. In the second edition, Marx adds:

> The labour...that forms the substance of value, is homogeneous human labour, expenditure of one uniform labour-power. The total labour-power of society, which is [expressed] in the [values] of all commodities, *counts* [*gilt*: is valid] here as one homogeneous mass of human labour-power, composed through it be of innumerable individual units. Each of these units is the same as any other, so far as it has the character of the average labour-power of society, and takes effect as such; that is, so far as it requires for producing a commodity, no more time than is needed on an average, no more than is socially necessary' (Marx, 1983, pp.46-7; emphasis HR).

These sentences appear, before Marx's presentation of the form of the appearance of value in exchange, on the first pages of the introduction of the category of value, where 'everything is said about the labour embodied in linen' that is later expressed in exchange.

Surprisingly Marx uses the expression 'is valid' in this context. Surprisingly because validity in its strict sense is tied to subjects, for whom something has validity – without subjects no validity – irrespective of how one might conceive the genesis and mode of existence of the valid thing. One therefore finds the various formulations of 'validity' and 'to be valid' only when Marx focuses on the value form – as in the appendix to the first edition. Here the relationships of value to one another are explicitly posed. One might suspect that Marx is not in the position to offer a more precise understanding of the category value without recourse to the process of exchange (and that therefore the physiological determination of abstract labour as 'expenditure of brain, muscle, nerve', amounts in the end to an act of theoretical violence (*theoretischer Gewaltakt*)).

We cannot offer here a detailed interpretation of this change between the first and second edition. However, as already emphasized: Marx only went half-way and did not fully develop the implications of the concept of validity. How might one resolve the central problem of economic theory – commensurability, addition of abstract, objective values – without presupposing a substantialist category of value? I leave it open whether such a continuation of the critique of economics can be conceived of as a reconstruction. If it were really just a matter of critical reconstruction, one would then have to presuppose that a unitary interpretation of Marx's work is in principle possible. I do not see this to be the case, however. One therefore has to start with Marx's critique of economics as the most developed form of consciousness, but at the same time – as Jürgen Habermas (1976, p.9) put it in his *Reconstruction of Historical Materialism* – one has 'to tear the theory apart and put it together in a new form to reach the goal that it has set itself better'. The goal is to overcome *aporias* in and through a genetic unfolding of economic categories. We therefore go back to the thought process of the *Grundrisse* and combine it with the concept of validity in the first edition of *Capital*.

Let us then return one more time to the 'genuinely dialectical' conceptions of value and money and let us start with a formulation from a philosopher who neither shied away from the risk of falling short of scientific criteria, nor was afraid to be excluded from the scientific community. '*Money* is the material, **existing concept**, the form of unity, or the possibility of all things' (Hegel, 1974a, p.334, bold emphasis HR). This formulation was not an early, speculative adventure. Hegel repeats the same thought in his lectures on the philosophy of law. As an 'existing concept', money is at the same time characterized as the 'existing universal' (Hegel, 1974b, p.229) and he adds 'here value exists as such', and 'money is the real existence of the universal. This universal is not only an external, objective universal, but also a subjective universal, a universal of a wholly different sort' (ibid., p.230). Hegel was not able to develop this thought any further. What is important, however, is that this universal of a 'wholly different sort' is subjective and at the same time objective, and as an objective it is an 'existing universal', that is, totality and abstraction, both at the same time. It is like the 'I' as an existing concept: 'transition(s) from undifferentiated indeterminacy to differentiation, determining and positing of its determination (§§ 5 and 6 of *The Philosophy of Right*). But it is like the 'I' not as an 'I' but as a thing.

Are only philosophers allowed to discover in economics this universal *in re* (in the thing) because, as thinkers of the universal, it is their task to think speculatively? Or can the scientist think such thoughts as well? We find formulations similar to Hegel's in the young Marx, for example in the *Paris Manuscripts*: 'money, as the existing and active concept of value...' (Marx, 1959, p.124). Also in the *Grundrisse*, he speaks of money as an existing universal:

> This totality exists in money itself as the comprehensive representation of commodities. Thus, wealth (exchange value as totality as well as abstraction) exists, individualized as such, to the exclusion of all other commodities, as a singular, tangible object, in gold and silver. Money is therefore the god among commodities (Marx, 1973, p.221).

Money '*as the individual* of general wealth' (ibid., p.222), is not only a form, but at the same time content itself.

> The concept of wealth, so to speak, is realized, *individualized* in a particular object...In money...the price is realized; and its substance is wealth itself in its totality in abstraction from its particular modes of existence (ibid., pp.218-21).

In the first edition, where the dialectical method is already 'very much hidden', one still finds, in the context of the development of the general equivalent form, a passage that is completely erased from the second edition:

> In form III, which is the reflected second form and therefore contained within it, linen appears however as the *genus form* of the equivalent for all other commodities. It is as if besides and next to lions, tigers, hares and all other real animals that make up the animal kingdom grouped in different genders, species and sub-species, families, etc., there exists also *the animal*, the individual incarnation of the whole animal kingdom. A singular that contains within itself the real species of the same thing, is a *universal*, like *animal, god*, etc. (Marx, 1983b, p.37).

Marx's conceptions of the existing universal, from the earliest economic works to *Capital*, are almost identical to Hegel's. How, however, can one conceive of this existing abstraction as something that is carried out in the practice of exchanging subjects? Although he clearly saw the problem, Hegel does not give us an answer. We can however find an answer in Marx's *Grundrisse*, which was, in part, carried over into *Capital*.

In his *Critique* of 1859, Marx criticizes Adam Smith, according to whom money was introduced as a medium, as a general means of exchange, in order to reduce the complexity of exchange where many owners of different commodities engage with each other to exchange their particular product with a multiplicity of other products that meet their needs. This conception of money that is still dominant in contemporary economics, sees in money a 'cleverly devised' thing. And

> proceeding from this quite superficial point of view, an ingenious British economist has rightly maintained that money is merely a material instrument, like a ship or a steam engine, and not an expression of a social relation of production, and hence is not an economic category. It is therefore simply a malpractice to deal with this subject in political economy, which in fact has nothing in common with technology (Marx, 1971, p.51).[20]

In the *Grundrisse* he still appreciates the positive side of this idea, since he presumes that the development of money started with the simple exchange of products that then expanded: 'The product becomes a commodity; the commodity becomes exchange value; the exchange value of the commodity is its immanent money-property; this, its money-property, separates itself from it in the form of money, and achieves a general social existence' (Marx, 1973, pp.146-47, see also pp.145, 165). Traces of this argument can still be found in *Capital*:

---

[20] An analogue critique of economic functionality/technology can be found in Alfred Amonn's (1911, p.330ff) assessment of Joseph Schumpeter's methodological individualism.

> In the direct barter of products, each commodity is directly a means of exchange to its owner, and to all other persons an equivalent...The articles exchanged to not acquire an [independent] value form...The necessity for a value form grows with the increasing number and variety of the commodities exchanged. The problem and the means of solution arise simultaneously. Commodity-owners never equate their own commodities to those of others, and exchange them on a large scale, without different kinds of commodities belonging to different owners being exchangeable for, and equated as values to, *one and the same special article*. Such last mentioned article, by becoming the equivalent of *various* other commodities, acquires at once, though within narrow limits, the character of a general social equivalent. This character comes and goes with the momentary social acts that called it into life. In turns and transiently it attaches itself first to this and then to that commodity. But with the development of exchange it fixes itself firmly and exclusively to the *particular* sorts of commodities, and becomes crystallized by assuming the *money-form* (Marx, 1983, pp.91-2).[21]

At the same time he argues that their *quantitative exchange relations* are 'at first quite a matter of chance' (ibid., p.91), and that their exchangeability rests on 'the mutual desire of their owners to alienate them' (ibid.), and that they therefore – and this sentence can be found only in the first edition – '[acquire] the form of exchangeability before they are developed as values' (Marx, 1983b, p.54). Their 'fixation as value magnitudes' comes later. Originally, it is thus the 'most marketable commodity' (cf. Menger, 1950) that first takes on the function of money.

> [Money] arises naturally out of exchange; it is a product of the same. *At the beginning*, that commodity will serve as money – i.e. it will be exchanged not for the purpose of satisfying a need, not for consumption, but in order to be re-exchanged and circulated as an object of consumption, and which is therefore most certain to be exchangeable again for other commodities, i.e. which represents within the given social organization of wealth (*par excellence*), which is the object of the most general demand and supply, and which possesses a particular use value. Thus salt, hide, cattle, slaves. In practice such a commodity corresponds more closely to itself as exchange value than do other commodities (a pity that the difference between *denrée* and *marchandise* cannot be neatly reproduced in German) It is the particular usefulness of the commodity, whether as a particular object of consumption (hides), or as a direct instrument of production (slaves), which stamps it as money in these cases. In the course of further development precisely the opposite will occur, i.e. that commodity which has the least utility as an object of consumption or instrument of production will best serve the ends of *exchange as such* (Marx, 1973, pp.165-66).

How can this be understood? Marx rebukes functional conceptions of money and at the same time agrees with the economists that money has its origin in exchange? Marx introduces the above quotation by saying that 'money does not arise by convention, any more than the state does' (ibid., p.165). This is the solution to the riddle. The targets of his rebuke are those who emphasize only the conventional side of the argument, that is, those who absolutize the notion of a conscious-intentional solution on the part of the participants to the common problem of

---

[21] Marx's emphases can only be found only in the first edition (1983b, p.55).

exchange. Within this 'problem solving' process, another process comes to the fore, which Marx explicates as the positing of forms, that is, a process in which the participants posit a 'form of equivalence' (Marx, 1987b, p.21) that is identical with the 'form of immediate exchangeability'. Form-positing is however value-positing. Whenever the participants exchange products, they posit them as qualitatively equal. In so doing, they posit difference-in-unity, that is, they posit the many as identical in the form of value. Thus he argues in the section on fetishism:

> Whenever, by an act of exchange, we equate as values our different products, by that very act, we also equate as human labour, the different kinds of labour expended upon them. We are not aware of this, nevertheless we do it. Value, therefore does not stalk about with a label describing what it is. It is value, rather, that converts every product into a social hieroglyphic (Marx, 1983, pp.78-9).

Let us leave aside for the moment Marx's assumption that Men, by reducing their labour to abstract labour, engage in this process of abstraction in the way that Marx himself conceives of this abstraction as an understandable abstraction. What can be stated is this: the process of equalization that transforms products into values, this 'natural and thus unconscious instinctive operation of the brain' (Marx, 1983b, p.46), operates like a hinge in the real development of a process of increasing social irrationalization that can no longer be deduced from understandable social acts. Marx's biologization of this process is not very helpful. It distracts from the insight that we are dealing here with a thought process whose logical unconsciousness occurs in the same way in the exchange actions of each of the participants. The distinctive specificity of the equivalent form is that it posits unity in the form of equivalence – the natural form of the product, the matter, is valid (*gilt*) as something immediately exchangeable. In the equivalent form, we have an immediate unity of validity (*Geltung*) and being (*Sein*): value *is* because matter, the natural form of the product, is *valid* as value.

The expression 'valid', thus, refers to an act of exchange that is no longer consciously understandable. It posits the difference of the two products in the form of a unity. Only now do the products obtain in the commodity form, that is, by virtue of their 'comparability' as 'equally valid', 'undifferentiable' products in the act of exchange. Marx saw the condition of their quantitative comparison in their reduction to their common characteristic as 'coagulations', as 'crystallizations' of abstract labour, which the products already possessed before the act of exchange. It seems that he neither wanted nor could concede that this positing of unity ensued in the process of the positing of equivalence itself. Conceding this would have questioned his basic materialist position.

In contrast to Marx's structure of presentation, which always depends upon a presupposed category of value, no pre-monetary value has to be presupposed. But the question that needs answering here is how this thought process of positing unity, that each individual unconsciously does, can be welded together. The two processes – the logically unconscious positing of unity that every individual engages in by virtue of the act of exchange between two different products, and the commonly agreed conscious selection of that product which is the 'most exchanged object of needs' (cf. Marx, 1983b, p.46) – these two processes have to be conceived as *uno actu*, that is, as distinct processes contained within the one act. Marx expounds this in the second chapter of *Capital*.

The first chapter of the first edition concludes with the statement that value has thus far been examined analytically, 'sometimes from the perspective of use value, sometimes from the perspective of exchange value'. The further examination will however have as its objective 'the real relationship between the commodities to one another', and that is, their 'exchange process' (Marx, 1983b, p.51).[22] In the 'analytical approach' to the commodity, the theoretical goal was the development of the equivalent form from the perspective of exchange value, an equivalent form that corresponds in its generality to the generality of the category of value.[23] The presentation of the 'real relationship', that is, the presentation of the reality of the genesis of money, the relationship between use-value and exchange value, must be examined. The development of the general form of equivalence has to ensue *uno actu* with the 'selection' of a corresponding use-value. In this context a note in the second chapter, whose theoretical significance has as yet not been recognized in the literature, is important. Marx emphasizes here that 'a particular commodity cannot become the universal equivalent except by a social act' (Marx, 1983, p.90). This refers to the use value of money as a commodity, and the social act is the conscious selection of an object suitable to perform the function of money.

Thus, the charge of functionality hits only when this act is made an absolute, that is, when the conception of the origin of money is restricted exclusively to the conscious-intentional decision to reduce the complexity of exchange relations. If one endorses this view, then money is a functional medium that rests on its general acceptance as a certain useful thing. However general acceptance is not the same as general validity. General validity is tied to general acceptance. The 'particular usefulness' that 'stamps' an object 'as money', generalizes and at the same time standardizes all positing of equivalence on the part of interacting exchange subjects. Immediate exchangeability assumes the form of a universal equivalent – the unity of all commodities exists as a particular next to the many. Money is a sensuous-supersensible, as a valid (*Geltendes*) it *is*, and it *is* only because it is *valid*, the matter is valid as value-objectivity, value-objectivity exists – as object.

In the Appendix, Marx characterizes the development of the universal form of equivalence in the following terms:

> This *exclusion* can be a *purely subjective process*, e.g. a process of the owner of linen who evaluates his own commodity in many other commodities. On the other hand, a commodity finds itself as the general form of equivalence (Form III), because and inasmuch as it is *excluded from all other commodities as form of equivalence*. From the perspective of the excluded commodity, this *exclusion* is a process independent from it, an *objective process*. In the historical development of the commodity form, the general equivalent form might therefore be at times this, at times that commodity. But a commodity never functions *really* as general equivalent, except on the condition that its

[22] Marx erased this methodologically most important last sentence from the second edition of *Capital*. It can be found however in the *Critique* of 1859.

[23] 'Only through its *general* character does the *value form* correspond to the *category of value*' (Marx, 1983b, p.643).

> exclusion and therefore its form of equivalence is the result of *objective social processes* (Marx, 1983b, p.646).

Marx's definition of economic categories as both 'subjective' and 'objective', as 'objective forms of thought' has to be read prior to this passage from the Appendix. The 'subjective' process that ensues 'in the head' of the owner of linen who posits his linen equivalent to all other products (a process in which all other products become – naturally only in thought do they exist or are valid as such – forms of equivalence) does not become an objective process in the sense that it strays, as it were, from the brain into the world and thereby materializes itself in a mysterious manner. The objectivity of the process resides in the inversion through which a commodity becomes the universal form of equivalence. This, however, is still a thought process – the 'thought form' becomes objective. Tellingly, Marx speaks about an objective *social* process that synthesizes in a single notion both the objectivity of inversion and the selection of the particular use value that is suitable as the form of money. Marx summarizes the unity of both processes, the constitution of general validity and the creation of general acceptance, in the concept '*general social validity*' (Marx, 1983b, p.647).

> One sees, the actual money-form generates in-itself no difficulties. Once the general equivalent form is revealed, it does not cause any difficulty to understand that this equivalent form fixes itself to a specific commodity like gold, much less since the general equivalent form, by its nature, necessitates the social exclusion of a particular commodity by all other commodities. This exclusion has to achieves objective social consistency and general validity, thus is neither taken on by different commodities nor limited in scope to local spheres of commodity exchange' (ibid., p.648).

The general form of equivalence that exists in a particular useful form, that is, as a universally valid, immediate form of exchangeability, displays that sort of inversion which Marx conceives of in the first edition as the defining characteristic of a universal and which he terms, in concise Hegelian, an '*Einbegreifens*' (a concept that as a single contains the many within itself). 'A singular that *contains within itself* all really existing species of the same thing, is a universal, like animal, god, etc.' (Marx, 1983b, p.37). The particular is not subsumed under an abstract-general, but is '*contained within*' (*einbegriffen*) – and it therewith is both an abstraction and a totality. The so-called real-abstraction (*Realabstraktion*) is something objectively conceptual. As an immediate unity of validity and being, it goes beyond the conventional idea of objectivity as something endowed with inter-subjective validity, and for the most demanding philosophy, it is sufficient that the universal is at the same time an existing universal. It is – identical with Hegel's formulation – 'the existing concept of the value of all things'. What, however, is to be understood by 'existing concept'? Nothing else then the 'I', this movement that is within itself a movement of opposites – the unity of the 'limitless infinity of absolute abstraction' and the 'transition from undifferentiated indeterminacy to differentiation, determining and positing of a determinate', as Hegel expounds it in §§ 5 and 6 in his *Philosophy of Right*. However, this 'I' is here not an 'I' but a thing – better: it is tied to objects and thus an objectivity (*Gegenständlichkeit*) that subsists in and through this movement of thought. Marx is much closer to Hegel than is conventionally assumed. And this means that Marx's early take on the Hegelian concept of appearance, as we know it from his early works, has to be abandoned. One has also to abandon the idea of value as a substitute for the missing self-conscious unity of social labour, as Marx expounds it in the fetish section of *Capital*, illustrated by the examples of Robinson and the association of free human beings. The central axis of bourgeois society is only established with the form of universal, immediate exchangeability. This form is, in a strict Hegelian sense, the form of self-consciousness – a consciousness tied to objects, the objectified self of consciousness.

Some Implications

How, then, can one bring labour into the reckoning? Within the constitution process of the form of general, immediate exchangeability, the natural form is valid immediately as value, and that also means that the 'quantity of matter' is valid as value quantity, gold quantity is immediately valid as money quantity. The particular labour, here the gold labour, is therefore immediately valid as general labour, and in the equivalence of all concrete labour with gold labour, through which the particular labour in gold production is valid as general labour, all particular forms of labour are valid as particularizations of labour in general. In this way we arrive at a dialectical concept of general labour – labour as totality and abstraction – a conception that is discernible in some of Marx's early formulations. This conception is also implied in the money form that develops itself in exchange. Inasmuch as this form is an existing universal, so too the particular labour. Marx emphasized this in precisely this sense in the first edition:

> like the linen became the *singular equivalent*, by virtue of other commodities relating to it as the form of appearance of value, the linen becomes the common form of appearance of value for all other commodities, that is, their *general equivalent, general value body, general materiality of abstract human labour*. The *particular* labour materialized in linen is valid therefore now as the *general form of realization* of human labour as *general labour* (Marx, 1983b, p.648).

He argues here in the context of his conception of the 'necessary, internal unity' between substance of value and value form. This highlights the importance of the choice of words in the last sentence. He speaks about validity, which, ultimately, can only relate to the positing of unity in exchange, and he uses the phrase 'general labour', which has other connotations than the expression of abstract-general labour, or abstract-human labour. As general labour, it is the 'embodiment' (*Inbegriff*) of all particular forms of labour, abstraction and totality. This, however, obtains only in the positing of equivalence in the process of exchange and the development of the general form of equivalence. Therefore, general labour exists itself in a particular form alongside the many particular forms of labour. Let us assume, as indeed it is the case only in developed competitive capitalism, that products are exchanged according to socially necessary labour time. Under this condition, the social product can indeed be conceived as *one*: as objectified collective labour. Marx focuses this point in a brilliant formulation in his *Critique* of 1859:

> Furthermore, in exchange-value the labour-time of a particular individual is directly represented as *labour-time in general*, and this *general character* of individual labour appears as the *social character* of this labour. The labour-time expressed in exchange-value is the labour-time of an individual, but of an individual in no way differing from the next individual and from all other individuals in so far as they perform equal labour; the labour-time, therefore, which one person requires for the production of a given commodity is *necessary* labour-time which any other person would require to produce the same commodity. It is the labour-time of an individual, *his* labour–time, but only as labour-time common to all; consequently it is quite immaterial *whose* individual labour-time this is...[It is] as if the different individuals had amalgamated their labour-time and allocated different portions of the labour-time at their joint disposal to the various use-values. The labour-time of the individual is thus, in fact, the labour-time required by society to produce a particular use-value, that is to satisfy a particular want (Marx, 1971, p.32).

Tellingly, the *Critique* does not speak about the double character of labour as abstract-general and concrete-sensuous labour. Instead, we still find here genuinely dialectical formulations, which point towards a universality that extends over and encompasses within itself all individual labours.

In the *Critique* Marx still conceptualizes the unity of labour and its quantitative expansion as 'general labour-time' – a determination that only achieves its full meaning in capitalism when, mediated through competition, labour-time is constantly reduced to its necessary measure. This insight is presupposed in the *Critique* and in *Capital*. How, then, can one think the relationship between general labour, necessary labour-time and equivalent-exchange in the pre-industrial era? Without further ado Marx assumes in his late works that before competitive capitalism profit rested on taking advantage of the buyer, and that therefore no equivalent exchange took place. This has important connotations for the theoretical exposition. The double meaning of simple circulation in the *Grundrisse* implies, as already mentioned, that the genetic development of categories, which starts with the exchange of products, does not have to return (*zurückführen*) the value-magnitude to socially necessary labour. This is, for Marx, a side issue; he is adamant that the real issue is the development of forms.

> Production is not only concerned with the simple determination of prices, i.e. with the translation of exchange values of commodities into a common unit, but with the creation of exchange values, hence also with the creation of the *particularity* of prices. **Not merely with positing the form, but also the content**. Therefore, while in simple circulation, money appears generally as productive, since circulation in general is itself a moment of the system of production, nevertheless this quality still only exists *for us*, and is not yet *posited* in money (Marx, 1973, p.217; bold emphasis HR).

What does this mean? The price form is of course always also defined in quantitative terms; but corresponding with his differentiation between exchange-value positing relations and labour creating exchange-value in the *Grundrisse*, the quantitative dimension assumes significance only with the genesis of capital and then the transition to industrial capital. Money as productive within simple circulation refers to the autonomization of value (the contradiction between the absolute form of wealth and its quantitative limitation as the bad-infinity of value expansion within the change of forms itself). This autonomization can only be sustained through the constant expansion of consumption – 'its disappearance must disappear, and must itself be merely a means for the emergence of a greater exchange value...*productive consumption* (Marx, 1987a, p.492) – and that is, the inversion of production to an end in itself – 'production for the sake of production'.[24] The transition from simple reproduction to industrial capital ensues thus when Marx tackles this question: how is it that the autonomization of value and its expansion that takes place through a constant change of forms in the sphere of circulation does not lead to the 'implosion of value'.

However, his argument presupposes that exchange process is always already based on equivalent values, a circumstance that has not always been the case historically. Marx thus faces a dilemma: if, as in the *Grundrisse*, he continues the development of forms, then he would be able to introduce the two determinations of labour as general labour and necessary labour-time separately. If he were to do that, however, an 'elegantly' argued dialectical transition into production would not be possible: the exposition would then no longer look like an 'a priori construction', as he put it in the Afterword to the second edition'.[25] If, however, he

[24] Despite the 'concealment of the dialectical method', one can still find, in the *Critique*, concise references to the unity of dialectical exposition and real inversion. In relation to the third determination of money, one reads 'while clinging to wealth in its metallic corporality the hoarder reduces it to a mere chimera. But the accumulation of money for the sake of money is in fact the barbaric form of production *for the sake of production*, i.e., the development of the productive power of social labour beyond its limits of customary requirements. The less advanced is the production of commodities, the more important is hoarding – the *first* form in which exchange value assumes an *independent existence as money*' (Marx, 1971, p.134, emphases HR).

[25] In the *Urtext*, Marx offers the following rudimentary conception of this issue and he does so by emphasizing the dialectical method of presentation as the 'necessary form' for the understanding of the historical becoming of a class of free wage labourers: 'That the possessor of money...*finds* labour capacity on the market...this premise from which we here proceed...is evidently the outcome of long historical development...and implies the decline of other modes of production (other social relations of production) and a determined development of the productive forces of social labour. The determined past historical process contained in that premise will be formulated even more determinately in the subsequent examination of this relationship. But this historical stage in the development of economic production – whose product itself is already *the free worker* – is the premise for the emergence and even more so for the being of capital as such...**It is made quite definite at this point that the dialectical form of presentation is right only when it knows its own limits**. The examination of the simply circulation shows *us* the general concept of capital...The exposition of the general concept of capital does not make it an incarnation of some eternal idea, **but shows how in actual reality, merely as a *necessary* form, it has yet**

posits both determinations together right at the beginning, then he has to presuppose developed capitalism, and the dialectical presentation of forms, at least until the abstract category capital, would have to presuppose the genesis of capitalism's own categorical presuppositions in the constituted form of capitalism itself.[26]

Marx chose the second option, but let us remain with the first and let us also assume that the law of value exacts itself only in capitalism and that the necessary categories for its existence are to be developed as 'valid forms' in the context of simple circulation. Only now will it be possible to think developments, such as changes in the quantity of money, velocity of circulation, development of paper money and changes in the purchasing power of money, in a unitary context and to formulate adequate theories of their laws of motion. What do these laws look like?

In his comprehensive study, Hans-Georg Backhaus (2000) has alluded to the double character of Marx's concept of critique: Critique as development of the real categories, and critique as critique of economic theory. Within this double character of critique, Marx is said to have also developed the constitutive conditions of theory production and shown how categorical unconsciousness continues to shape economic science. Its theoretical endeavour rests on unreflected presuppositions. With its opaque naturalization of the commodity to a sheerly sensuous thing (from fixed capital to machinery and instruments of production) and its conception of money as a mere 'given', economic thought renders the appearance of simple circulation a theoretical absolute. The categorical-unconscious positing and discovery of the money-form as an *uno-actu* process (in Hegel's words: the money-form is posited as presupposed) manifests itself theoretically in the form of an unbridgeable gap that is typical of two-world theory where the many commodities, which are one-sidedly perceived as sensuous things, stand in an external relation to their unity, that is money. Characteristically, economic theory calls sensuous things goods, and money is 'externally taken from the empirical world'. As Marx argues, this is the way in which economics deals with its categories on the whole. That is, economic theory is, as it were, condemned to construct equilibrium relations between externally related quantities. Say's politically useful formula expresses this in paradigmatic terms: the quantity of money determines prices and money determines the circulation of commodities. Economic theory can only be a theory of quantities. It thus has to presuppose value as a macro-economic category and is no longer able to understand value as a form of social practice. Its conception of value is underhanded. See for example, David Hume who 'quite contrary to the principles of his own philosophy uncritically turns unilaterally interpreted facts into general propositions' (Marx, 1971, p.163). Hume's theory of circulation can be summed up in three such general sentences:

> 1. Commodity-prices in a given country are determined by the amount of money (real or token money) existing therein. 2. The money circulating in a given country represents all commodities which are in that country. As the amount of money grows, each unit

---

to flow into the labour creating exchange value' (Marx, 1987a, p.505; bold emphases HR).

[26] In this dilemma we might find one of the motifs that let Marx to hide his method.

> represents a correspondingly larger or smaller proportion of the things represented. 3. If the volume of commodities increases, then their prices fall or the value of money rises. If the amount of money increases, then, on the contrary, commodity-prices rise and the value of money falls (ibid., p.162).

The principle of this theory is thus: 'commodities without price and gold and silver without value enter the process of circulation. He, therefore, never mentions the value of commodities and the value of gold, but speaks only of their reciprocal quantity' (ibid., p.164). That this is not an unusual view is indicated by Alfred Marshall's shell example that repeats this same thought: '[Let us suppose] there be a million such shells, and the income of the country be sixty million bushels of corn, a shell will be worth...six bushels' (Marshall, 1871, p.168).

This type of theory is (in itself, as Hegel would say) the formulation of the appearance of simple circulation, the 'abstract sphere' of the whole process that Marx also called surface appearance. This whole process, however, does not consist of a naturalistically imagined production process that achieves, with the help of money, a general synthesis *post-festum*. Instead, it comprises interlocking circuits of capital, that is, the metamorphoses of value. It moves, maintaining and expanding itself, through production and circulation. Starting with the development of value in its first form as universal immediate exchangeability and from there to the further development of this 'existing universality' to the concept of capital, Marx has not only developed a theory that pursues exchange value arising from circulation to its attempted 'self-perpetuation' (cf. Marx, 1987a, p.498). He also showed that 'the intransience for which money strives as it negatively sets itself with respect to circulation...is acquired by capital in that it preserves itself by precisely giving itself up to circulation' (ibid., p.487). Thus, 'the process of becoming independent appears not only in the form of capital that confronts circulation as an independent abstract exchange value – money – but also in that circulation is simultaneously the process of its becoming independent' (ibid., p.486). The process of this becoming of independence is the process of inversion that makes the whole world in its own image. The 'supersensible' maintains itself in that it both constantly drags the 'sensuous' into and ejects it from this process of inversion quâ autonomization. The initial immediate unity between sensuous-concrete thing and supersensible validity autonomizes itself in the form of the inverted world of capital, in which each thing subsists as a transitory moment of this – inverted – supersensible unity. Capital as circulating capital 'exists in the form of the *objectivity* (*Gegenständlichkeit*), but it is indifferent to whether it is the objectivity of the money and or the commodity' (ibid., p.499). It is simply the change of form of the autonomized value in circulation, the change between particular form (the commodity) and universal form (the money). Each capital is a process of this movement. Each capital, thus, is this second, Hegelian supersensible world, the unity between the sensuous and the first supersensible world. Each individual capital is at the same time *the* capital. As a processual moment of the metamorphosis of value, each individual capital is the same as all the others, they are as alike as two peas – thus each individual capital is 'capital in general'.

In this second supersensible inverted world, the law of motion is characterized, as already mentioned, as the 'retention of the universal in and through the constant disappearance of the particular'. In contrast to Hegel's conception of the category of 'force', where the law of motion can never be brought into conformity with appearance (thus securing the further development of appearing knowledge), Marx proposes that appearance is the expression of social laws, and reality is appearance of social laws. However, we have to differentiate. In so far as we are discussing the laws of circulation, the first categories – price form, means of circulation, coin, money as money – must be conceptualized as precipitations of the specific forms of circulating value. It has to be shown how those money functions that appear separate from each other in their surface operation are, in fact, immanently interlocked. Instead of defining money in terms of its functions, without being able to offer any theoretical justification whether there should be three or even sixteen different money functions, the form and content of money functions must be brought out immanently. With this presupposition, Marx is able to explain particular forms of appearance. He does so not by posing a hypothesis that then has to be verified empirically. Instead, he traces respective forms of appearance back to the general law of supersensible existence, an existence that contains within itself all its particularizations.

Thus we see that with the critique of economic categories, the Hegelian concept of appearance obtains as more than just a figure of thought in the first materialist attempts of penetrating and expounding the experience of an inverted, autonomized world. It is crucial to the development of the concept of society. However, the redeeming of this concept of appearance is only achievable on the basis of a theory of value, money, and capital that elaborates the concept of validity that Marx's work thematized only in rudimentary terms. Such an endeavour has to guard itself against those left-Hegelian temptations that ultimately still inform Marx's conception of value in *Capital*. The Robinson example in the fetish section makes clear that Marx's holds on to this early left-Hegelian understanding of a social essence that, by way of practical abolition (*Aufhebung*), has to be liberated from its inverted forms of appearance. This then invites the question whether the early conception of dialectics was not itself taken in by the socially produced appearance (*Schein*) that Marx's critique of economics deciphers. Were we to look at this closely, we would have to start with the elaboration of Feuerbachian thoughts in the *Critique of Hegel's Philosophy of Right*. As I already suggested, one finds here, aided by a Rousseauian conception of radical democracy, a chiasm that brings the constitutive subjects to the fore as passive victims of a world they themselves created. This conception of democracy renders bourgeois subjectivity absolute: its presupposition is the equality and the freedom of all subjects who relate to each other on the basis of a social contract. This presupposition, too, enters Marx's critique: in principle each individual subject is *the* subject, and each subject is thus also an unfree appendage of an undecipherable social autonomization that the subjects themselves produce and reproduce but which turns against them. The two poles of this argumentation are constitutive subjectivity and the no longer decipherable, autonomized objectivity. However, is it the case that Marx here really develops the autonomization of society through its genesis, or does he merely articulate, with the help of this dialectics, the experience of such an autonomized world?

At least with the precise understanding of the double character of simple circulation, and its deciphering as a sphere of appearance, Marx should have asked himself whether his early critique was not taken in by that appearance which he later reveals *as* appearance. The basic figure that underlies every economic and political – social-nominalist (Adorno) – construction is always the atomized free and equal subject that is rendered absolute and whose universalization is the mere reverse of the developed capitalist system.

> Equality and freedom are thus not only respected in exchange based on exchange values but, also, the exchange of exchange values is the productive, real basis of *equality* and *freedom*. As pure ideas they are merely the idealized expressions of this basis; as developed in juridical, political, social relations, they are merely this basis to a higher power (Marx, 1973, p.245).

In accordance with the double character of simple circulation, and without the complete subsumption of production to exchange relations, these 'ideas' can already be developed to a certain degree – as Marx tries to show by means of an example in relation to the definition of the slave in Roman law.[27] With capital's encroachment into, and transformation of, the sphere of production, this 'system of freedom and equality' reveals itself as its exact opposite, or as the unity of both. The most developed version of this central thought can be found in the *Grundrisse*, where Marx shows, in the context of the development of categories, how freedom and equality have to be conceptualized together with the development of the whole system that is at the same time a class society. Marx's critique thus looks in two directions: critique of a political and economic consciousness that in its ideas of political and economic praxis is taken in by the appearance of circulation; and critique also as the genetic deciphering of this appearance within the context of the development of categories itself.

> What this reveals...is the foolishness of those socialists (namely the French, who want to depict socialism as the realization of the ideals of *bourgeois* society articulated by the French revolution) who demonstrate that exchange and exchange value etc. are *originally* (in time) or *essentially* (in their adequate form) a system of universal freedom and equality, but that they have been perverted by money, capital, etc. Or, also, that history has so far failed in every attempt to implement them in their true manner, but that they have now, like Proudhon, discovered e.g. the real Jacob, and intend now to supply the genuine history of these relations in place of the fake. The proper reply to them is: that exchange value or, more precisely, the money system is in fact the system of equality and freedom, and the disturbances which they encounter in the further development of the system are disturbances inherent in it, are merely the realization of

[27] 'In Roman law, the *servus* is therefore correctly defined as one who may not enter into exchange for the purpose of acquiring anything for himself (see the *Institutes*). It is, consequently, equally clear that although this legal system corresponds to a social state in which exchange was by no means developed, nevertheless, in so far as it was developed in a limited sphere, it was able to develop *attributes of the juridical person, precisely of the individual engaged in exchange*, and thus anticipate (in its basic aspects) the legal relations of industrial society, and in particular the right which arising bourgeois society had necessarily to assert against medieval society' (Marx, 1973, pp.245-46).

> *equality and freedom*, which prove to be inequality and unfreedom. It is just as pious as it is stupid to wish that exchange value would not develop into capital, nor labour which produces exchange value into wage labour. What divides these gentlemen from the bourgeois apologists is, on the one side, their sensitivity to the contradictions included in the system; on the other, the utopian inability to grasp the necessary difference between the real and the ideal form of bourgeois society, which is the cause of their desire to undertake the superfluous business of realizing the ideal expression again, which is in fact only the inverted projection [*Lichtbild*] of this reality (Marx, 1973, pp.248-49).

These are two sides of the same coin that do not appear *as* two sides. Perception ensues from within the subjects who confront each other, make contracts in the sphere of circulation, where they deal in mysterious economic forms with so-called 'goods', and who have always already perceived each other as equal and free subjects of law, and who, prior to this thinly veiled perception of themselves as independent subjects, experience class society as one of inequality, exploitation and rule by an autonomized system. This experience of the system's real facticity articulates itself more and more vividly and differently with the development of the system itself. But it remains an experience that never penetrates the concept of the whole. Human sensuous practice subsists through its supersensible existence in the autonomization of society as both the object and subject of its perverted (*verrückte*) social practice. Its class practice ensues thus through perverted social forms, as well as in them and against them. This, however, also means that class is not an affirmative category but, rather, a critical concept of Marx's conception of reality (Gunn, 1992).

References

Adorno, T.W. (1971), *Drei Studien zu Hegel*, in *Gesammelte Schriften*, Vol. 5, Suhrkamp, Frankfurt.

Adorno, T.W. (1972), *Soziologische Schriften*, in *Gesammelte Schriften*, Vol. 8, Suhrkamp, Frankfurt.

Adorno, T. (1978), *Minima Moralia. Reflections from Damanged Life*, trans. E. F. N. Jephcott, Verso, London.

Amonn, A. (1911), *Objekt und Grundbegriffe der theoretischen Nationalökonomie*, Böhlau, Wien and Leipzig.

Backhaus, H.G (2000), 'Über den Doppelsinn der Begriffe "Politische Ökonomie" und "Kritik" bei Marx und in der Frankfurter Schule', in S. Dornuf and R. Pitsch (eds.) *Wolfgang Harich zum Gedächnis. Eine Gedenkschrift in zwei Bänden*, Vol. I, Müller & Nerding, Munich.

Cassirer, E. (1953), *Substance and Function*, trans. W. C. Swabey and M. C. Swabey, Dover Publications, New York.

Feuerbach, L. (1957), *The Essence of Christianity*, trans. G. Eliot, Harper & Row, London.

Feuerbach, L. (1975), 'Vorläufige Thesen zur Reform der Philosophie', in H. Reichelt (ed.) *Texte zur materialistischen Geschichtsauffassung*, Ullstein, Berlin.

Gadamer, H.G. (1976), *Hegel's Dialectic*, trans. and intro. by C. Smith, Yale University Press, New Haven.

Gunn, R. (1992), 'Against Historical Materialism: Marxism as First Order Discourse', in W. Bonefeld, R. Gunn and K. Psychopedis (eds.) *Open Marxism*, Vol. II, Pluto Press, London.

Habermas, J. (1976), *Zur Rekonstruktion des Historischen Materialismus*, Suhrkamp, Frankfurt.

Hartmann, K. (1970), *Die Marxsche Theorie*, de Gruyter, Berlin.

Hegel, G.W.F. (1974a), *Jenenser Realphilosophie. 1. Die Vorlesungen von 1803/04, Frühe politische Systeme*, ed. and intro. G. Göhler, Ullstein, Berlin.

Hegel, G.W.F. (1974b), *Philosophie des Rechts nach der Vorlesungsnachschrift von K.G. von Griesheim 1924/25*, in *Vorlesungen über Rechtsphilosophie 1818-1831*, Vol. 6, ed. K.H. Ilting, Fromann-Holzboog, Stuttgard-Bad Camstadt.

Hegel, G.W.F. (1977), *Phenomenology of Spirit*, trans. A.V. Miller, Clarendon Press, Oxford.

Liebruck, B. (1970), *Sprache und Bewußtsein*, Vol. 5, Akademische Verlagsgesellschaft, Frankfurt.

Marshall, A. (1871), *Essays on Economic Theory*, in *The Early Economic Writings of Alfred Marshall*, Vol. 1, ed. J.K. Whitaker, Macmillan, London, 1975.

Marx, K. (1841), *Difference between Democratean and Epicurean Philosophy of Nature*, in *Collected Works*, Vol. 1, Lawrence & Wishart, London.

Marx, K. (1843), *Contribution to Hegel's Philosophy of Right*, in Collected Works, Vol. 3, Lawrence & Wishart, London.

Marx, K. (1845), 'Theses on Feuerbach', in D. McLellan (ed.) 1977.

Marx, K. (1959), *Economic and Philosophic Manuscripts of 1844*, Lawrence & Wishart, London.

Marx, K. (1961), 'Letter to Engels, 9.12.1881', in *Collected Works*, Vol. 41, Lawrence & Wishart, London.

Marx, K. (1971), *A Contribution to the Critique of Political Economy*, Lawrence & Wishart, London.

Marx, K. (1973), *Grundrisse*, Penguin, London.

Marx, K. (1976), *Theories of Surplus Value*, Part 1, Lawrence & Wishart, London.

Marx, K. (1979), *Das Kapital*, vol. I, MEW, Vol. 23, Dietz, Berlin.

Marx, K. (1981), *Zur Kritik der politischen Ökonomie*, MEW, Vol. 13, Dietz, Berlin.

Marx, K. (1983a), *Capital*, vol. I, Lawrence & Wishart, London.

Marx, K. (1983b), *Erstausgabe des Kapitals*, MEGA, Vol. M/II.5, Dietz, Berlin.

Marx, K. (1987a), *From the Preparatory Materials, Economic Works, 1857-61*, Collected Works, Vol. 29, Lawrence & Wishart, London.

Marx, K. (1987b), *Ergänzungen und Veränderungen zum ersten Band des Kapitals*, MEGA, Vol. II.6, Dietz, Berlin.

Marx, K. and F. Engels (1974), *The German Ideology*, ed. and intro. C.J. Arthur, 2nd ed., Lawrence & Wishart, London.

McLellan, D. (1977), *Karl Marx. Selected Writings*, Oxford University Press, Oxford.

Menger, C. (1950), *Principles of Economics*, Free Press, Glencoe.

Reichelt, H. (1970), *Zur logischen Struktur des Kapitalbegriffs bei Karl Marx*, EVA, Frankfurt, revised ed., Ça ira, Freiburg, 2001.

Reichelt, H. (1995), 'Why did Marx Conceal his Dialectical Method?', trans. G. Finlayson, in W. Bonefeld, R. Gunn, J. Holloway and K. Psychopedis (eds.) *Open Marxism*, vol. III, Pluto, London.

Reichelt, H. (2002), 'Die Marxsche Kritik ökonomischer Kategorien. Überlegungen zum Problem der Geltung in der dialektischen Darstellungsmethode im *Kapital*', in I. Fetscher and A. Schmidt (eds.) *Emanzipation als Versöhnung. Zu Adornos Kritik der*

'Warentausch'-Gesellschaft und Perspektiven der Transformation, Verlag Neue Kritik, Frankfurt.
Schrader, F.F. (1980), *Restauration und Revolution. Die Vorarbeiten zum "Kapital" von Karl Marx in seinen Studienheften 1850-1858*, Gerstenberg, Hildesheim.
Stamatis, G. (1999), 'Über einige Goethe's "Faust" entlehnte Marxsche Wendungen' in *Beiträge zur Marx-Engels Forschung, Neue Folge 1998*, Argument Verlag, Hamburg, pp. 235-38.

Translated from German by Werner Bonefeld

Chapter 4

Social Critique and the Logic of Revolution: From Kant to Marx and from Marx to Us

Kosmas Psychopedis

I

A critical social theory must explain how exploitative and oppressive social relations can be changed, how new norms can be established as the autonomous achievement of acting subjects, so that social relations lose their unconscious character and are transformed into relations of freedom and justice. Such norms will be revolutionary insofar as they put into relief established norms in a manner that cannot be foreseen from within those established norms themselves. The new revolutionary norms will, for example, make possible collective decision-making about the allocation of social resources or the distribution of social wealth or will establish direct democratic participation in political processes in place of merely formal representation.

One of the most important problems for a theory of revolution was the analysis of causal consequences of social acts in the context of a logic of social preconditions and revolutionary goals. In the concept of 'socialist' revolutions of the kind that was typical in the twentieth century, it almost went without saying that the establishment of central economic means was the 'precondition' for bringing about free social relations. With this precondition established, the primary revolutionary task seemed to be to secure this economic means, typically through the organization of a political apparatus devoted to this purpose. In this way, however, the revolution inevitably ran the risk of cancelling itself out insofar as it proclaimed political power as the means of eliminating political power. This problem was already encountered by dialectical idealist philosophies. Kant, for example, saw that the most important problem for the transition to a free and rational society was that of coordinating the social relations based on egoistic private action and markets with the teleology of morality, that is, the teleology of moral action that endeavours to realize rational practical purposes. In Kant's view, a proper relation between both moments cannot be produced mechanically; rather, in order to establish such an idea, he had to have recourse to God! Hegel too addressed the problem of the transition from mechanical and irrational relations to relations of freedom as a question that had to be treated within the framework of his dialectical presentation of bourgeois society and its state. Therewith, however, a latent positivism made its way into the idealist dialectical treatment of the problem of revolution – and one that ran counter to the idea of revolution and that itself had to be revolutionized.

The central question to be answered about revolution conceived as a transition to freedom is the problem of the violence that would be necessary to coerce counter-revolutionaries to accept the revolutionary transformation of society.[1] In contrast to the closed logic of idealist-dialectical theories, more revolutionary vigour seemed to be contained in another Kantian idea, namely, that the rational *citoyen* can affirm the results of revolutionary processes (e.g. norms such as freedom, equality, justice), without, however, having to accept those disgraceful conditions that are caused and made possible by them, like for example, revolutionary terror. This means that revolutionary theory can assume that relevant emancipatory results could have been attained through means other than inhumane, undignified or cynical practices. But how? – we must ask. Kant would answer: through rational practical actions which themselves presuppose a 'revolution in the mode of thought'.

In the context of the sensualist materialism of his early works, Marx conceived of revolution as the radical explosion of the alienated relations produced by and reproduced through money and private property. This early notion entails on the one hand the idea that in revolution people will indeed transcend their particular interests in the form of universal human interests *sans phrase*; yet, on the other hand, it also means that, in the post-revolutionary period, this transcendence will be rescinded and replaced by relations based on human individuality. In important analyses in his later works Marx showed how the social forces of production are, by necessity of capitalism's constituted logic, transformed into forces of destruction. He showed how the working class forms and organizes itself in reaction to capitalism's destructive logic, and seeks to establish means of social protection against the capitalist forms of appropriation that endanger the conditions of social life. These norms, however, cannot be stabilized and secured within the framework of capitalist society. This means, then, that the maintenance of social life itself presupposes the revolutionary transcendence (*Aufhebung*) of capitalist social relations.

In contrast to the Hegelian dialectic, Marx insisted that the revolution had to be carried further until it reaches the point where Hegel's separations and mediations (e.g. the separation of *bourgeois* and *citoyen*, of society and state, and the fundamental separation between classes) would be transcended (*aufgehoben*). But Marx leaves undetermined the particular conditions and the concrete steps that such a transition and transcendence entails. Particularly, he left open what new values and norms must be adopted in the process of the revolutionary transformation of the old values and norms.

---

[1] [Translator's Note: The German original speaks of *Gewalt*. This can be translated as either violence or force. Since 'violence' and 'force' carry different meanings, the translation uses one or the other according to what seems contextually appropriate.]

Most of these questions found no satisfactory answer during Marx's time – nor in the twentieth century. In the epoch of generalized conflicts and crises, of the total mobilization of the economic and state mechanisms with the deployment of means (e.g. nuclear weapons) that result in catastrophes and in constant changes in the conditions of life on a global scale, it has become especially difficult to decide which criteria legitimize radical socio-political and cultural changes and how such changes can be brought about. To revolutionaries, it seemed almost impossible to decide rationally which political purposes and which means are the right ones – and especially what the proper relation is between emancipatory purposes and revolutionary violence. The question of the relationship between emancipation and violence is most important because it poses the issue whether it is justified or not to 'force people to be free', as Rousseau demanded. Several of these questions have been addressed by twentieth-century theoreticians: Walter Benjamin posed the question of the nature of violence and the relation between violence and revolution in the era of 'the second technology'; Hannah Arendt attempted to decipher the logic of the political as an 'exceptional situation' and to study the antinomies between the conception of a political, and that of a social, revolution.

These considerations lead to the question: Is there in the contemporary era of capitalist globalization and the new imperialism even room for revolutionary action; and if so, where? This question belongs together with the question, posed by dialectical social theory, of the 'determinate negation' of bourgeois society. The legitimation of the revolution has to do with practical action that bases itself on the social materiality as it already exists in today's society, and that seeks not only to defend human social values, which are being destroyed by the form of society, by power plays, exploitation, and the logics of control and discipline, but that also seeks to transform and realize them *in toto*, in a free and just society. Revolution amounts to a social praxis that struggles against the social irrationality resulting from the constituted instrumental rationality of capitalist social relations. And its struggle for a just and free society proceeds from the experience that no authentic overcoming of injustice can succeed if bureaucratic mechanisms are used as the means; for such mechanisms lead not to emancipation but to political tyranny.

One antimony is implicit here: the emancipatory revolutionary action organizes means for the realization of collective action and worldwide solidarity in order that the conditions of life and human dignity are not destroyed. But revolutionary praxis must simultaneously guarantee that the revolutionaries themselves do not fall into the trap of a logic of domination, but rather preserve, in the course of revolutionary transformation, critical thinking, distance, integrity, and humanity (the arsenal of Enlightenment values that are today deconstructed and denounced as dogmatic by the prevailing relativistic ideologies). Revolutionary logic and the standpoint of dogmatism belong to different worlds. Dogmatism fights against indeterminacy, relativism, instability, etc, but in reality it seeks to incorporate relativism into its dogmatic stance. The revolutionary opposes conditions of 'stability' that are produced by illegitimate rule.

Revolution is the process of transcending the coherence of systems that endanger values such as the preservation of social life, freedom, or solidarity. However an inversion of the 'determinate negation' of social relations occurs frequently in real history; and the result of this inversion is a festishizing of the values of life, freedom, and solidarity in organizational forms that endanger that which they supposedly advocate (for example: warlike action in order to protect human rights that allegedly are not respected in a particular society can endanger life and destroy the freedom of people whose rights it is supposed to protect and preserve). Revolutionary in this case is to carry the struggle against both projects, namely: it is necessary to oppose both the suppression of values of life and human dignity and the mechanisms that, in the name of the struggle against oppression, create new oppression and suffering. Revolutionary is the praxis that blocks both oppressive projects and it does so by blocking the conditions that render them possible.

But this raises the question of how this double struggle can be coordinated. Connected with this question is that of the binding norms of this struggle and coordination. These norms that are supposed to guide revolutionary action can themselves only come from values that are constantly endangered by the ongoing antagonistic, atomized, and fragmented form of society, namely: from values that respect life, human dignity and demand the elimination of injustice and exploitation on a global scale.

II

To inquire about the meaning of revolution today entails reflection on the relation between revolution and the Enlightenment. The Enlightenment understood itself as a philosophy that had to be realized in practice; it demanded the revolutionizing of reality so that reality becomes worthy of philosophy. Rousseau considered the constitution of reality as a process that transcends current social nature and brings into being of a new nature. According to him, the task of thought and of praxis consisted first of bringing about an internal break in the historical, and then of reproducing those relationships that illuminate history's normative and emancipatory nature. Several elements of political reality that exist as *volontes particulieres* must 'be forced to be free' (*forcer d'être libre*), to become parts of a whole that is subjected to the normative principles of theory. This revolutionary thought leads directly to the theory of the assemblies in the fourth book of the *Contract Social*, which is concerned with the question of whether the existing state is an expression of a *volonte generale* or whether it only represents a *volonte particuliere*. In the latter case, the state should be forced to transform itself, to adapt itself to the *volonte generale* (these analyses thus pose the problem of revolution as the central problem of political philosophy).

In the Kantian version of the Enlightenment, it appears that revolutionary force is to be rejected and countered with the positive values of truth, critique, and public discussion. Always present and efficacious at the heart of this position, however, is the mechanism of the formation of judgment, which makes possible *a priori* synthetic judgments, and which enables revolution to be expressed in the language of critical philosophy. The conditions of the possibility of experience are here presented as conditions of the objects of experience themselves. But those conditions are subordinate to the primacy of praxis. Reality must satisfy the transcendental subject's claims to freedom and is therefore understood to be in constant transformation in order to satisfy those claims.

Already in the period before the *French Revolution*, Immanuel Kant's political philosophy conceptualized history as progress towards freedom and equality before the law. In Kant's view the development of these values was guaranteed by the development of the intellectual and sensual powers of the human species itself. According to Kant, the species learns, through antagonisms and conflicts, that it is in its own interests to establish a bourgeois political constitution with universally valid laws and freedom. The economic antagonism (mobilized through the instrumental rationality of the understanding) leads to the establishment of a state based on the rule of law (*Rechtsstaat*) for which the universal rule of law (i.e. the form of reason itself!) is characteristic. The categories of the critique present in their re-arrangement a theoretical model of an enlightened and free civil society whose realization is presented as a practical duty.

Such an ideal of progress is, for example, expressed in Kant's essay, 'Idea for a Universal History in Cosmopolitan Perspective' (1784), and it is reformulated and specified in his essay 'Conflicts of the Faculties' (1798). In the time that passed between both texts, the great *French Revolution* had begun, and this experience put its stamp on the structure of argumentation in the latter text. Here Kant comes to speak again of the problem of the progress of the human species; and he maintains that it is impossible to establish empirically whether or not progress toward the better is embedded in a given historical situation. The criteria of historical progress must therefore be sought in the 'non-empirical'. They are to be derived rather from the *a priori* standpoint of reason (the standpoint of freedom and the universal rule of law). Proceeding from the non-empirical, rational criteria of evaluation, 'historical signs' can be found that satisfy these criteria. Such signs elucidates whether the 'revolution of a gifted [*geistreiche*] people which we have seen unfolding in our day may succeed or miscarry' (Kant, 1979, p.153). According to Kant, this revolutionary event, which can verify philosophical principles, entails characteristics such as the open and universal nature of reflection about its results, the unselfish moral sympathy for the realization of law as the purpose of reason, and finally the enthusiasm of the observer who is in conformity with the law (cf. Kant 1979). Good purpose, universal form, subordination of the emotional to the rational norm – these are the determinations of the intellectual and practical-spiritual powers of the Kantian transcendental subject.

For the logic of revolution Kant's analyses contain an important methodological insight. His thesis is that revolution is to be affirmed insofar as it realizes a constitution based on natural rights (freedom, equality before the law), but not in terms of the violent means that may have contributed to that realization. According to Kant, then, the value of its rational content is to be affirmed on the condition that the indeterminacy of its causation is maintained. According to this formulation, the decoupling of the rational constitution of social reality (wherever it has been attained) from the unfree, undignified and terrorist prerequisites of its possible realization is revolutionary. This means, however, that that causation is revolutionary which presupposes rational critique and which suppresses and transcends mechanisms of violence and structures of blind domination. The importance of this logic was never clearly recognized in either the post-Kantian tradition of dialectical idealism or dogmatic Marxism.

Kant's revolutionary logic brings indeterminacy into the reckoning of reason. This logic also lay at the heart of Kant's position in the controversy with Benjamin Constant on the use of force and deception in politics.[2] May one lie for a good purpose – if, for example, someone inquires after the whereabouts of my friend and I assume that the questioner is an enemy who wants to murder my friend? In a world of lies, the murderer could discover where my friend is hiding precisely because he does not believe my lie – just as, if I had told the truth, he could assume it was a lie and thus not discover my friend's hiding place. Kant, however, refuses to accept that speaking the truth, that not deceiving can be the true cause of a deleterious effect. The world of deception and violence ought not be countered with more betrayal and counter-violence; it should rather be transformed into a world in which lies are not told and in which power does not become naked violence, but is bound to norms. The norms originate in the critique that rejects tyrannical violence, but that simultaneously refuses to affirm that violence which fights against tyranny – for this would entail the perpetuation of the relations of violence. Critique attempts to bind the rulers to guarantee just norms, and these norms can also protect the ruled from their own unjust action. Such norms are those that originate among the ruled so that the separation of rulers and ruled would disappear.

That the instrumental rationality of the rulers will adapt itself to the postulates of reason – this is a premise that results from the possibility of harmonization those capacities of the human species (reason, understanding, sensuality) whose interaction forms history. But the determination of the direction of this interaction does not follow some sort of automatic logic; rather its direction is determined through the constant struggle of reason against irrational forces. Whether the mechanism of egoistic actions conforms to rational norms and moral practice is uncertain and cannot be scientifically affirmed. But in order to guarantee that this will be the case, Kant had recourse to the idea of God. Kant adopts the conception of the Enlightenment that, if people act *egoistically* a 'natural intention' (or the 'invisible hand') coordinates their actions in such a way that their results conform to rationality and justice. His recourse to God, however, also supports the counter-thesis, namely that if people act *morally*, the world will remain healthy and not collapse. Thus, it could well be that the coordination of action on the level of the entire society runs amok and that moral action could therefore lead, not to happiness, but to misery and catastrophes.

If one abandons this idea of the harmony of reason and understanding that was typical of the early Enlightenment (and this is typical of the deconstructionist critique of the Enlightenment since Nietzsche), then 'good' action runs the risk of becoming irrational, a force of destruction. In this case one would be dependent on a logic (and a politics) of responsibility on a global level that could protect us from this risk. But such a logic is not Kantian. Moreover, such a logic cannot replace the

[2] See also his 'On the Alleged Right to Lie out of Love for Humanity' of 1797.

Kantian God. Kant's recourse to God means that his thought is premised on the indeterminacy of the action of the historical actors. It is impossible for the actors to predict the exact course of events. But it is precisely on this indeterminacy that the possibility of critique is based. Critique rejects the standpoint of the dogmatic fanatic and terrorist revolutionary; they both assume to have complete knowledge of reality in its particular forms and that they can therefore 'correct' or 'improve' reality by destroying those of its parts that they designate as 'evil'. Against this concept of revolution, which might well increase rather than reduce evil, Kant insists that social relations and the consequences of actions must remain indeterminate as long as they are connected to conditions that are violent, exploitative, and beneath human dignity. But this does not answer the question of how the motto, 'critique instead of violence', can be integrated into a theory of revolution.

III

The programme of Kant, the reformer who limited revolutionary action, was rejected by German Jacobins. In his book on the right of the people to make a revolution, for example, the neo-Kantian Jacobin Johann Benjamin Erhard gives four reasons that in his view justify revolution: a) so that injustice will be ended; b) so that justice will be realized; c) so that infringements on human rights cease; d) so that the Enlightenment will be completed. (The text was published in 1795, and immediately censured and confiscated.)

The German Jacobins were disappointed by Napoleon's expansionist politics, and found themselves again confronted with the contradiction between ideal and reality. Without understanding this contradiction, we cannot understand dialectical thinking, and least of all Hegel's dialectical thinking. Neither the experience of the *terreur* nor the mistrust in the ability of the revolution to erect stable institutions made Hegel an opponent of revolution. Hegel was always in favour of the destruction of the institutions of the *ancien regime*, which for him meant the destruction of a system that was already internally destroyed because it was characterized by misery, injustice, and alienation from rights. Enthusiastic about the prospect of realizing freedom and founding political institutions grounded in freedom, Hegel's *Geist* rose against the *ancien regime*. But revolution cannot solve precisely this problem of freedom, a problem posed by revolution itself, when it confronts individual historical institutions with an abstract ideal of freedom. In order to solve this problem, Hegel thought that revolution must first of all be established within philosophy itself; it must become the organizational principle of its concepts, of the dialectical categories. A new totality is meant to arise that is not romantic or organic, but one which presupposes a break with all contents and historical rights that contradict the principle of freedom. The presentation of the institutions of the law and state in the *Philosophy of Right* presupposes this revolutionary break. The dialectical presentation coordinates the contents that conform to the principle of freedom so that in the *Philosophy of Right* every contents 'comes to its right'. Here, the concept of freedom concurs with the totality of all presented moments and with the power that prevents the regression to traditional, historically contingent relations. In this sense the revolution always takes place internally within the dialectical concepts themselves. This internality is prerequisite of their constitution and of their relationship to one another.

The particular socio-economic interactions are coordinated with the systems of binding norms in such a way that they realize the social purposes of the consciously interacting *citoyen*, rendering social well being and justice in bourgeois society effective. In this way, the revolutionary ideal, that Kant had entrusted to God, is to be realized through political action. The conscious citizens, the philosophers and the officials who care for the whole, act in the place of God and effect concrete freedom on earth. The dialectical system of philosophy, which leads to freedom as the absolute idea, guarantees that the concrete steps in the realization of freedom proceed in the proper direction and sequence. The presentation of the categories of the philosophy of right, which implies the logical transition from necessity to freedom, proves itself to be revolutionary. However, this presentation also sublates (*aufheben*) the intermediary moments of property, particularity of private interests and market-socialization – and that means, they continue to exist as positive values; and, as parts of the absolute, they are even accorded additional dignity.

IV

In the *Economic-Philosophical Manuscripts* of 1844, the young Marx criticized Hegel for considering objectivity (*Gegenständlichkeit*) as such as something alien, as a human relation that does not correspond to the human essence. In Hegel's view, then, reappropriation entails the sublation (*Aufhebung*) not only of alienation, but also of objectivity, that is: reappropriation is suggested as the restoration of Man[3] according to and in the idea of Man. Rather than being put off by the alienation of a particular form of objectivity, Hegel found the objective character of the object as itself repugnant (Landshut, 1964, p.276). Marx, however, sees perceptions and passions as ontological affirmations of both the human essence and nature. In contrast to Hegel, Marx appreciates the objective character of the objects because they are, however alienated, affirmations of Man's sensuous being. It is therefore necessary to pay attention to the form in which objectivity is affirmed: individual gratification does not derive from the individual's relationship to the object but rather consists in the affirmation of the object by another person! The developed form of gratification/affirmation occurs in developed industry where, albeit mediated through private property, the ontological essence of human passion appears in its totality, in its 'humanity'. Marx therefore concludes that sensuous private property, separated from alienation, is the essential object for Man, both as object of gratification and activity (ibid., p.296).

These considerations may be understood as theorems of Marx's early conception of revolution: the goal of the revolution would then be the

---

[3] [Translator's Note: Man with a capital 'M' indicates here and throughout *Mensch*.]

reappropriation of the objective from its alienated form. Objectivity is here conceived as a form of human gratification, mediating the relationships between individuals. This mediation is historical; it develops (in inverted, alienated form) in modern industrial society. Revolution is thus the termination of alienated forms of gratification and activity. Revolution changes the historical direction of activity so that it becomes an ontological affirmation of the human essence and nature.

This notion of revolution as a sensual struggle that leads to the overcoming of alienation is also characteristic of *The Holy Family*. Here Marx states that 'every mass-type "interest" that asserts itself historically goes far beyond the real limits in the "idea" or "imagination" when it first comes o the scene and is confused with human interest in general'. Thus the French Revolution served the interest of the bourgeoisie, but not the real interest, the 'true life-principle' of the masses 'whose real conditions for emancipation were essentially different from the conditions within which the bourgeoisie could emancipate itself and society'. In the principles of previous revolutions, 'the most numerous mass...did not have its real interest in the principle of the Revolution' (Marx and Engels, 1975, pp.81, 82).

The enemy of the masses are the autonomized conditions that produce self-degradation, self-deprecation, and self-estrangement. Rather than understanding and confronting these conditions as necessary conditions of alienated social relations, the masses seek to overcome their condition on the basis of these conditions themselves, as if their degradation were really just a matter of their own shortcomings as individuals. They should not see their degradation as a mere externalization of their self-consciousness (as Hegel does in the *Phenomenology of Mind*); rather they must comprehend their condition as a necessary one that must be overcome through external, sensual struggles. Revolution thus becomes a sensual struggle against the autonomization (*Verselbständigung*) of the products of human labour. The revolutionary struggle leads to the elevation of sensuality to sensual activity and thus overcomes the separation of sensuality and intellect. In this sense Marx demands in the first thesis on Feuerbach that passive observation be transformed into sensual human activity, into praxis.

On the basis of these texts, it is possible to define revolution as the separation of sensuality from the existing abstract social forms, allowing Man to re-appropriate and restore society to himself. Revolutionary would then mean the development of a society whose materiality does not abstract from the social individual, that is, a society whose material form does not contradict Man's sensual social existence. Materiality would then exist in the form of the 'species-being', that is on the one hand as the unity of *sociality* that is no longer ruled by abstractions and on the other hand *individuality* without mediation through egotistical atomism. Abstraction from alienated mediation and coordination of the objective and subjective sides of objectivity are necessary moments of the revolutionary process. But here there arises an antinomy in the question of how this 'coordination-in-revolution' is be conceived. If this is to take place through means of *political* action, then splits and separations will occur in the post-revolutionary reality. This new reality will therefore not be one of general human emancipation, and the necessity of revolution would continue.

Let us turn now to the analysis of *The German Ideology*. In the Feuerbach chapter Marx lists the conditions of revolution.

> In the development of the productive forces there comes a stage when productive forces and means of intercourse are brought into being which, under existing relations, only cause mischief, and are no longer productive but destructive forces (machinery and money) (Marx and Engels, 1976, p.52).

He continues, 'a class is called forth which has to bear all the burdens of society', a class which stands 'in the sharpest contradiction to all other classes'. This 'class forms the majority of all members of society and from which emanates the consciousness of the necessity of a fundamental revolution'. The *revolutionary struggle* is direct against the conditions under which the 'the forces of production are applied', and these conditions 'are the conditions of the rule of a definite class of society'. The anticipated revolution is called the communist revolution: In contrast to all *previous revolutions* which leave the mode of activity untouched, the *communist revolution* abolishes this *mode of activity, labour, classes* and their rule. This revolution will change the people, especially the revolutionary class, the class will 'found society anew' (ibid., pp.52, 53).

This motif of changing the relationships and also people themselves in the course of the revolutionary process is at the centre of the controversy between Marx and Stirner, which Marx addresses in the *German Ideology* with the differentiation between revolution and rebellion. Stirner rejects Marx's concept of revolution, which calls for the overthrow of the existing conditions of the state and society through a social and political act that founds society anew. Stirner advocates rebellion by which he means 'the refusal to respect the holy' and the rejection of any canonization of social relation' (ibid., p.377). Rebellion, according to Stirner, does not proceed from the transformation of the condition, but expresses 'dissatisfaction with oneself' (cf. ibid., p.379). The goal of rebellious dissatisfaction is not at a new form of society, but 'new arrangements'. 'Rebellion leads to a position' where we 'arrange things for ourselves (ibid.). It is not a struggle against the existing society, because what exists will break down on its own, once rebellion prospers. '[S]ince my aim is not to overthrow something that exists, but for me to rise above it, my aim and action are not political or social, but *egoistical*' (Stirner, quoted in ibid., p.377). Marx counters Stirner, insisting that had he 'concerned himself with actual individuals "existing" in every revolution...he would have come to the understanding that every revolution, and its results, was determined by these relations, by needs, and that the "political act or social act" was in no way in contradiction to the "egoistical act"' (ibid., p.378).

Through his opposition between revolution and rebellion Stirner sought to call attention to the possibility that revolution might not achieve the *coordination* between, on the one hand, the realization of new modes of social organization and, on the other, the autonomy of the individual as a free person. Marx, on the one hand, seems to assume that the social and political action of founding of a new society is not in contradiction with egoistic-individual action that preserves freedom and spontaneity. Thus, he suggests that the coordination between the freedom of the individual and the revolutionary founding of a new society ensues without contradictions: the revolutionary process is seen to effect relationships as well as people and will therefore *lead to the harmonization* of subjective needs and those new social and political structures through which alienation is overcome. Marx objects to Stirner's category of rebellion arguing that it is psychological, that it reduces revolution to the individual discontent, moods etc. of the participants and their good will to change the existing relations (voluntarism). Marx believes that his conception of revolution is much better founded because it proceeds from the actual people in their social relations. And he points out that Stirner's notion of self-arrangement presumes a common 'we' in action (Marx and Engels, 1976, p.379), a social 'we' with which each individual has to go along and which emphasises the necessity of common action.

Marx explicates his critique of Stirner's concept of the constitution by introducing a political-economy type of argument in place of Stirner's institutionalism. In contrast to Stirner's demand for the *transcendence of the constitution* (*Aufhebung der Verfassung*), Marx wants to show that the given constitution is a result of the social division of labour and that only the communist revolution will transcend the division of labour and ultimately the political institutions. But this upheaval is to be determined, not in relation to the political institutions, but in relation to the forces of production. Moreover, the 'senselessness' (ibid., p.378) of the rebel's endeavour 'to be *without a constitution*' (Stirner, in ibid., p.380) is revealed in his embrace of human rights: '"if the community treats me unjustly, I rebel against it"' (Stirner, in ibid., p.403). But, Marx says, this is insurrection (he refers to right of insurrection of the *droits de l' homme* of 1793), 'a human right that, of course, bears bitter fruit for him who tries to make use of it at his "own" discretion' (ibid.). Marx is thinking here of the Declaration that was composed by Robespierre and that claimed: 'When the government infringes on the right of the people, rebellion is the holiest right and the unconditional, indispensable duty of the entire people and of every single one of its parts'. Marx's argument does, however, encounter difficulties when he warns against rebelling 'according to one's own discretion' and instead favours, as the appropriate measure, the adaptation of emancipatory actions to the level of development of the forces of production. For such an adaptation could reproduce the reification of the social relations within the revolution, making the overcoming of alienation dependent on the development of the social forces. The embarrassment of Marx's analysis is obvious in expressions such as 'the revolt of modern productive forces' (Marx and Engels, 1996, p.18) that are fettered by the social relations of production – expressions that can still to be found in Marx's late works (Marx, 1983, p.715). Marx thus did not answer the question that Stirner's indirectly posed, namely, how the transition from the fetishized conditions to emancipatory practice might be conceived. This however is the question of revolution, not only in terms of the appropriate conditions for the development of freedom, but also in terms of the appropriate means of revolution so that those conditions of enslavement do not perpetuate themselves within the emancipatory project.

V

Marx develops the most important themes of his early conception of revolution in his later work. Here the important issues are: a) the critique of the alienated forms of social materiality and its emancipation from alienation; b) the demonstration that in capitalism the social forces of production become forces of destruction; c) the elaboration of the sort of change required, in the capitalist social relations and the people themselves, to make revolution possible in practice.

The dialectical presentation of the categories in Marx's late works seeks to inscribe this revolutionary programme into the concepts themselves. The categories of the critique of political economy are critical concepts of the human condition that exists in the mode of being denied, that is, in the form of alienated objectivity, as relations between things. Each category thus affirms the existence of human dignity as dignity denied. These categories thus affirm the material content of society at the same time as they criticize the alienated, or capitalist, form of this content. The destructiveness of social forces derives from their capitalist form. This categorial dialectics seeks to reconstruct the capital relation as a social relationship between humans. The purpose of this reconstruction is to render Man visible in his alienation and thus to demonstrate how the social forces revolutionize themselves, and in this process shed their alienated form, and thereby producing conditions for emancipated human relations. Marx's concepts entail therefore 'a tension within the concepts'. Use-value is a product of social labour but assumes social existence only in the form of exchange value, that is, through the mediation of an alienated form; the labour-process subsists as a valorization process; human sensuous activity exists in the form of a labouring commodity, wage labour, and the means of subsistence required to satisfy the needs of the labouring population pertain through the category of variable capital, etc. However, his dialectical presentation is not simply a matter of contrasting the 'bad form' with the 'good contents'. Rather, it confronts the form with its social-historical materiality, and shows that this form poses a real threat to the continued existence of this materiality. Today, this threat is a real possibility. Its form-determined constitution and movement is self-contradictory. The continued existence of society requires what its capitalist form constantly thwarts, namely: survival, protection of the weak, solidarity, development of the sensual and intellectual powers of all and every single human being. Already under capitalist conditions, the development of this material side of social being has become a necessary condition of the reproduction of the whole of society. For this reason, the state has become involved in developing norms and regulations to protect these material conditions. Revolution is the result of the failure of these regulations; revolution, then, is an attempt of preserving the conditions of life – and above all those conditions, which society itself has already institutionalized, thereby admitting in practice their necessity for its own survival. And yet the capitalist form of society destroys what it itself requires for the sake of its own reproduction.

There are many places in *Capital* where *this logic of revolution* can be reconstructed (cf. Psychopedis 2000). In the eighth chapter of the first volume, for example, Marx sought to demonstrate that the labouring substance of society is threatened through capitalist exploitation, that its 'life-force' (*Lebenskraft*) has been 'seized' by its roots. The expression of the social reaction to the threatened annihilation of the basis of social reproduction is the implementation of legal norms that regulate the working day. A parallel example of the tendency to introduce conscious social regulation to preserve society from the threat emanating from its capitalist form can be found in the thirteenth chapter of the first volume that discusses factory regulation. On the one hand it is a necessary product of large-scale capitalist industry; on the other hand it represents 'the first conscious and methodological reaction of society against the spontaneous developed form of the process of production' (Marx, 1983, p.451). Marx's analyses demonstrate that regulation, such as that for the protection of health, for universal education, the equality of the sexes, are functional prerequisites for the continued existence of the capitalist economy itself. At the same time, however, the antagonistic economic form prevents the positive consequences of such regulations. In order to increase productivity, the capitalist economy requires adaptable workers, who adopt with great flexibility to the demands of work and whose multi-directional mobility renders advanced methods of production profitable.

The development of multi-talented people, education etc., is a *functional condition* of capitalist reproduction. At the same time, this development promotes new social contents that potentially transcend the capitalist mode of production; only a future communist society can fully develop these contents. Marx shows that the tendencies to protect life and health, the demand for humane development and the development of personality by means of poly-technical education, requisites of a creative and adaptable labour-force, come into conflict with the profit-driven interests of each individual capitalist, requiring the state to legislate against their interests in order to secure the capitalist development of the forces of production on the basis of political regulation.

Marx, however, assumes that all these regulations must remain *unstable*, because in the long run capital cannot tolerate regulations that reduce the profit margin – even though the purpose of these regulations was to secure its conditions of production. If one pursues this logic, the only possibility of guaranteeing the reproduction of modern society would therefore be the *conquest* of political power by the proletariat (cf. Marx, 1983, p.458). That is, the political sphere – in consequence of the logic that Marx follows here – is doubled into: a) a *system-immanent normativity* which preserves from within its own laws of development, the substance of society and develops its social forces and individuals in accordance with the requirements of the new technologies of modern capitalism; b) *system-transcending action* (the seizure of political power) which protects emergent new social contents from the dangers to which any system-immanent normativity is susceptible (dangers caused by the antagonistic constitution of society, that is by the profit-oriented behaviour characteristic of capitalism). The logic of Marx's conception of revolution in his late work can be reconstructed along this line.

A 'blind spot' is contained in this logic – and indeed at precisely that point where, according to the development of the forces of production, the 'many-sided individuals' are meant to free themselves from their conditions of existence through practical (revolutionary) action, creating new, emancipatory conditions of life. Instead of proceeding to the delineation of the processes of this praxis, the analysis jumps immediately to the moment of the capture of power. Action remains therewith thoroughly dependent on, and in conformity with, those conditions determined by the logic of the forces of production. The capture of power mediates the transition from the practical precondition of revolution to its realization in the realm of freedom. This view runs contrary to the logic of his dialectical presentation of categories. This dialectics suggests that the revolutionary moment subsists in the tension between form and content. With this tension, the 'material' element is not reducible to a technical relation. Marx had defined materiality in terms of the possibility of a labour process that would consist, not of an alienated form, but of solidarity and free cooperation. Materiality referred to the possibility of separating human relations from their alienated form of existence, that is: it pertained to the possibility of praxis.

Marx's dialectical presentation endeavoured to show the conditions of social reproduction in the light of their possible practical transformation, that is, he sought to show their practical contents that could be realized through revolutionary practice. His conception of transition from the functional requirements of reproduction to conquest of power is a step back from this dialectical formulation of the problem. In this regard, the question that Kant had posed – the question of praxis not just as positing, but also as determining, or revealing, those conditions that present emancipatory points in the hidden form of a technical-mechanical process – is therefore posed anew.

In the Marxist tradition after Marx, this ambivalence in the relationship of the conditions to social practice favoured the dogmatic resolution to the dilemma of praxis. Such a dogmatic version of the dialectic was characteristic of the ideologies of 'really existing socialism'; it is based on the assumption that the seizure of power by the proletariat would be followed by a schematic sequence from mechanical to teleological phases of development, that is: first, the mechanical system (development of the forces of production) would be developed to its logical conclusion, and then, on this basis, social goals such as freedom and self-determination would be realized. In this ideology, the problem of creating the prerequisite for the transcendence of the capitalist organization of social life and for the realization of free and cooperative social relations is resolved schematically: a) the revolutionary seizure of power; b) the socialist phase in which the conditions (mechanisms) for overcoming the old society and developing the social forces of production; c) the communist phase where freedom, true democracy and the self-determination of the citizens is real (which is the 'final purpose' of the whole development).

In this conception, the mechanical process is laid on the teleological process, and operates as its prerequisite. This conception overlooks the fact that a cooperative process of solidarity (i.e. a 'teleological' process – one of evaluation and of the practical realization of the theoretical and practical purposes of the actors themselves) has always to be presupposed so that the priorities of this revolutionary development can be established. Furthermore, the logic of the second socialist phase (separation of planning and execution) excludes *a priori* the possibility of the transition to the communist phase that is fundamentally opposed to this separation. Thus, 'revolutionary' means in this context something quite different from schematic versions of transition. It means social practice as a practice of self-determination, of social autonomy; it conceives of society not as something that is separated from itself, but as a form of sociability where the development of the forces of production are not separated from the producers, but rather where this separation is overcome and guaranteed in practice.

VI

From Kant to Marx, revolution implies the transformation of the conditions of human life through praxis. Praxis is initiated by the autonomous logic of social mechanisms. But it can also render itself autonomous of these mechanisms. Marx saw that social change is mediated by situations in which the mechanisms of the forces of production become destructive; that is, in Kantian terms, social 'understanding' can injure the rational contents (materiality) of social life.

In this way action is confronted with destruction and crisis; it becomes revolutionary insofar as it is able to oppose such emergency situations with confidence in its own purpose, a confidence that emerges through and relies on mutual trust, sense of justice, and solidarity. To be sure, the action that is supposed to eliminate destructive practices requires an instrument, an organization of power that can, however, itself become an obstacle to solidarity, trust, etc. among the revolutionaries. For this reason, the typical Kantian question of how the result of action is related to the conditions of action poses itself anew for post-Marxian modernity. Walter Benjamin and Hannah Arendt are the thinkers of our times who placed this question in the centre of their thinking about revolution.

Benjamin's analysis presupposes a new approach to history: the historical is that which Man has not experienced; it is the lack of fulfilment and justice in all previous history. Humanity of today must 'save' its past; it must fulfil *ex post facto* those same conditions that have hitherto constituted this lack of happiness. History exists only as redemption. History possesses thus a 'weak messianic power'. According to Benjamin, the way in which this redemption occurs can be described in the language of historical materialism: His conception of historical materialism implies an inversion of the traditional views of the historical role of the redeeming powers of the proletariat. In this perspective, class struggle is not a 'war for booty', not the appropriation of material wealth and the imposition of rule and ideologies; in this struggle, rather, elements such as 'faith, hope, trust' are present together with humour, courage, and cunning. The new revolutionaries must distance themselves from dogmas, and must possess above all detachment from their own individual interests. Benjamin's programme aims at saving the prehistory of thought itself, namely that of enlightened thinking, from its own instrumental modes of deployment. As Kant demanded knowledge and courage ('*sapere aude*') of enlightened thought, Benjamin demanded the courage to think and to act so that the postulate of historical materialism can be realized.

This new conception of historical materialism contains a critique of the idea of progress that had been adopted in the theory and practice of Marxism and social-democracy. This idea of progress presupposes an 'objective' movement of the disciplined, homogeneous, and coherently organized masses in the form of the labour movement. This, then, is a politics that seeks to incorporate social relations into the functional, objective processes, causing the subordination and disciplining of social relations. In Benjamin's view this attempt at incorporation is common to both Social Democracy and fascism. The conformist social-democratic politics of the period between the two world wars combines in an unreflected manner technical-economic progress with proletarian interests. Factory labour is posited as equivalent to political action. Labour means wealth, and wealth means freedom. This logic, however, fails to consider the form of this process, namely: the private character of the appropriation of the products of labour and the exploitation that goes with it. The form-element sublates (*aufheben*) progress; it constitutes, in Benjamin's words, negative progress. It is therefore the sublation of this form itself that constitutes the real possibility of human history. This utopia of a new beginning demands the re-constitution of historical knowledge (see Benjamin, 1974, p.698). The subject of historical knowledge is the suffering and enslaved class that struggles and transforms its lack of happiness into revolutionary might. The means and ends of this struggle, however, (and precisely herein lies the utopian dimension of his conception) are not incorporated again into the logic of power, a logic that belongs to linear conceptions of historical time as 'progress'.

The historical materialist is revolutionary. He seeks to destroy the conditions that make up *reality* – a reality of suffering, sacrifice and indignity. He does not recognize the elements of this reality as conditions of emancipation. Rejecting recognition of these elements today is for him the condition that the coherence of the false totality of the present will become fragile in the future. For that reason, the historical materialist understands the exception in history, the emergency situation or the crisis in reality, as history's actual rule. What differentiates Benjamin's position from classical Marxism is the emphasis on the particular, the break with the continuity of the historical, the accentuation of the momentary and the fragmentary. The *experience* of the historical materialist is based not on the repetition and perpetuation of events, but on reversing their causal sequence, on negating their currently valid constellations, and on the mobilization of the individual, the unique (to which relativist historicism had also appealed) for purposes of critique.

Important analyses of the problem of revolutionary violence are contained in Walter Benjamin's works, especially the 'Critique of Violence' (Benjamin, 1996) and the notes to 'The Work of Art in the Age of Mechanical Reproduction' (Benjamin, 1968). Benjamin is interested in the 'natural' violence that stands behind institutions. Violence is posited in legal form and poses a threat to its form of institutionalization. The violence of the great criminal who is admired by the masses is confronted with the violence of the class struggle. Class struggle presupposes legal regulation (for example, the legal regulation of labour struggles, strikes, etc.) and class struggle constantly calls existing forms of social regulation into question. Benjamin's notion of violence goes back to Marx's conception of 'original accumulation', that is, the forced separations of the worker from the means of production that constitutes modern class relations. The transcendence of these separations becomes visible in the revolutionary general strike. This strike presents a simultaneous mobilization in all socio-economic areas and its purpose is the downfall of the legal order – or at least the demand for decisive concessions in favour the working class. The general strike unveils the nature of violence as a power that can found and modify legal conditions (Benjamin, 1996, p.240). Critique is charged with deciphering the function of violence as a power that posits legal relations: the existing institutions presuppose organized police violence. The 'normality' of the modern political system presupposes that violence appears within certain limits as 'normal', 'neutral' or 'non-violent'. This is especially true for parliament, the space of discussions, deliberations and the building of consensus. The separation of powers, the structure of representation, and the guarantees of property – all arrangements that are defended with violence if necessary – are constitutive of this institution.

Benjamin's central thought is that the structured social reality presupposes violence to keep its elements separate from each other. Bourgeois reality in particular presupposes the constant separation of life and the means of life (*Lebensmittel*). This separation is guaranteed through violence. For the actors themselves it seems rational to accept the established rules because they fear those who render them effective. 'Revolutionary' means the repudiation of this logical chain of 'fear, violence, and rule'; but through their revolutionary action, the actors, seeking to preserve themselves as just beings, put their own life in danger (cf. Benjamin, 1996). Benjamin's social theory conceives of revolutionary condition in which the 'mythical' institutions of violence, the authoritarian containment of society, the encrusted institutions, the state monopoly of violence is constantly destroyed by the revolutionary actors. For the actors understand that these mechanisms, while protecting their lives, simultaneously threaten their autonomy. But by destroying these mechanisms of protection they constantly put their own lives at risk. Even if they succeed in doing away with the authoritarian institutions, they must at every moment be able to mobilize themselves in order to render impossible the threats against their lives and against the level of social and cooperative relations of solidarity that has been attained. That is: to accomplish this they must be able to use force, and this ability is a dimension of their freedom. The conventions that regulate the scope and boundary of this force are limited by nothing other than the actors' own responsibility – we already found this idea in Stirner.

In Benjamin's essay, 'The Work of Art in the Age of Mechanical Reproduction' (Benjamin, 1968), the problem of the revolution is indirectly posed – linked to his (by now matured) conception of the transformation of social relations and of the conditions of contemporary technology. In this work Benjamin formulates more precisely his thoughts in relation to the problems of modern technology and mass democracy. Benjamin rejects the traditional aesthetic values of creativity, genius, the mystery of art, etc. and demands a new *revolutionary aesthetic*. This new aesthetic presupposes the overcoming of previous forms of technology, which are based on the domination of nature and which subject Man to the logic of this domination. The new aesthetic is conceived as a *second* technology that expresses the relationship between Man and nature in the form of a playful exchange. Humanity learns to develop means of exchange that presuppose variety, experiment, play, sincerity, honesty, and recognition of and kindness towards fellow human beings. It thus represents transition from enslavement and necessity to freedom. This new logic of technology contains a new logic of *revolution*.

Contemporary art that removes itself from the aesthetic of the beautiful illusion, breaks the false unity of the aesthetic experience and puts the unity of humanity and materiality back into play. By means of technology, the portrayal is rendered independent of that which is portrayed and also of the audience. For that reason it can be critically perceived by the masses; but at the same time it is impossible for the masses to influence directly or to control the action to which the picture refers. The masses are only capable of this after capitalist relations have been overcome. Until this occurs, the revolutionary possibilities of the masses to control political praxis are transformed into a counter-revolutionary force. These analyses (points XI and XII and the notes) contain an anticipation and critique of the modern forms of the (formal) democracy of mass media (Benjamin, 1968). In the twelfth note, Benjamin formulates a critique of mass democracy that can be understood as a modern theory of revolution. The masses, he writes, are constituted as such through the lack of class-consciousness. Insofar as class-consciousness is developed, the class constitutes itself as a class and this constitution is synonymous with the dissolution of class as a social mass. Masses only react and are subjected to impersonal laws. Class-consciousness overcomes this coherence of the masses as a mass. The establishment of a coherent mass is synonymous with the establishment of the programme of fascism; the overcoming of this coherence is synonymous with revolution.

Hannah Arendt's *On Revolution* represent a radical inversion of Benjamin's programme. Her analyses of the problem of revolution intended to separate the revolutionary project from the Marxist tradition that viewed revolution as a means of producing substantial social justice.[4] For Arendt, revolution is synonymous with a new beginning that will lead to the establishment of new institutions of liberty. Arendt's position can best be elucidated through her comparison of the *French Revolution* with the *American*. Arendt criticizes the French Revolution for having defined itself as a revolution aimed at overcoming *poverty and misery*. Robespierre sacrificed the ideal of freedom in favour of the social rights of the people (overcoming of hunger). But, she argues, precisely this sacrifice had to lead to the *Terror*. The goal of the revolution was not the freedom of the people, but their happiness. Arendt puts Marx too into this tradition. In her view, Marx falsely identified the revolution against suffering with the revolution that creates relations of freedom. This identification led in turn to theories that legitimize unfree, tyrannical regimes with the argument that they contribute to the overcoming of inequality and injustice, to economic growth, etc., all of which are perceived as constituting 'real freedom'. Arendt contrasts this with the American Revolution,

[4] On Arendt's critique of Benjamin, see Weber (2000).

which in her view created 'truly' revolutionary relations. She goes beyond the establishment of *bills of rights* because their sole purpose was to limit state power, not to create new institutions. The American idea that the people give themselves a constitution is, in Arendt's view, revolutionary. The American Revolution created new political relations not through the concentration, but through the decentralization of power (the federalist principle). Furthermore, the constitutional branches of power balance each other out (checks and balances). This strengthens the entire constitution as each branch controls, supports, and protects all the others. The *new power* that emerges from these parts is stronger than the sum of its parts. The American Revolution represents an entirely new experience in creating free political institutions that is without historical precedent.

The realization of Arendt's political ideals presupposes the separation of the political from social contents and the exclusion of the latter from the realm of political deliberation. For social questions cannot be solved through decentralization, but only through redistribution, which can, however, entail the use of force. To Arendt, every attempt to eliminate poverty with political means seems dangerous to the existence of society and therefore counter-revolutionary. The result is an anti-social political programme that rejects any form of 'sympathy' (Rousseau). Arendt naturalizes this political programme and stylizes it as destiny. She contrasts substantial goodness, for which in her view no rational criteria can be found, to the 'naturally evil' on the one hand and to the law on the other. Arendt finds an exemplary representation of this relation in Melville's novella *Billy Budd*. Here, evil is personified in Claggert, a character who is opposed to the speechless, natural goodness represented by Billy Budd. According to Arendt, the law, represented by Captain Verse, is to be given primacy over the good. Evil will be punished by natural goodness; but because this punishment occurs without judicial process and legal procedure, the good must, in turn, be punished by the law. Since its options cannot be settled by rational means, the law presents itself as tragedy. But in Arendt's rendition, precisely the essential dimension of Melville's story is lacking, namely, that the legality represented by Captain Verse is that of an emergency situation (*Notzustand*). His is the legality that, in the interest of preserving the endangered society, suspends justice – the norms of a just life. This becomes clear in the eighteenth chapter of *Billy Budd* where the emergency nature of the situation (mutiny in the navy) is underlined. In this situation special courts assume jurisdiction and these do not inquire whether actions were committed intentionally ('material law operating through us'). Arendt, thus, renders law irrational and links it to the naked logic of decision-making under martial law. The good is speechless and cannot be represented as a rational norm. Social justice is excluded from the realm of the good, and of legality, only the decision remains. A transition from the value of the good (for example, nobody should be hungry) to the norm is not possible.

In contrast to Hannah Arendt, a critical theory of society will inquire into the ground rules of substantial justice and also into the possibility of establishing a rational connection between these rules and their social deployment. Such deployment seeks to mediate the human value-content of action with the existing form of society and is thereby confronted with the problem of violating positive rights (revolution). Arendt renders this process of development irrational. Revolution then becomes the spontaneous creative act, an act that she discovers in the council-movement in which people participate directly in decision-making and create living institutions. Arendt, however, did not consider the danger that 'spontaneous' creation *ex nihil*, that is, uncoupled from socially just institutions, might be inverted into anti-democratic political solutions and counter-revolution.

VII

Kant's notion of revolution contains two ideas that are of decisive significance for the way in which we think of radical praxis today: *first*, the idea of the indeterminacy of the causal relation that occurs through domination and exploitation; *second*, the idea that the pursuit of emancipatory goals becomes ineffective when its means of realization deceptively disguise its purposes and intensions. Kant's idea that no good can come from untruth says something about modern society. Here the pursuit of strategic action cannot be one of certainty because no exact calculation of all causal factors can be provided and strategic action can therefore not determine how the manipulation of an individual factor might influence the end result. If one pursues the implications of Kant's reflections, one must conclude that the core-logic of terrorism and fanaticism rests on such a strategic calculation – which, however, is completely unsuitable as a revolutionary logic in the contemporary world.

Marx imagined the revolution as a kind of re-establishment of the sensual essence of the species through the overcoming of its alienated, capitalist form of existence. The emancipation of the sensual contents could succeed, not on the individual, but only on the social level. Stirner made Marx take notice of the problem that if revolution is to result in the intended overcoming of social relations, it must also distance itself from the given instrumental causal conditions that revolutionary action confronts. The unsatisfactory solution of this antinomy is expressed in Marx's analyses that either demand 'the seizure of power' by the exploited, or represent revolution as the action of the unconscious 'masses'.

Walter Benjamin pushed this question into the centre of his thinking. He criticized the concepts of 'progress' and the 'masses' whose coherence is an expression of non-attained critical consciousness. In this regard, Adorno's critique of 'mass culture' in the *Dialectic of Enlightenment* is also in part a theory of revolution. Benjamin's critique demands that revolutionary action simultaneously protects and reproduces the conditions of life threatened by their capitalist form of existence, and preserves the autonomy of the actors. Such a revolution, however, would only be possible in the context of a new form of technology that integrates the playful and the experimental, and where social reproduction no longer depends on mechanical repetition and compliance with technical commands. This critical utopia is directly opposed to those theoretical undertakings, which, like Hannah Arendt's, deprive revolution of its social contents, naturalize the practical value-contents of social theory, and treat revolutionary action as irrational.

Throughout its historical development, the theory of revolution has experienced several transformations and variations of meaning. These variations are associated with attempts to realize the protection of the citizen from the arbitrariness of state power, but also with overcoming of social inequality, exploitation, and misery. They are associated with creating the institutions that would guarantee political freedom; but in order to assure that this freedom would be grounded in universal consent, the theory of revolution initially accepted the legitimacy of property titles. As a consequence of the historical development of bourgeois society in the nineteenth and twentieth century, revolutionary theory came to demand the abolition of property, the ending of poverty, the social administration of wealth. Finally, revolutionary theory raised the theme of rebellion against the bureaucratic administration of collective goods – a demand that postulates the autonomy of the citizen as a social individual.

Since revolutionary activity seeks to transform the present, it affects not only the life-conditions of the revolutionaries but also of those who are opposed to such change. A theory of revolution must therefore confront the question of the revolutionary ends, that is, the *proper arrangement* of the social relations that it strives for, not only through persuasion, but also through *violence*. This, then, implies the further questions about how such violence might be legitimate.

Kant recognized as revolutionary only the transformation of violence into rational discourse and into critique, and rejected any revolution that ends discussion and issues a call to arms. A truly revolutionary action would be one in which the actors organize their own *conditions of life* in an *autonomous* manner. Autonomy is guaranteed by collective power. The negation of this collective power eliminates freedom, and introduces *tyranny*. In such a case the task of the actors would certainly be the 'prevention of all obstacles to freedom' (cf. Kant, 1979). The question of the legitimate use of violence obviously cannot be excluded from this complex problematic.

The 'legitimation' of the violence of fascist and Stalinist concentration camps was not in any way based on rules of reason, but on the 'right' that the administrators of the 'revolution' claimed for themselves, to punish those whom they declared the enemy. On the basis of the constitutions of western bourgeois societies, violence is legitimized when the constitutional order is threatened. The use of violence is legitimate as a means of re-establishing values such as freedom, equality before the law, justice and liberty. This legitimation is bound up with the tradition of natural law. Complementarily, yet also in part contradictorily, this legitimation brings to the fore social values that are of fundamental importance for social actors for these are values of social survival – such as the fight against poverty and sickness, the deployment of technology for humane purposes, the prevention of war and environmental disasters, etc. Moreover, and this was already true in Marx's time, the rules of substantial justice and the establishment of relations of trust and solidarity still come into contradiction with the antagonistic form of society, with the rights that guarantee property, or with the organizational principles of 'socialist' bureaucrats.

These intertwined contradictions demand a new arrangement of social relations on a global level. They demand 'revolution' – yet its character is still to be determined. In societies that suppress the right of critique and the free expression of thoughts, a right whose exercise is necessary to render threats to the conditions of life public, destructive forces can be unleashed that endanger social existence. Where profit interests and class advantages block information about dangers to the environment or dangers arising from the self-absorbed use of technology, movements demanding democracy and the free exchange of knowledge are the guarantors of the continued existence of social life as such. Is action on the part of the threatened, an action that breaks the law and might perhaps also involve the use violence, legitimate? They rise up because their conditions of life are endangered by the profit-oriented action of others. Surely, such movements cannot be condemned, even more so if the possibilities of protecting life and freedom by means of critique and the building of consensus are structurally precluded.

Against the background of an almost universal reduction of existing guarantees of social security and global instability, these questions have become ever more pressing. In the past, revolutionary action sought to force the state to guarantee the security of life and freedom. These traditional state mechanisms have lost much of their meaning. Multinational companies that present networks of political and economic interests, have taken on political functions, as have criminal networks, including the mafia. There are then no institutions that could guarantee the conditions of life, health, freedom, etc. on a global level. In their place step organizations that guarantee means of well being only selectively for limited groups and persons – the proprietors of money and wealth. Organizations such as these establish means of worldwide communication and delivery of information; they operate without any responsibility to those whose life conditions they determine; and they do so without any form of democratic accountability and democratic legitimation.

The question of revolution, then, is posed as the question of the self-determination of the actors whose conditions of life are determined by alien powers. Revolution means the break with the positive rules and conditions that disdain human life and human dignity and that render the rule of unfreedom possible. Revolutionary actions, thus, emerge along the lines of the international division of labour and at those points where the mechanisms that destroy the conditions of life are reproduced.

Under the guise of instituting human rights in the third world, profit and power driven action amounts to economic extortion and political aggression, tolerating and exacerbating environmental destruction and destroying social nets of cooperation. Wherever this destructive action is effective, counter-forces emerge, new aggression and the willingness among those without hope to let themselves be used for the violent and terrorist purposes of fanatics and fundamentalists. Yet, this is not the whole story. On all fronts possibilities of action become visible that are grounded in solidarity between those who bear the brunt of the destruction and those who however integrated in the mechanisms of domination in the first world, reject those same mechanisms because they can no longer tolerate injustice. These actions, of course, require support from other movements, both local and international. The power of the whole movement for freedom increases with the growth in the solidarity among the various parts – an idea that Hannah Arendt explicated on the example of the American Revolution. Coordination between the means and purposes of these movements is needed to tackle the mechanisms of economic profit, the monopolizing of power, the destruction of the conditions of life, and terror. However, coordination of emancipatory actions cannot be base on harmonious principles of integration – as expressed in Kant's idea of God. Rather, coordination remains an open project and as such is synonymous with revolutionary praxis.

Is a revolution as it has been described here a utopia or does it represent a real possibility for humanity? Following Rousseau's 'Second Discourse on Inequality', one can imagine a worldwide process of revolutionary restructuring to achieve forms of coexistence. Restructuring would take the form of a dialogical process between the rulers and privileged, on the one hand, and the poor and enslaved on the other. Here the threat of violence would be the means of persuasion. The rulers always use violence in order to achieve their goals, secure their position, and increase their influence. They must however reckon with blind reactions to their violence by the hopeless and the enslaved, an uncontrolled violence that would not arise if profit- and control-oriented action could be confronted with conscious counter-action based on compassion, understanding and reason. The utopia of revolution would thus contain the idea of reason as a principle of social organization, a principle if affected before the catastrophe that is before us, that would engender social relations, not based on conquest, but on mutual trust. This bit of utopia seems however to be that which remains of the old worthy idea of revolution that was passed on from Kant to Marx and from Marx to us.

References

Arendt, H. (1990) *On Revolution*, Penguin, London.

Benjamin, W. (1968), 'The Work of Art in the Age of Mechanical Reproduction', in *Illuminations*, trans. H. Zorn, ed. and introd. Hannah Arendt, Harcourt, Brace & World, New York.

Benjamin, W. (1974), 'Über den Begriff der Geschichte', in R. Tiedermann and H. Schweppenhäuser (eds.) *Gesammelte Schriften*, Vol. I.2, Suhrkamp, Frankfurt.

Benjamin, W. (1996), 'Critique of Violence', in M. Bullock and M. W. Jennings (eds.) *Selected Writings*, vol. I, Belknap Press, Cambridge MA.

Horkheimer, M. and T. Adorno (1979), *Dialectic of Enlightenment*, Verso, London.

Kant, I. (1979), *The Conflict of the Faculty*, trans. and introd. M. J. Gregor, Abaris Books, New York.

Landshut, S. (1964), *Karl Marx: Die Frühschriften*, Kröner Taschenbücher, Stuttgard.

Marx, K. (1959), *Economic and Philosophical Manuscripts*, Lawrence & Wishart, London.

Marx, K. (1983), *Capital*, Vol. I, Lawrence & Wishart, London.

Marx, K. and F. Engels (1975), *The Holy Family*, in *Collected Works*, Vol. 4, Lawrence & Wishart, London.

Marx, K. and F. Engels (1976), *The German Ideology*, in *Collected Works*, Vol. 5, Lawrence & Wishart, London.

Marx, K. and F. Engels (1996), *The Communist Manifesto*, Pluto, London.

Psychopedis, K. (2000), 'New Social Thought: Questions of Theory and Critique', in W. Bonefeld and K. Psychopedis (eds.) *The Politics of Change. Globalisation, Ideology and Critique*, Palgrave, London.

Weber, T. (2000), '"Der Seltsame Marxist" Hannah Arendt's Benjamin-Porträt', *Das Argument*, no. 250, pp.282-290.

Translated from German by Joe Fracchia

Part II
Social Autonomy: Time, Experience and Means

Chapter 5

Beyond the Muck of Ages

Michael A. Lebowitz

'Only in a revolution', *The German Ideology* (Marx and Engels, 1846, p.53) argued, can the working class 'succeed in ridding itself of all the muck of ages and become fitted to found society anew'. Revolution is necessary not only to overthrow capital but also to transform human beings 'on a mass scale'. Both to transform the existing modes of distribution and production and also for 'the production on a mass scale of this communist consciousness' – the consciousness of the '*all-round* dependence' of each upon each, this consciousness of the power of social labour, the communist revolution is essential.

This conception of 'revolutionary practice' – the coincidence of the changing of circumstances and self-change, which Marx introduced explicitly in his *Theses on Feuerbach* (Marx, 1845, p.4), is the guiding red thread in the work of these revolutionary thinkers. 'You will have to go through 15, 20, 50 years of civil wars and national struggles not only in order to bring about a change in society but also to change yourselves, and prepare yourselves for the exercise of political power' – here was the position Marx presented to workers in 1850 (Marx, 1853, p.403). In the same year, Engels described how the struggle over the Ten Hours' Bill had transformed workers: 'The working man, who has passed through such an agitation, is no longer the same as he was before; and the whole working class, after passing through it, is a hundred times stronger, more enlightened, and better organized than it was at the outset (Engels, 1850, p.275). Two decades later, Marx's understanding of the self-development of the working class through its struggles remained unchanged – following the Paris Commune, he observed that workers know that 'they will have to pass through long struggles, through a series of historic processes, transforming circumstances and men' (Marx, 1871, p.76).

What could be clearer? Their own activity is essential if workers are to rid themselves of the muck of ages. 'The continual conflicts between masters and men', Marx stressed (Marx and Engels, 1979, p.169) in 1853, are 'the indispensable means of holding up the spirit of the labouring classes...and of preventing them from becoming apathetic, thoughtless, more or less well-fed instruments of production'. Indeed, without strikes and constant struggle, the working classes 'would be a heart-broken, a weak-minded, a worn-out, unresisting mass'. His position on the centrality of struggle was the same in 1865 when responding to Citizen Weston's argument against the effectiveness of the wage struggle. Should workers renounce the struggle against capital's tendency to lower wages? 'If they did, they would be degraded to one level mass of broken wretches past salvation'. Workers who give way in daily struggles 'would certainly disqualify themselves for the initiating of any larger movement' (Marx, 1865, p.148).

Yet, for Marx the muck of ages did not disappear simply as the result of the daily struggles of workers against capital. Why else would there be a need for theory? Why would Marx have considered it necessary to sacrifice his 'health, happiness, and family' in order to complete the first volume of *Capital* (Marx and Engels, 1987, p.366)? To understand why Marx wrote *Capital*, we need to understand that muck of ages.

The Muck of Capital

Look back at *The German Ideology*. 'One of the chief factors in historical development up till now,' Marx and Engels (1846, pp.47-8) proposed, is the 'consolidation of what we ourselves produce into a material power above us'. Here, indeed, is the muck of ages: 'man's own deed becomes an alien power opposed to him, which enslaves him instead of being controlled by him'. All the wealth produced by workers ('the social power, i.e., the multiplied productive force, which arises through the co-operation of different individuals') appears as 'not their own united power, but as an alien force existing outside them'. What is needed to shovel away this muck?

The central point that Marx subsequently attempted to communicate in his critique of the political economy of capital was the essence of that power above us. *What is capital*? What is this money that we sell our labour-power for, these objects of labour upon which we work, these tools, machines, instruments that we use in production? What are these products that sit in stores and which we work to obtain? His answer was unequivocal: they are the workers' own product which has been turned against them, a product in the form of tools, machinery – indeed, all the products of human activity (mental and manual). His answer was the same as that given in *The German Ideology*. Our power does not look like our power. Because it *is not* our power.

Why the workers' 'social power' becomes the power of capital over them and *why* they do not recognize that product as their own is at the core of *Capital*. Insofar as workers sell their capacity to work in order to satisfy their needs, they surrender all property rights in the products they produce. By purchasing the right to dispose of the worker's power, the capitalist has purchased the right to exploit the worker in production; and the result of that exploitation goes into the accumulation of more means of production. What you see when you look at capital is the result of past exploitation. In capitalism, the 'association of the workers – the cooperation and division of labour as fundamental conditions of the productivity of labour – appears as the productive power of capital. The collective power of labour, its character as social labour, is therefore the collective power of capital' (Marx, 1973, p.585). Simple.

But, why doesn't everyone recognize this? The key, Marx emphasized, is that the exploitation of workers is not *obvious*. It doesn't look like the worker sells her ability to work and that the capitalist then proceeds to get all the benefits of her labour. Rather, it looks like the worker sells a certain amount of her time (a day's work) to the capitalist and that she gets its *equivalent* in money. So, clearly the worker must get what she deserves – if her income is low, it must mean that she didn't have anything very valuable to sell, nothing much to contribute to society. On the face of it, in short, there is no exploitation. Marx was very clear on this point – the very way that wages are expressed as a wage for a given number of hours of work, the wage-form, extinguishes every trace of exploitation – 'all labour appears as paid labour'. This disappearance of exploitation on the surface, he insisted, underlies 'all the notions of justice held by both the worker and the capitalist, all the mystifications of the capitalist mode of production...' (Marx, 1977, p.680; Lebowitz, 2003, pp.172-75).

Obviously, if there is no inherent exploitation, capital cannot appear as the result of exploitation, i.e. cannot be recognized as the workers' own product. So, where must all that wealth come from? What is the source of machinery, science, everything that increases productivity? *It must be the contribution of the capitalist.* Having sold their power to the capitalist, the social productivity of workers necessarily takes the form of the social productivity of capital. Fixed capital, machinery, technology, science – all necessarily appear only as capital. Marx commented, '[t]he accumulation of knowledge and of skill, of the general productive forces of the social brain, is thus absorbed into capital, as opposed to labour, and hence appears as an attribute of capital' (Marx, 1973, p.694; Lebowitz, 2003, pp.156-57). This is the mystification of capital. The more the system develops, the more that production relies upon fixed capital, on the results of exploitation which take the form of instruments of labour – the more that capital (and the capitalist) appear to be necessary to workers. Indeed, Marx proposed that capitalism tends to produce the workers it needs, workers who treat capitalism as common sense:

> The advance of capitalist production develops a working class which by education, tradition and habit looks upon the requirements of this mode of production as self-evident natural laws. The organization of the capitalist process of production, once it is fully developed, breaks down all resistance (Marx, 1977, p.899).

The very nature of capitalist relations, in short, spreads the muck and does so more deeply the fuller the development of the capitalist mode of production. Of course, workers do resist particular characteristics of capitalism, and Marx never questioned that. Workers struggle over wages, the length and intensity of the workday and working conditions in general. But if they do not recognize the nature of exploitation and do not understand that capital is their own product, what exactly are they struggling over? Injustice. Unfairness. These are struggles for justice *within* capitalist relations but not justice *beyond* capitalism; they are struggles not against exploitation as such but for a 'fair day's work for a fair day's pay'. In short, a 'trade union' or social-democratic consciousness – a perspective bounded by a continuing sense of dependence upon capital – ensures that those struggles do not challenge the logic of capital.[1] As long as workers think capital is necessary, look upon its requirements 'as self-evident natural laws', then even if workers 'win the battle of democracy' a state in their hands will be used to provide the conditions for the expanded reproduction of capital (Lebowitz, 2003, pp.189-91). Here, in a nutshell, is the sorry history of social democracy – which, despite the subjective perspective of some of its supporters, ends by reinforcing the rule of capital.

How do you go beyond a struggle for fairness? Given that the appearance of non-exploitation is 'reproduced directly and spontaneously, as current and usual modes of thought,' Marx (1977, p.682) insisted that 'the essential relation must first be discovered by science'. Of course struggle is essential. But it is not enough. Marx (1865, p.148) warned that 'the working class ought not to exaggerate to themselves the ultimate working of these every-day struggles'. Workers need to understand the system. They need to learn where capital comes from. And, that is precisely what Marx attempted to communicate to workers in *Capital*. Through his critique of the political economy of capital, Marx demonstrated how and why 'man's own deed becomes an alien power opposed to him, which enslaves him instead of being controlled by him'. He offered workers a weapon that could help them go beyond capital, the weapon of criticism.

But; is *Capital* enough? To dispel the muck of ages, workers need more – the belief that another world is possible. 'They ought to understand that, with all the miseries it imposes upon them, the present system simultaneously engenders the *material conditions* and the *social forms* necessary for an economical reconstruction of society' (Marx, 1865, pp.148-49).

There is an Alternative

Marx envisioned a clear alternative to the rule of capital – a communist society, one in which social wealth, rather than accruing to the purchasers of labour-power, is employed by freely associated individuals. In the society of associated producers, the cooperation of the collective worker and the absence of alien mediators demonstrate that 'to bear fruit, the means of labour need not be monopolized as a means of dominion over, and of extortion against, the labouring man himself' (Marx, 1864, p.11). In this new, reconstructed society, that 'multiplied productive force, which arises through the co-operation of different individuals' is 'their own united power'. This would be 'a society of free individuality, based on the universal development of individuals and on their subordination of their communal, social productivity as their social wealth' (Marx, 1973, p.158). Expending 'their many different forms of labour-power in full self-awareness as one single social labour force' (Marx, 1977, p.171), they produce in accordance with 'communal purposes and communal needs' (Marx, 1973, pp.158-

[1] To acknowledge this critical point is not at all to presume a particular form of instrument – as the acceptance of the point by both Kautsky and Lenin suggests.

59, 171-72) and simultaneously produce themselves as members of a communal society.

Such a society, at last, would permit the full development of human potential. 'What is the aim of the Communists?' asked Engels in his early version of the *Communist Manifesto*, and he answered, 'To organize society in such a way that every member of it can develop and use all his capabilities and powers in complete freedom and without thereby infringing the basic conditions of this society' (Marx and Engels, 1976b, p.96). In Marx's final version of the *Manifesto*, this goal was further represented as indivisible – as the 'association, in which the free development of each is the condition for the free development of all' (Marx and Engels, 1848). In contrast to capitalist society, where the worker exists to satisfy the capitalist's need to increase the value of his capital, communist society would be 'the inverse situation in which objective wealth is there to satisfy the worker's own need for development' (Marx, 1977, p.772).

In short, the removal of all fetters to the full development of human beings was at the heart of Marx's conception of the society of free and associated producers. Here would be the creation of real wealth – the 'development of the rich individuality which is as all-sided in its production as in its consumption' (Marx, 1973, p.325). What, indeed, is wealth, he asked (1973, p.488), 'other than the universality of individual needs, capacities, pleasures, productive forces'? Indeed, the most important products of this society of freely associated producers would be rich human beings able to develop their full potential – i.e., the 'absolute working-out of his creative potentialities,' the 'complete working-out of the human content,' the 'development of all human powers as such the end in itself' (Marx, 1973, pp.488, 541, 708). In communism as it has developed upon its own foundations, the productive forces have 'increased with the all-round development of the individual, and all the springs of co-operative wealth flow more abundantly' (Marx, 1962, p.24).

But, where is the description of this alternative in *Capital*? It's not there – even though for Marx it was imperative that workers understand that their collective power could be their own power, that 'their communal, social productivity' could be their own social wealth. That alternative of a communist society is not developed in *Capital* but it is *Capital*'s premise! That 'inverse situation' in which their social power is not alien to the associated producers is not elaborated because it is the implicit perspective from which Marx views the inversions of capitalism. Understanding this premise explains why he describes the fact that means of production employ the worker as an inversion 'peculiar to and characteristic of capitalist production' (Marx, 1977, p.425). An inversion of *what*? Simply, an inversion of the relation between producers and their communal, social productivity in a society that has gone beyond the muck of ages. To really understand *Capital*, we need to recognize Marx's premise. Grasp Marx's understanding of real wealth as human wealth, as human capacities and capabilities (Lebowitz, 2003, pp.130-33), and you cannot fail to feel his condemnation right at the outset of *Capital* of a society in which wealth appears as an enormous collection of commodities.

Capital's premise is only hinted at in Marx's reference to that 'inverse situation' and in his occasional comments about the inversions of capitalism. Yet, it is important to recognize that contained within (and going beyond) his critique of the political economy of capital is another political economy, the political economy of the working class. That other political economy points beyond the muck of capital.

The Political Economy of the Working Class

Although Marx is often described as opposed to political economy as such, it is important to remember that in the 'Inaugural Address' of the First International he called attention to the existence of *not one political economy but two* – the political economy of capital and the political economy of the working class. 'Two great facts,' he noted, went counter to the general pattern of decline in the English workers' movement after 1848. Two victories had been achieved for 'the political economy of the working class'. One was the Ten Hours' Bill, the first time that 'in broad daylight the political economy of the middle class succumbed to the political economy of the working class'. 'A still greater victory of the political economy of labour over the political economy of property,' however, was the emergence of the co-operative movement, especially the co-operative factories. These demonstrated that large scale production could be 'carried on without the existence of a class of masters employing a class of hands' (Marx, 1864, pp.10-11).

What is this political economy of the working class that contests the political economy of capital – and which encompasses both victories? In *Beyond Capital: Marx's Political Economy of the Working Class* (Lebowitz, 2003), I have attempted to make explicit some elements of this theory that are implicit within *Capital.* Perhaps the most central proposition concerns the nature and effect of social labour. This can be expressed in the following proposition: *any co-operation and combination of labour in production generates a combined, social productivity of labour that exceeds the sum of individual, isolated productivities*. Thus, when producers co-operate by working together side by side performing similar operations or engage in different but connected processes or where they produce differing use-values which correspond to social requirements (the division of labour within society), the effect of their combined, social labour is increased productivity. Their co-operation results in 'the creation of a new productive power, which is intrinsically a collective one' (Marx, 1977, p.443).

This greater productivity of social labour had been noted in the *Grundrisse* where Marx (1973, p.528) commented that the combination of individuals to build a road is more than just an addition of their individual labour capacities: 'The unification of their forces increases their *force of production*'. This 'association of workers – the cooperation and division of labour as fundamental conditions of the productivity of labour' is independent of any particular form of production (Marx, 1973, p.585). Further, the principle clearly extends beyond a particular workplace to the division of labour within society. For example, insofar as some producers are active in the production of means of production that increase the productivity of others who work with those means of production, total social productivity is higher than it would be in the absence of this division (or, more appropriately, *combination*) of labour within society. Indeed, the growth of social productivity increasingly depends upon the extent that science, intellectual labour, 'the general productive forces of the social brain' are embodied in means of production (Marx, 1973, pp.694, 704-6). Here, too, the unification of different workers yields higher productivity for the producers as a whole, which is a social productivity: 'This development in productivity can always be reduced in the last analysis to the social character of the labour that is set to work, to the division of labour within society, and to the development of intellectual labour, in particular of the natural sciences' (Marx, 1981, p.175). What we are describing here is the productivity of the collective worker – that aggregate worker (some of whom 'work better with their hands, others with their heads, one as a manager, engineer, technologist, etc.') whose cooperation and combination of labour is the fundamental condition of social productivity (Marx, 1977, p.1040). But, that collective worker is involved in more than the so-called 'productive sector'. From the perspective of the political economy of the working class, which proceeds from the side of workers, the labour that is relevant is not only the labour mediated by capital (the only labour considered by the political economy of capital). It includes the labour, which provides 'that which is needed for the common satisfaction of needs, such as schools, health services, etc', and it encompasses the labour 'absolutely necessary in order to consume things' – i.e., the labour unproductive for capital that Marx included under the costs of consumption (cf. Lebowitz, 2003, chs.8, 11). All this is part of the collective worker.

In short, recognition of the interdependence of all limbs of the collective worker is at the core of the political economy of the working class. After all, we have to ask, what is the real product of the collective worker? It is not specific products or use-values. Rather, from the side of the worker, all products and activities can be seen as mere moments in a process of producing human beings; this is what the productive organism comprised of the collective worker yields as its real result:

> When we consider bourgeois society in the long view and as a whole, then the final result of the process of social production always appears as the society itself, i.e., the human being itself in its social relations. Everything that has a fixed form, such as the product, etc appears as merely a moment, a vanishing moment, in this movement (Marx, 1973, p.712).

From the perspective of the political economy of the working class, accordingly, the divisions within the collective worker between mental and manual, 'productive' and 'unproductive', waged and unwaged can be seen as an inversion characteristic of a capitalist society – as the artificial constructs of a society in which capital rules (and of its corresponding political economy). When we think about that productive organism that is the collective worker, we begin from the recognition that it is the combination of producers that generates wealth; thus, the starting point is 'the social power, i.e., the multiplied productive force, which arises through the co-operation of different individuals' that *The German Ideology* identified in its discussion of 'the muck of ages'.

But, why is that social power an alien force? Marx's critique of the political economy of capital revealed, as we have indicated, that the capitalist's purchase of the worker's ability to produce is central to the explanation of where capital comes from. Yet, the political economy of the working class explicitly identifies the necessary condition of existence for capitalist exploitation. A second proposition proposed in *Beyond Capital* focuses upon the nature of social relations characteristic of that collective worker. It states that, in any society, *separation and division in social relations among producers allow those who* ***mediate*** *among the producers to capture the fruits of co-operation in production.*

How the capture of those fruits occurs in capitalist production is easy to see; capital mediates between 'individual, isolated' owners of labour-power 'who enter into relations with the capitalist, but not with each other' (Marx, 1977, p.451). In this process, 'the individual workers or rather labour capacities are paid, and paid as separate ones. Their cooperation, and the productive power which arises therefrom, is not paid for'; i.e., the increase in productive power resulting from co-operation 'costs the capitalist nothing' (Marx, 1988, pp.260, 321). Thus, having purchased labour-power and thereby secured the property rights to the products of labour, the capitalist captures the fruits of co-operation in production. 'The social productive power which arises from co-operation is a *free gift*' (Marx, 1988, p.260).

Why are the producers *themselves* not able to capture the fruits of co-operation in production? Marx's answer was clear: their situation depends upon the degree of separation among them. E.g., comparing rural and urban workers within capitalism, he pointed out that 'the dispersal of the rural workers over large areas breaks their power of resistance, while concentration increases that of the urban workers' (Marx, 1977, p.638). Similarly, he noted that 'in the so-called domestic industries this exploitation is still more shameless than in modern manufacture, because the workers' power of resistance declines with their dispersal' (Marx, 1977, p.591). The workers' power of resistance rises to the extent to which they are able to unite. This second proposition implies that the extent of the surplus extracted by those who mediate among producers (i.e., the extent of exploitation) is a function of the degree to which producers are separated.

If workers can reduce the degree of separation among them, they thereby mount a challenge to capital's condition of existence. Within the sphere of direct relations with specific capitals, their unity (through, e.g., trade unions) can lead to increases in real wages and a reduction in the length and intensity of the work they perform for capital; i.e., they can drive the rate of exploitation down. Yet, as discussed in Chapter 5 of *Beyond Capital,* the ultimate power of capital resides in its right to the ownership of the products of labour, and the struggle against this is not one that can be conducted successfully by the institutional forms appropriate to the struggle against particular capitals. Rather, this struggle calls for higher forms of unity in order to confront capital as a totality. To the extent that workers can eliminate the divisions among them (and defeat capital's never-ending efforts to divide them), the fruits of social labour can be captured by the producers.

But, we are talking here not simply of the unity of commodity producers. It is the unity of all those who produce the collective worker, a unity which dissolves capital's divisions and which is based upon the principle that 'the worker's own need for development' must prevail rather than that 'inversion, indeed this distortion, which is peculiar to and characteristic of capitalist production' in which human beings exist to ensure the valorisation of capital.

Solidarity based upon recognition of their differences and of their complementarity can remove capital as the mediator between and over the various limbs and organs of the collective worker; it can put in its place, finally, the cooperative society based upon the common ownership of the means of production, a world without mediators – one where that collective worker expends its 'many different forms of labour-power in full self-awareness as one single social labour force', where 'the veil' is 'removed from the countenance of the social life-process' and production stands under the 'conscious and planned control' of associated producers (Marx, 1977, pp.171, 173). 'Social production controlled by social foresight,' Marx noted, 'forms the political economy of the working class' (Marx, 1864, p.11).

Building a World without Muck

This social form that corresponds to social production can only be created through struggle. Only through revolutionary practice, that simultaneous changing of circumstances and self-change, do the producers become fit to found society anew. Yet, as argued above, 'every-day struggles' are not enough to remove the muck of ages. To be able to go beyond capital, the producers need to grasp that capital's requirements are not 'self-evident natural laws'; they need to understand that capital is not necessary.

Marx's critique of the political economy of capital is essential for dispelling what is 'reproduced directly and spontaneously, as current and usual modes of thought'. But, the political economy of the working class needs to be developed and articulated explicitly in order to complete that critique. What it brings to the struggle is a guide to 'the *material conditions* and the *social forms* necessary for an economical reconstruction of society'. It points to a world without muck. As in any labour process, the collective worker must begin to build that structure in its imagination before it erects it in reality.

References

Engels, F. (1850), 'The Ten Hours' Question' in K. Marx and F. Engels, *Collected Works*, Vol. 10, International Publishers, New York.

Lebowitz, M.A. (2003), *Beyond **Capital**: Marx's Political Economy of the Working Class*. Revised Edition, Palgrave, London.

Marx, K. and F. Engels (1846), *The German Ideology*, in K. Marx and F. Engels, *Collected Works*, Vol. 5, International Publishers, New York.

Marx, K. and F. Engels (1848), *The Communist Manifesto,* in K. Marx and F. Engels, *Collected Works*, Vol. 6, International Publishers, New York.

Marx, K. and F. Engels (1976), Marx and Engels, *Collected Works*, Vol. 6, International Publisher, New York.

Marx, K. and F. Engels (1979), *Collected Works,* Vol. 12, International Publisher, New York.

Marx, K. and F. Engels (1987) *Collected Works,* Vol. 42, International Publisher, New York.

Marx, K. (1845) *Theses on Feuerbach*, in K. Marx and F. Engels, *Collected Works,* Vol. 5, International Publisher, New York.

Marx, K. (1853) *Revelations Concerning the Communist Trial in Cologne,* in K. Marx and F. Engels, *Collected Works,* Vol. 11, International Publisher, New York.

Marx, K. (1864), 'Inaugural Address of the Working Men's International Association', in K. Marx and F. Engels, *Collected Works,* Vol. 20 International Publisher, New York.

Marx, K. (1865), *Value, Price and Profit,* in K. Marx and F. Engels, *Collected Works*, Vol. 20, International Publisher, New York.

Marx, K. (1871), *The Civil War in France,* in K. Marx and F. Engels (1971), *On the Paris Commune*, Progress Publishers, Moscow.

Marx, K. (1962), *Critique of the Gotha Programme*, in K. Marx and F. Engels, *Selected Works*, Vol. II, Foreign Languages Publishing House, Moscow.

Marx, K. (1973), *Grundrisse*, Vintage Books, New York.

Marx, K. (1977), *Capital, Vol. I*, Vintage Books, New York.

Marx, K. (1981), *Capital, Vol. III*, Vintage Books, New York.

Marx, K. (1988), *Economic Manuscript of 1861-63*, in K. Marx and F. Engels, *Collected Works,* Vol. 30, International Publisher, New York.

Chapter 6

The Untimely Timeliness of Rosa Luxemburg

Joseph Fracchia

Introduction: Mind In and Out of Time

Evaluating Rosa Luxemburg's historical significance, her most authoritative English-language biographer, J.P. Nettl, somewhat sentimentally relegates her to

> [t]he world that ended in August, 1914, [which] was essentially Rosa's world as much as Bebel's, Victor Adler's and the emperor's. Protest, even negation, had always been based on understanding the essential processes of that world, had been a part – if an extreme part – of it. The Lenins, the Hitlers, with their tight ideological blinkers, had been in it but not of it – but they inherited the future (Nettl, 1969, p.326).

This largely correct assessment that the person and her thought were rooted in the pre-war world seems to render hopelessly anachronistic any discussion of Luxemburg's relevance to our world so much different from hers. I would argue, however, that though Luxemburg's thought was very much a *product* of the pre-war period (and, I contend, Lenin's as well),[1] the relegation of her thought to that period has less to do with the *validity* of her ideas themselves than with the particular way they were conceived in the pre-war period and received and dismissed in the post-war context – a context consisting of impatient revolutionary expectations that were disappointed by the failure of the Socialist parties to live up to their anti-war claims and confounded by the success of the Bolshevik revolution in an underdeveloped capitalist nation. In this context, ironically, Luxemburg's critique of imperialism as capitalism in decline helped create, and seemed to justify, the revolutionary expectations that contributed to the post-war dismissal of her ideas as a naïve theory of 'spontaneity', supposedly rendered obsolete by the success of Lenin's tightly-organized vanguard party.

Against this dismissal of the Luxemburg's lingering validity, Istvan Mészáros, certainly one of her most authoritative theoretical interpreters, maintains that she

[1] Lenin's acute awareness of Russian underdevelopment and his condemnation of Stalin as too rude, boorish, and dogmatic are two quite diverse examples of the degree to which he too inhabited the pre-war world. The crucial point is not that Lenin inherited the future but that the future inherited Lenin as monstrously transformed by Stalin, while Luxemburg's legacy was ignored.

'entered the historical stage with her radical ideas far too early, remaining desperately out of phase with her time, and even with ours'. And he concludes that 'we can recognize in her fate the tragedy of someone whose time has *not yet* come' (Mészáros, 1995, p.284). Though I fully agree with Mészáros's refutation of the premature dismissal of Luxemburg's thought, I would slightly modify his formulation as well. For I do think that, in a subjunctive sense, the time had come for Luxemburg's insights into the relation between party and class, the role of organization, and the self-emancipation of the exploited, that is: if those ideas had guided the politics of socialist parties before the first world-war, had Second International rhetoric that the international working class would strike, not fight, in event of war been complemented by a commensurate politics of the kind Luxemburg advocated, the barbarism of the war itself and much of the twentieth century may have been reduced, if not avoided. Because, however, few of the pre-war socialist leaders were so inclined, her time had 'not yet come'.

With these modifications, Nettl's and Mészáros's seemingly diametrically opposed evaluations of Rosa Luxemburg may be viewed as complementary; for each evaluation accurately depicts a dimension of her life and thought and both must therefore be considered in order to understand how she may help us avoid the tragic outcome of the two historical possibilities that she, following Marx and Engels, so succinctly summarized in the choice of 'Socialism or Barbarism'.[2] If willingness to put Luxemburg's theories into practice is the measure, then their time has still not come and the tragedy of Rosa Luxemburg persists. And given the rapid increase of barbarism in the world over the past two years that Mészáros sketches in his own more recent book, *Socialism or Barbarism* (2002), their time is now.

In this essay I shall elaborate the tragedies surrounding the untimely timeliness of Rosa Luxemburg. I shall focus on the development of her theories of the party-class relations in response first to the 'revisionism debate' prompted by Eduard Bernstein, and then in sympathy with Lenin's revolutionary commitment, but through a critique of his notions of organization and revolution. I shall also show how her theory and historical evaluation of imperialism created revolutionary expectations that, against the background of Second International failure and Bolshevik success in 1917, profoundly yet adversely affected twentieth-century Marxist thinking about working-class subjectivity and the nature of a properly revolutionary organization. Most notably, this climate of unfulfilled expectations set the stage for the emergence of a 'Western Marxist' theoretical tradition for which the first article of faith, allegedly proven by Lukács, was the reification of working-class consciousness – in another tragic irony, a standpoint against which

[2] Though not so succinct, the language of *The Communist Manifesto* clearly implies a future of 'socialism or barbarism'. Engels's conclusion in 'European War Inevitable' (*Neue Rheinische Zeitung*, March 2, 1849) is still not as succinct, but more explicit: 'The war will come, it must come. It will divide Europe into two armed camps, not according to nations or national sympathies, but according to the level of civilization. On the one side the revolution, on the other the coalition of all outmoded estate-classes and interests; on the one side civilization, on the other barbarism' (*Collected Works*, Vol. 8, p.457).

Luxemburg had spent most of her life struggling. In concluding, finally, I shall suggest why and how Rosa Luxemburg remains, to paraphrase Ernst Bloch, 'a co-worker in the space of the present'.

The Revisionism Debate and Luxemburg's Dialectic of Reform and Revolution

Rosa Luxemburg's first significant contribution to Marxist theory, 'Social Reform or Revolution' (1899), appeared as a rebuttal of Bernstein's 'revisionist' separation of social reform from revolution and as a revolutionary alternative to Kautsky's commitment to revolutionary waiting. Bernstein launched the revisionism debate by daring the party to appear as what, in his view, it actually was, namely: a social-democratic reform party.[3] This dare was grounded in his conviction that history had proven wrong the two fundamental pillars of Marx's critique of capitalism. Though Marx had predicted increasing proletarian immiseration, Bernstein pointed to contemporary working class life as evidence that capitalism had produced sufficient wealth to improve the material conditions of working-class life; and though Marx had (supposedly) predicted that capitalism's immanent contradictions would produce a great and final economic collapse, Bernstein argued that capitalism had proven itself sufficiently adaptable to prolong its existence indefinitely. Since history had allegedly proven Marx wrong, the party should concern itself with furthering the reform-process and the improvement of working-class life; and it should drop its revolutionary rhetoric which only frightened the established orders and made them unsympathetic to needed and possible reforms.

Bernstein's dare threw the SPD into an uproar. There was certainly a good deal of support for his position, though most supporters agreed with Ignaz Auer's council for subtlety ('My dear Ede, what you demand – one does not mention it, one simply does it')[4] in severing ties with the entrenched Marxist tradition that had sustained the Party through the years of illegality. The centre of the Party, especially Bebel and Kautsky, found Bernstein's position blasphemous, if not heretical. At Bebel's urging, Kautsky responded with a series of counter articles that carefully articulated a position of theoretical outrage and political passivity.[5] He insisted that the party maintain its Marxist heritage, its conviction that capitalism was self-destructive, and its socialist commitment, but his suggestions, or lack thereof, for revolutionary politics led Dieter Groh (1971) rightly to characterize his position as '*revolutionärer Attentismus*' (revolutionary waiting).

Luxemburg's task was thus to counter Bernstein's affront and confront Kautsky's revolutionary complacency with a viable critique of capitalism and

---

[3] From 1896-98 Bernstein published a series of articles on 'Probleme des Sozialismus' in *Die Neue Zeit*. These were published in bookform in 1899 as *Die Voraussetzungen des Sozialismus und die Aufgabe der Sozialdemokratie*.

[4] Auer cited in Gerhard Ritter (1963, p.201).

[5] First published in *Die Neue Zeit*, these appeared in bookform in 1899 as *Berstein und das Sozialdemokratische Programm*.

theory of revolution. She viewed Bernstein's dare as a matter, 'not of this or that tactic, but of the entire existence of the social-democratic movement'. Bernstein's insistence that 'the [socialist] goal is nothing, the movement everything', was a 'question of the being or non-being' of Social Democracy (I/I, p.370).[6] 'The socialist goal', she countered, 'is the only decisive moment separating the socialist movement from bourgeois democracy and bourgeois radicalism'. Certain that the cause of Bernstein's reformism was his facile understanding of Marx, Luxemburg sought to confirm the *raison d'être* of Social Democracy by rehabilitating Marx's critique of capitalism and rejuvenating the party's revolutionary commitment. Pursuing a double theoretical strategy, she first exposed the fallacies in Bernstein's 'naive' belief in capitalism's adaptability by fortifying Marx's analysis establishing the inevitability of capitalism's collapse and the 'objective necessity' of socialism (I/I, p.376); on this basis she then delineated the dialectical relation between reform and revolution.

Luxemburg argued that what Bernstein considered the means of capitalism's adaptability were, from a Marxist viewpoint, thoroughly predictable responses to, and intensifications of, its own internal contradictions. The recent economic reforms were enabled by a necessarily momentary economic upswing, but were unsustainable and would be rescinded with the next economic crisis. Luxemburg denied neither the importance nor the necessity of parliamentary and union struggles, and fought hard for the kind of reforms that would improve the economic conditions and enhance the political power of the working class. But she insisted that such improvements were illusory. Most importantly, reforms could not abolish the wage-labour relation, which is the locus of exploitation. Consequently, she categorically rejected a reformist politics that dismissed the socialist end-goal. Viewed in terms of the unity of Marx's theory of capitalist breakdown and political practice aimed at a socialist transformation of society, 'the great socialist meaning' of union and political struggles is revealed as the means to 'socialize the knowledge, the consciousness of the working class' – or, in short: 'the reform struggle is the recruiting school for the revolutionary struggle' (I/I, pp.401-2). The purpose of the struggle for reform is as a means to expose the limits of capital's flexibility and to prepare workers to overthrow capitalism and build a new society; it is a means to the end of social revolution.

After having presented in that first major essay a general theory of the lengthy process of social transformation, Luxemburg quickly moved to give it concrete content. She had already begun, in her writings on the Belgian struggle for universal suffrage (1901-02), to mention the mass strike as a specifically socialist form of struggle. Impressed by the seemingly spontaneous strikes during the Russian Revolution of 1905, she undertook in 'Mass Strike, Party, and Unions' (1906) the theoretical articulation of the mass strike as the dialectical link between reform and revolution; on that basis she then articulated her conception of the

[6] Unless otherwise noted, all citations of Luxemburg are my translations from: Rosa Luxemburg, *Gesammelte Werk*, 5 volumes (1974). Volume and page number of the source are given in parentheses following the quotation.

relation between party and class and of the role of organization in the socialist workers' movement.

Luxemburg first explained that Marx's and Engels's rejection of the mass strike was of its anarchist version that, as formulated by Bakunin, is to be planned, organized, and launched by a decision of a central committee. But, she argued, the mass strikes of 1905 meant 'precisely the historical liquidation of Anarchism' (II, p.95) and pointed toward the course of future revolutions. Initiated by the workers themselves, the Russian events taught that the mass strike has nothing to do with an 'executive decision', that it cannot be 'artificially "made", nor decided out of the blue, nor "propagated"' (II, p.100). One need only observe the concrete history of the Russian Revolution in order to understand that the workers' mass strike is 'not a sly means cleverly invented for the purpose of some more powerful effect of the proletarian struggle; rather it is...the form of appearance of the proletarian revolutionary struggle' (II, p.125). For this reason, 'not even a decision from the highest level of the strongest social-democratic party can simply unleash it by decree', nor is 'the greatest enthusiasm and impatience of the social-democratic troops sufficient to bring to life a true period of mass strike as a living and powerful popular movement'. The mass strike is by definition a revolution from below in which 'the spontaneous element' plays a great role. In Russia, 'the spontaneous element played such a dominant role, not because the Russian proletariat is "unschooled", but because revolutions cannot be taught' (II, p.132). As the actual praxis of proletarian revolution, these strikes obliged party leaders and intellectuals theoretically to catch up with actual historical development by rethinking the mass strike in historically up-to-date terms. Only in this way could theory again become relevant to praxis.

Once the historical significance of the 'modern' mass strike is understood, it is possible to develop a 'general view point' which is the measure of organization and tactics. This viewpoint has three elements: the mass strike must not be seen as 'a single act', but as a 'general concept denoting a years-long, perhaps decades-long period of class struggle'; the economic and political moments of the struggle are inseparable; and the mass strike is inseparable from revolution – as in Russia where 'the history of the mass strike...is the history of the Russian revolution' (II, pp.125-29). From this general viewpoint, she proceeded to explicate the relation between party and class as a dialectic of spontaneity and organization.

Though the outbreak of the mass strike is the outbreak of the revolution, it is only the beginning: the revolution must be completed by the open confrontation with, and assumption of, state power. In order to insure that it follows its proper course, an appropriately concentrated power is required that can 'take over the political leadership in the middle of the revolutionary period' and whose knowledge and organization can fuse the various separate actions of the proletariat and direct them toward the revolutionary transformation of society. This, of course, is the task of the social-democratic party. At the crucial moment, success depends on the willingness of the party to develop 'a decisive, forward-moving social-democratic tactic [that] calls forth in the masses the feeling of safety, self-confidence and will to struggle' (II, pp.133-34). In the revolutionary moment, in short, an organic unity of party and class must be forged that can then overthrow the existing order.

The construction of this unity, however, is not a foregone conclusion; it depends rather on whether the appropriate preparations have been made 'in peaceful times'. For the unity of party and class to be achieved, everyday tactics must aim at its construction. Even if the party is 'the most enlightened, class-conscious vanguard of the proletariat', it cannot be concluded that its relation to the proletariat is a traditional, hierarchical one between leadership and rank-and-file, nor that the party-organization is the crucial question. For 'the overestimation and the false estimation of the role of organization in the proletarian class struggle is usually complemented by the underestimation of the unorganized proletarian masses and of their political ripeness' (II, p.144). If, as Marx insisted, the emancipation of the proletariat must be its own work, then the task of the party is not to lead the proletariat, but to help it to power. Accordingly, the party must focus on the cultivation of worker experience and the formation of a revolutionary class-consciousness: 'in a period of strong political actions the liveliest and most efficacious revolutionary class feeling will grasp the broadest and deepest levels of the proletariat, and indeed all the quicker and all the more strongly, the more effectively the party has previously carried out the educational work' (II, p.145).

For Luxemburg, then, the rejuvenation of Marxist theory depended on proving that capitalism's immanent contradictions established the limits of its adaptability and on developing a praxis to facilitate proletarian self-emancipation. As the form of the proletarian revolution, the mass strike is the measure of organizational form, strategy, and tactics. The so-called 'spontaneous' element in her thought is nothing more than the recognition that a revolutionary period cannot be called into being by executive decision, but will emerge, unplanned, out of socio-economic developments and workers' actions.[7] The insistence that workers must be the agents of their own emancipation establishes the limits of the efficacy and therewith leadership role of the social-democratic organization and points to a new and specifically proletarian relation between party and class. The party could and should play a role in helping to prepare workers to be the agents of their own history, and the better it carried out this preparatory work, the better the chances of a successful revolution. But it could not 'make' the revolution.

Despite her deeply democratic commitment to overcoming the separation of party and class, there is a certain blindness in Luxemburg's theory that resulted from the battle over the role of the unions. From roughly 1906-1909, a struggle was waged between the leaders of the SPD and the German unions over the question of the latter's independence from the Party. As Carl Schorske (1955) has chronicled, the eventual result was the *de facto* independence of the unions hidden

---

[7] As Oskar Negt argues, Luxemburg's notion of spontaneity was always a mediated one: spontaneous worker politics would emerge 'against the bureaucratized apparatus of the proletarian parties and unions; and the spontaneous mass strike 'necessarily emerges out of the production process under specific conditions; it is mediated through the entire social context that is determined by the contradictions of the capitalist mode of production at a historically concrete level of development' (Negt, 1974, pp.154-55).

behind a thin veneer of rhetorical solidarity with the Party. Luxemburg became increasingly frustrated with this inversion of roles that had transformed the party into a 'recruiting school for the unions' (II, p.162). This produced 'the strange situation' in which 'the same union movement that below, in the broad proletarian mass, is unified with Social Democracy, above, in the administrative superstructure of the unions, is sharply separated from Social Democracy and has established itself in opposition as a second independent great power'. Seeing a double 'tendency to oligarchy' (cf. Michels, 1968), she depicted the German workers' movement as having 'acquired the peculiar form of a double pyramid whose base and body consists of a single mass, but whose summits are far apart' (II, pp.167-68). This schizophrenic element introduced by the union leadership into the workers' movement required a double loyalty from workers and thus fragmented proletarian power.

Luxemburg explained this inverted and counterproductive bifurcation of the workers' movement as 'an artificial, albeit historically determined product' of the exigencies of a period of capitalist upswing (II, p.155). This division, however, would only be temporary; for with the onset of a revolutionary period and the appearance of the masses 'on the battlefield, the splintering of the economic struggle and the indirect parliamentary form of the political struggle will disappear', as will 'the artificial separation between unions and the social-democratic party as two distinct and entirely independent forms of the workers' movement'; it will then become clear that the unions' economic struggles and the party's political struggles are not 'two parallel actions, but simply two phases, two steps of the workers' struggle for emancipation. The union struggle encompasses the present interests, the party struggle the future interests, of the workers' movement' (II, p.155). In the meantime therefore both party and unions should orient their tactics toward educating workers to understand the unity of the two movements. All tactics must be directed toward 'giving the average worker the feeling that to be a member of a union is also to be a member of a social-democratic party'; for, the appeal of the unions lay not in their appearance of neutrality', but in 'their social-democratic essence' (II, p.160). Thus, the most pressing task was 'to reintegrate the unions into Social Democracy' as the necessary prerequisite of a consistent strategy rooted in the dialectic of reform and revolution (II, p.169).

Luxemburg's theoretical call for the politicizing of the workplace and the economic struggle was, however, muted by the concrete politics of the conflict over control of the unions. The politicizing of the workplace was displaced onto the struggle between the party and union bureaucracies over who had the right to establish the unions' goals and tactics. This resulted in an insistence on party primacy that, by default if not design, effectively widened the gap between the political and economic struggles and between party and unions and forced workers to choose between their present economic and future political interests. The focus on the question of control of the unions thus produced a degree of myopia toward the question of modes of political organization in the workplace itself – which is crucial to realizing Luxemburg's stated goals of overcoming the separation of the political and economic struggles and of establishing a dialectic of reform and revolution that enables workers to be the subjects of their own history.

Luxemburg's Critique of Lenin and her Dialectic of Party and Class

Despite this practical diversion issuing from the party-union struggle, Luxemburg further elaborated her notion of the party-class relation through her critique of Lenin. First, however, it must be emphasized that the post-war encapsulation of the relation between Luxemburg and Lenin as spontaneity versus organization is false and misleading. As Marcel Liebman (1975, p.32) has insisted, 'the divergence between Luxemburg's "belief in spontaneity" and Lenin's criticism of spontaneity was not so wide as has been alleged'. Their generational affinities lay in their theoretical and practical commitment to revolutionary praxis. Their expressions of mutual respect, moreover, were clearly more than lip service. Luxemburg praised Lenin for his 'opposition to opportunism, carried through to the smallest detail of the organization question' (1/2, p.435); and after the Bolshevik revolution she wrote that Lenin's 'unforgettable historical accomplishment' was 'for the first time to have proclaimed the socialist goal as the immediate programme of practical politics' (IV, p.341). Lenin, in his more acerbic tone, appreciated Luxemburg's opposition to the 'stinking corpse' of Social Democracy and praised her commitment to revolution as the only positive remnant of the SPD. Finally, they were in remarkable formal agreement on several issues. Both insisted on the need for a revolutionary organization and saw the party as the 'vanguard', the 'most enlightened core' of the socialist movement; both insisted that the party must await the revolutionary upsurge from below; and both provided theoretical explanations explaining the objective ripeness of the situation for socialist revolution.

The vast differences in theoretical content are, however, more significant than their formal similarities. Yet to specify those differences, it is necessary to go beyond the false polarization of spontaneity versus organization, which incorrectly depicts their differences as an affirmation or negation of organization, and thereby occludes their crucial differences on the party-class relationship. Liebman (1975, p.32) alludes to this difference by noting that 'Lenin did draw a clear distinction between the "organization" and the "movement", and thought that the activity of the masses belonged essentially under the latter heading'. In this section I shall summarize Lenin's thought on the relation between organization and movement, between party and class, which determined the particular type of organization he proposed; then I shall focus on Luxemburg's relation between party and class which had already emerged from her critique of reformism, but was significantly refined through her critique of Lenin.

Behind Lenin's and Luxemburg's theoretical differences on these issues lay not the generational difference noted by Nettl, but rather a geo-historical *Ungleichzeitigkeit*. Like Marx, Luxemburg derived her conceptions of revolution and the relation between party and class from advanced industrial capitalism and a state in which workers could organize legally. Lenin, however, was constrained to work within an underdeveloped capitalist country and against the czarist political police. It is not coincidental that Lenin saw the coming revolution against the *ancien regime* in Russia as a bourgeois revolution on the model of the French Revolution of 1789, nor that he defined the Marxist revolutionary as a 'tribune of the people' and elsewhere as 'a Jacobin allied with the proletariat'. Consciously adapting Marxism to the underdeveloped conditions of czarist Russia, Lenin defined revolution unambiguously as an armed seizure of power. As Liebman (1975, p.103) put it,

> Leninism and Bolshevism are a theory and a form of organization, but they are also a type of political commitment focused on the idea of battle and insurrection...It is impossible to understand anything about Leninism if one ignores the fact that it accords primordial importance to the idea of armed, organized insurrection as indispensable, decisive form of political struggle – its highest form.

Or in Trotsky's succinct formulation: 'Lenin was warlike from head to foot' (cited in Liebman, 1975, p.99).

Unlike Luxemburg who felt obliged to articulate a notion of socialist revolution against reformism, Lenin's had no such need.[8] Assuming that revolution is armed insurrection, he already knew 'What is to be Done?' Thus, his first major theoretical treatise would have been more appropriately entitled 'How is it to Be Done?' – for the question he addressed was *how* to accomplish that insurrection and seize power. His answer was to sketch the kind of organization that could best attain that goal given the conditions in czarist Russia. Following Kautsky, Lenin insisted that the workers on their own could only develop a 'trade-union consciousness' and thus not go beyond the economic struggle. But he also realized that even if they wanted to, they could not succeed in an open, mass struggle, which would make them vulnerable to the police. Given the frequent arrests, exile, and execution of revolutionaries, Lenin concluded that the only possibility of success lay with a small, tightly knit, and clandestine organization of professional revolutionaries who could avoid capture while awaiting the proletarian protests that would provide the context in which the party could seize power. The only means to proletarian emancipation was to smash the state; and given Russian conditions, the proletariat would only be able to so if led by an appropriately revolutionary and disciplined party.

Since the party was committed to workers' best interests, Lenin imagined a harmonious and symbiotic relation between party and class.[9] He envisioned workers as scornful of economistic reformists who could not teach them anything they did not already know and desirous of the leadership of 'their' vanguard party that would lead them to political revolution. He insisted that workers be recruited into the party and cultivated as professional revolutionaries. And he felt that in revolutionary moments the party should be expanded 'in order to be able to keep

---

[8] Only shortly before the Bolshevik revolution did Lenin articulate, in *State and Revolution* (September, 1917), his theory of revolution.

[9] See Lenin's elaborate and remarkable, imagined sketch of the relations between workers and socialist revolutionaries in *What is To Be Done?* (Lenin, 1988, pp.72-74).

up with the stream of popular revolutionary energy' (Lenin, cited in Liebman, 1975, p.46). Marcel Liebman sympathetically views this seeming flexibility as evidence of a 'libertarian Leninism' saturated in a 'deeply democratic inspiration' that in 1917 effected the (momentary) fusion of party and class:

> The terms of the relation between class and party, between the guided class and the guiding party, the class that is led and the party that leads, were reversed, the Bolshevik organization having at last agreed to submit itself to the revolutionary proletariat..."Libertarian Leninism" was made possible because the traditional mediator between the masses and power, in other words, the Party...while becoming reinforced...ceased to be, in relation to the masses, an external body, an organ imposing itself as leader. An extraordinary osmosis took placed between the industrial proletariat of Russia and the Bolshevik – an interpenetration to which history knows no equivalent (Liebman, 1975, p.305).

Luxemburg was more critical and in my view more perspicacious than Liebman. She felt that Lenin's strict separation of organization and movement, party and class, was an untenable form of proletarian revolution.[10] Disturbed by Lenin's adoption of a bourgeois example, the French Revolution, as his model for socialist revolution, she rejected his qualitative differentiation of his socialist Jacobinism from Blanqui's putschism. Lenin was surely right in differentiating himself from Blanqui who felt that power could be seized by a small group of revolutionaries. Nevertheless, he was a kind of historically and politically astute Blanqui – who understood that the revolutionary seizure of power is more likely to succeed if the revolutionary organization has the patience to await the proper revolutionary moment when mass actions had paved the way. For Luxemburg, however, Lenin's demand for 'the blind subordination' of the entire party to a 'central power that alone thinks, creates, and decides for all' and for 'the strict separation of the organized kernel of the party from the revolutionary milieu surrounding it', was a 'mechanical transference of Blanquist organizational principles, its conspiratorial circles, onto the social-democratic movement of the working masses' (I/II, p.429). The centralized party organizationally separate from the working class perpetuated the traditional principle of hierarchy that prevents workers from becoming the subjects of their own history: Acknowledging the difficult Russian conditions, she nevertheless concluded that Lenin's conception of the party-class relation missed the whole point of the social-democratic movement. Leaping on Lenin's depiction of the revolutionary social-democrat as 'the Jacobin *allied* with the organization of class-conscious workers', Luxemburg noted that this turn of phrase captured his position precisely and precisely that was the problem: 'Actually, Social Democracy is not *allied* with the organization of the working class; it is rather the movement of the working class itself' (I/II, p.429); it is the first movement in the history of class societies which in all of its moments, in its entire course, is based on the independent and direct action of the masses' (I/II, pp.427-29).

---

[10] For an important collection of essays mostly written from standpoints close to Luxemburg's and critical of Lenin's conception of the relations between organization and movement, party and class, see Werner Bonefeld and Sergio Tischler (2002).

In *History and Class Consciousness* (that philosophical justification of Leninism considered, curiously, the founding work of 'Western Marxism') Georg Lukács (1985, p.284) accused Luxemburg of conceiving the proletarian revolution with the same structural forms as bourgeois revolutions. He pointed to the (Bolshevik) party, that Lenin himself called a 'party of a new type', as the form of organization appropriate for a socialist revolution. Both Lukács and Lenin, however, were blind both to the traditional nature of Lenin's party and the radical newness of Luxemburg's notion of the party-class relation and revolution. This is best exemplified by considering two fundamentally different formulations by Marx. In the Introduction to his *Critique of Hegel's Philosophy of Right* Marx wrote, in a traditionally hierarchical manner, that philosophy is the 'head', the proletariat the 'heart' of the emancipatory movement (Marx, 1978a, p.65). In introducing the Statutes of the First International, however, Marx supplanted his earlier, very traditional and elitist formulation with the insistence that 'the emancipation of the working class must be accomplished by the working class itself' (Marx, 1964, p.57).

Lenin in effect only slightly reformulated Marx's earlier and abandoned formulation and viewed the party as the head and the proletariat as the heart. The novelty of Lenin's 'party of a new type' lay not in having overcome the bourgeois principle of hierarchy, but in its single-minded commitment to armed insurrection and the seizure of power. Though Liebman insists otherwise, neither the quantitative expansion of the party nor its momentary fusion with the working class meant a qualitative change in Lenin's hierarchical understanding of the party-class relationship. Nor can the party's organizational separation from the working class be overcome simply by making it more accessible. Because the job of a 'professional revolutionary' is full-time, workers who join the party cease being workers and become first and foremost cadres (even if their agitational work is carried out in factories). As long as the decision-making power remains the privilege of the central committee, the quantitative expansion of the party rank-and-file effects no qualitative change in the party-class relation; it simply reproduces the hierarchical leadership-follower relation within the party – as is the case with the social-democratic and bourgeois parties.

Lenin's party, like bourgeois parties, was still based on the principle of representation, though with the proletariat's (post-revolutionary) maturation the party would ostensibly wither away. But given a hierarchical separation between organization and followers, representation almost invariably comes to mean substitution. In Lenin's case, the party as self-proclaimed representative of the proletariat retains the role of the thinking, decision-making subject, while workers are objects of party decision-making and their role is reduced to supplying the mass and the enthusiasm – the heart – required to initiate the revolutionary process. Aimed single-mindedly at the armed seizure of power, Lenin wasted no thoughts on the problem of attempting to build socialist forms of intercourse within the workers' movement – neither politically in regard to abolishing the hierarchical exercise of power nor economically in regard to abolishing hierarchical organization of the production process. It is therefore no surprise that the state did not simply 'wither away' as he imagined it would, nor that he envisioned the

Taylor system as the form of the socialist production process. Precisely because of his monotone concentration on the seizure of power, Lenin never questioned the hierarchical principle of the party-class relation – and ignored, it remained in effect.

Luxemburg, on the other hand, in both her definition of socialist praxis as a dialectic of reform and revolution and also in her conception of the party-class relation pointed in the direction of a new kind of politics carried out by a new kind of organization. Like Marx, Luxemburg felt that a successful and emancipatory socialist praxis, and the purpose of socialism in general, must be the enabling of workers to become the subjects of their own history – both in overthrowing capitalism and in the building of the new socialist society. Because socialism is 'the movement of the working class itself', an organization that reserves decision-making for itself and treats the working class as the rank and file, the followers, cannot, properly speaking, be a socialist party:

> Socialism will not and cannot be made by decree, not even by the most socialist of governments. Socialism must be made by the masses, by every proletarian. Where the chains of capital are forged – there they must be broken...The masses must learn how to use power by exercising power. There is no other way for them to learn (Luxemburg, cited in Mészáros, 1995, p.319).

In keeping with this notion, she directed all her theoretical and practical energies toward developing a party whose politics would aim at the party's own dissolution as workers themselves organized themselves as a political movement.

Here mention must be made of the council and soviet movements, whose importance as examples of political forms of organization in the workplace, at the site of the economic struggle, stands in inverse relation to their historical brevity. Precisely in order to overturn the existing order, and to ensure that workers in a socialist order would no longer be 'hands' in a socialist Taylor-system, but would be able effectively to democratize the workplace and efficiently to carry out production, some organizational form modelled on workers' councils is absolutely necessary. It would have certainly been interesting had Luxemburg lived to reflect on the council movement. But the premature deaths of the council movement and Rosa Luxemburg, however, combined with the collapse of the Second International and the Bolshevik Revolution, meant a clear victory for Lenin – not only over czarism, but also for his conception of the party-class relation. His conception was in the pre-bourgeois conditions of czarist Russia perfectly logical. Perhaps tempted by the lone success of his own party in the 'objectively ripe' situation, Lenin himself, despite his earlier hesitations, flirted with transforming the necessity of the underdeveloped moment into a historical-political virtue: 'at the present moment in history...the *Russian model* ["*the fundamentals of Bolshevik theory and tactics*"] reveals to *all countries* something – and something highly significant of their *near and inevitable future*' (Lenin, cited in Mészáros, 1995, p.324). History had apparently chosen Lenin over Luxemburg; and because of its success in a world of revolutionary failure, Lenin's model derived from socio-economically and politically underdeveloped conditions inherited the mantel of

Marxist orthodoxy. Both its supporters and its opponents were obliged to come to terms with this untimely theory. Its supporters felt they were riding the wave of 'the near and inevitable future', while many theoreticians opposed to Bolshevism, and already stunned by the collapse of the Second International, rejected both the proletariat and the party and felt that they had little choice but to retreat from politics into theory. Unfortunately, both sides ignored as an outdated theory of spontaneity the 'deeply democratic inspiration' behind and the political insights in Luxemburg's writings. In a further tragic irony, Luxemburg's theory of imperialism inadvertently contributed to the dismissal of her own insights.

Theories of Imperialism and Revolutionary Expectations

Marx occasionally remarked that 'the English possess all the necessary material preconditions for social revolution' (Marx, cited in Lukács, 2000, p.67) but were lacking in the class-consciousness necessary to make a revolution. A case might be made that this notion of 'objective ripeness' and 'subjective backwardness' is the most disastrous formulation in the history of Marxism. There is certainly enough evidence from twentieth-century Marxism indicating that it can lead to all too facile theoretical shortcuts in the analysis of subjectivity, which can have extremely dangerous political consequences. The obsession with proving the objective ripeness of the situation for capitalist collapse and socialist revolution was provoked by Bernstein's claim for capitalism's infinite adaptability: disproving Bernstein's claim became paramount for those attempting to rejuvenate the revolutionary movement. In 'Social Reform and Revolution' Luxemburg had already aimed at the heart of Bernstein's position and argued that precisely the 'adaptations' made in a period of rapid economic growth would intensify the contradictions, hasten the next, more serious economic crisis and initiate a revolutionary period. Crucial here is that she felt obliged to argue not only that the capitalism's immanent contradictions would lead to its breakdown, but that that breakdown was imminent. To strengthen this argument, especially in view of capital's immense growth in the pre-war decades, she turned her attention to capitalist globalization or imperialism. The several-hundred pages that she devoted to a careful analysis of *The Accumulation of Capital* (1913) had, as Nettl (1965, pp.89-90) noted, a directly political purpose, namely: to provoke social-democratic parties to develop revolutionary tactics commensurate with the proximity of capitalist collapse and the objective revolutionary ripeness of the present.

Luxemburg's argument, briefly, was that domestic demand is insufficient for the increasing supply of commodities produced by capitalist industry. The insufficiency of domestic demand indicated an approaching 'crisis of overproduction' that threatened the capitalism's existence. Recognizing this, capitalists 'opened', i.e. conquered, markets abroad. Imperialism is thus 'the political expression of the process of capital accumulation in its competitive struggle for the rest of the non-capitalist world milieu not yet occupied' (IV, p.391). The state would play a dual role in this process: first, as consumer of the products of industries producing arms and other accoutrements of warfare; and secondly, as the provider of military protection for the economic interests of its citizens abroad. Expanding international economic competition would increasingly imbricate national militaries and, as evidenced by the many skirmishes among European powers in Africa and Asia in the decades before the first world-war, exacerbate tensions among imperialist states.

More noticed than the specifics of Luxemburg's detailed analysis was her overall evaluation of imperialism's historical significance. Acknowledging capitalism's adaptability, she sought to establish the limits of that elasticity. Though foreign markets enabled capitalism to revive itself, the need for those markets, is already in itself a sign of capitalism's decay.

> The more powerfully, energetically and fundamentally that imperialism brings about the decline of non-capitalist cultures, all the faster does it pull the rug out from underneath the feet of capitalist accumulation. Imperialism is just as much a historical method of prolonging the existence of capital as it is the most certain means to establish most quickly and objectively its limit (IV, pp391-92).

Nearing this limit, capitalism is in its final phase which will be 'a period of catastrophes' (IV, p.392). The globalization of capitalism's systemic contradictions is fatal: capitalism is 'a living historical contradiction, its accumulation process is the expression, the continuing solution, and simultaneously the intensification of this contradiction [that] can only be solved by developing the foundations for socialism' (IV, p.411). Thus, in the very process of bringing the whole world into its own orbit, capitalism hastens its own demise. It need not ever reach its 'natural' limit before it will destroy itself, most likely in imperialist war.

A year after the publication of her treatise on imperialism the first world-war began. Two years later, Lenin wrote his brochure on 'Imperialism as the Highest Stage of Capitalism', which explained capitalist imperialism in terms of the logic of finance capital rather than the need for commodity markets, but evaluated its historical significance in exactly the same terms as did Luxemburg. In this context, revolutionary Marxist politicians and theoreticians inevitably interpreted the first world-war not only as confirmation of Luxemburg's and Lenin's thesis on the inseparable relation between capitalism and war, but, more fatefully, as the final collapse of capitalism and therewith the sign that the situation was objectively ripe for socialist revolution.

However logical their theoretical underpinnings, the notions of the 'historical ripeness' for the 'final collapse' of capitalism, the 'objective necessity' of 'socialism', and the socialist character of the coming revolution were dangerous illusions. One need not doubt Luxemburg's analysis of the relation between capitalism, imperialism, and the imminence of war and revolutions in order to acknowledge that the decisive finality of the verdict was premature. That the coming war would provoke social unrest and revolution, especially in Germany and Russia, and that the socialist parties would play a decisive role in those upheavals, could be expected. The verdict of capitalist collapse and socialist revolution was, however, a theoretically logical, but historically questionable metamorphosis of a passionate political hope into a revolutionary expectation. The logic of this metamorphosis of hope into expectation is easy enough to understand. Luxemburg clearly intended the notions of the 'final collapse' of capitalism and the 'end goal' of socialism heuristically rather than teleologically – that is, as a general explanation of why capitalism is barbaric and not self-sustaining and that socialism is the solution to capitalism's problems. Her practical impatience, however, led to the hasty and false syllogism that the imperialist war that had broken out was a sign that capitalism had finally collapsed and that the socialist end-goal was in sight. With so much empirical evidence of the links between capitalism, imperialism, and the descent of 'civilization' into the barbarism of war, Luxemburg's heuristically conceived notion of the 'final collapse' became more than a heuristic device; it attained the status of an objective fact. The problem, of course, is that it can only be known in retrospect whether any given collapse of capitalism is its 'final' collapse – that is, until an emancipatory alternative is realized. Pinning political strategies on the conviction that this or that crisis is the 'final collapse' is a recipe for defeat and disappointment. And it certainly had fateful consequences in the post-war period.

The Tragedies of Rosa Luxemburg and 'Western Marxism'

If the first tragedy of Rosa Luxemburg is, as Mészáros put it, that of 'someone whose time has *not yet* come', the second is the fate of her thought in the aftermath of the first world-war when she was seen as someone whose time had come and gone. The post-war climate in the 'West' was one of frustrated revolutionary expectations. The failure and/or lack of socialist revolutions in the 'objectively ripe' advanced capitalist countries, and Bolshevik success in underdeveloped Russia produced a loss of faith in both the 'subjectively backward' proletariat and in Luxemburg's theories of revolution, the party-class relation, and, most importantly, of workers as the subjects of their own history. The lack of 'spontaneous' revolution in the situation whose 'objective ripeness' Luxemburg had herself helped to prove was taken as obvious evidence that she had drawn the wrong political conclusions. Simplistically reduced to a discredited theory of proletarian spontaneity, her ideas were dismissed even as she herself was revered as a tragic heroine and martyr of the revolutionary working class.

As revolutionary impatience reinforced by theoretical guarantees gave way to disappointed revolutionary expectations, a collection of post-war theoreticians, making up what Maurice Merleau-Ponty (1973) misleadingly called 'Western Marxism', began a frantic search for an explanation of revolutionary failure in the objectively ripe capitalist countries. Seen by many as perhaps the best (and last) hope of reviving Marxism, 'Western Marxism' was quite the rage among left intellectuals in the 1960s and 1970s. But seemingly having by then run its course, it was quickly eclipsed by post-structuralist theories emanating primarily from France, and little has been heard of it for at least two decades. Since 'Western Marxism' was generally assumed to be the most sophisticated version of Marxist theory that had supplanted all competitors not only from the period before the first world-war, but also afterwards, its demise seemed to seal the fate of Marxism. But it is worth looking more closely at the uses of the term 'Western Marxism', and at its genesis, without automatically assuming that it had superseded all other versions of Marxist theory – and to do so from the viewpoint of Mészáros's insistence that the time for Luxemburg's ideas has 'not yet come'.

The first thing to note is that there are at least two problems surrounding the term itself. One is that it immediately establishes a false geographical opposition to an 'Eastern' Marxism or 'Leninism'. The problem with this geographic binary is most graphically exemplified in the person generally credited with having founded 'Western Marxism', Georg Lukács. Lukács's theory of reification and his designation of the communist party as the actual bearer of the revolutionary class-consciousness 'ascribed' to the working class is a proudly self-proclaimed, (excessively) philosophical justification of Leninism, i.e. 'Eastern Marxism'. A more serious problem involves a disjuncture between the definition of 'Western Marxism' and the timing of its emergence. Most commentators agree that 'Western Marxism' is best defined loosely and deployed generically to encompass a diverse range of thinkers who share a 'deeply democratic inspiration' (as Liebman said of Lenin) and an analytical concern with subjectivity and culture. Given especially the concern with subjectivity and culture, it is then common to assume that Western Marxism was a post-World War I development initiated by Georg Lukács, Karl Korsch, Antonio Gramsci, and including Theodor Adorno, Max Horkheimer, Walter Benjamin, Bertolt Brecht, etc. But if 'Western Marxism' is supposed to denote a deeply democratic tradition west of the Bolsheviks, then it ought to include those pre-war 'Western' thinkers who were both fundamentally concerned with questions of subjectivity and deeply democratic in their politics, most notably, of course, Rosa Luxemburg. I therefore suggest it is necessary to introduce a generational dimension into definitions of 'Western Marxism', that is: to begin with Marx and Engels, to view such pre-war thinkers such as Luxemburg as members of a second generation, and to classify theoreticians whose work began in the inter-war period as a third generation. I also suggest that it is necessary to understand how the maturation of this third generation was accomplished at the cost of ignoring or simplifying Luxemburg's insights and how this produced blindspots in 'Western Marxist' theory itself. And once this is acknowledged, we can gain a much clearer view of the contemporary relevance of Luxemburg's 'Western Marxism'.

Russell Jacoby (1981) and Perry Anderson (1976) correctly insist that what I call the third generation of 'Western Marxism' was born in the context of defeat and its maturation process was a 'dialectic of defeat', 'Western' defeat in any case defined the theoretical problematic that post-war Marxist theoreticians confronted. And in confronting what in their eyes was actually even worse than defeat – the apparent failure of the proletariat even to engage the enemy – the only possible explanation seemed to be the immaturity of proletarian subjectivity. Having thus written off the proletariat as the revolutionary subject and agent of its own emancipation, 'Western Marxist' theoreticians sought to explain the causes of proletarian backwardness. In so doing, several 'Western Marxist' theoreticians (most notably Lukács, Adorno, and Horkheimer) all too quickly and easily reshaped the question of why revolution failed where it should have succeeded, and succeeded where it should have failed, into a virtual indictment of the proletariat for having failed to fulfill its historical mission. To support this indictment, such thinkers began a systematic investigation of the backwardness of proletarian subjectivity.

The first, most influential, and in my view most misplaced and crippling explanation was Lukács's theory of the reified consciousness of the working class which became the bedrock of 'Western Marxist' theories. Lukács sought to ground his theory of reification in Marx's notion of commodity fetishism. But whereas Marx treats commodity fetishism as the specific form of bourgeois consciousness, Lukács (1985, p.150), based on his thoroughly unfounded claim that society in its immediacy is the same for the capitalists and workers,[11] universalized commodity fetishism into the concept of reification which he then posited as the form of the immediate consciousness of all inhabitants of capitalist societies. Once posited as the universal form of consciousness, he explained the reification of workers' consciousness in terms of their experience in the capitalist workplace, itself organized by the dictates of the valorization process. Lukács's insistence that reification is everywhere provided Adorno and Horkheimer among others with a research programme. It is not too much an exaggeration to say that the bulk of their theoretical production consisted of uncovering reification in every social nook and cultural cranny.

It is crucial to be precise here. My point is not to question the validity of their critiques of bourgeois society and culture, nor to deny the existence of reified consciousness, nor even to claim that working-class consciousness is free of reification. My point is rather methodological. The analysis of reification by Lukács, Adorno and Horkheimer consisted of two moves, the second of which is rather questionable. The first step was to analyze forms of bourgeois social and cultural objectivity in order to derive their objective meaning; and this produced many superb critiques of institutions and their intent, art forms, etc. The problem is that the second step was to ascribe to the working class the forms of subjectivity derived from and commensurate with these forms of social objectivity – without at all having analyzed directly the forms of working-class consciousness as they emerged from working-class experience. Rather, the assumption of the backwardness of working-class consciousness, itself a product of unwarranted and disappointed revolutionary expectations, served as a license simply to explain the already-assumed reification. The tragic irony here is that these iconic 'Western Marxist' thinkers are hailed for having restored the concern with consciousness to what had become an economically determinist and reductionist Marxism; but they actually introduced the question of subjectivity only in order to dismiss it with the assumption of the backward and hopelessly reified state of proletarian consciousness.

Having written off proletarian political efficacy, these thinkers were forced to confront the dilemma of praxis. The response generally took one of two forms: a justification of the vanguard party as the locus of proper proletarian class-consciousness (Lukács); or a retreat into theory that, as Adorno and Horkheimer

---

[11] See note 15 below.

put it, would preserve the promise of happiness whose moment of realization had passed or that, as Herbert Marcuse uncharacteristically put it, will hold onto the truth even when revolutionary practice diverges from its proper path.[12] These were all too easy political choices (however personally disconcerting they may have been) arising as they did from the deployment of reification as the all too easy explanation of the failure of the expected revolution. In this context it is worth noting that though Lukács, Adorno and Horkheimer were much influenced by Max Weber's work and surely knew Robert Michels's analysis of the bureaucratization of socialist parties, they completely avoided any serious inquiry into the problem of the bureaucratization of the SPD and the increasing separation of party and class. This issue was rather glossed over with the assumption, sometimes implicit, sometimes explicit, that the Party leadership was simply a mirror of working class consciousness, that the workers got the leaders they wanted – which is not only quite wrong but quite simplistic as an explanation of organizational sociology, the decisions of party leaders, and of the relation between party and class.

Concluding Remarks: The Time and Tragedy of Rosa Luxemburg

Sealed in the category of 'spontaneity' and left to collect historical dust, Luxemburg's insights could have proven quite timely well beyond her own untimely death, certainly in the inter-war period and definitely now. In order find a way out of and beyond the theoretically sophisticated dead-end in which 'Western Marxism' since Lukács has been trapped, it would be well worth the effort to go back beyond the time when 'Western Marxism' succumbed to a dialectic of defeat, to return to Luxemburg, to rehabilitate her insights, and rejuvenate them by reconsidering their theoretical consequences and practical implications.

It is safe to assume that had Luxemburg lived long enough to be able to reflect on the collapse of Second International resolve in August, 1914, and on the lack of socialist revolution in the advanced capitalist countries, she would not have been tempted by the easy answers that post-war 'Western Marxists' beginning with Lukács provided to some very complex questions. Even though the revolutionary expectations raised by her theory of imperialism contributed to it, she would have categorically rejected the blanket explanation of the inevitably reified and therefore backward state of working class consciousness – especially one derived from an analysis, not of worker experience and subjectivity, but of social objectivity. Nor would she have made the easy assumption that the decisions of the Second International leadership were representative of working-class opinion. In several articles written after the war began and until her death, she castigated the SPD-leadership for its failure, its lack of courage and conviction, for its weakness that was essentially a betrayal of the working class in a crucial situation.[13] Holding the

[12] See, Theodor Adorno (2003, p.128 et passim) and Herbert Marcuse (1962, p.282).

[13] See Luxemburg's essays: 'Die Krise der Sozialdemokratie', 1916 (IV, p.51ff, esp. pp.61, 147-52); 'Was machen die Führer?', 1919 (IV, pp.518-20); 'Das Versagen der Führer', 1919 (IV, pp.525-28).

party leadership responsible for more than just writing a party programme, she made a point of insisting during her speech at the founding of the *Spartakusbund* that 'it is not a matter of what is written in the [Party] programme, but how the programme is actively embraced [*lebendig erfasst*]' (IV, p.490). Understanding that socialist politics must be the active embracing of the promises and goals enumerated in party programmes, she could hardly been surprised, even if horrified, when, after a quarter-century of revolutionary proclamations being subverted by 'revolutionary *Attentismus*', the Second International failed to prevent the war which it had committed itself to stop. Having watched the majority of Second International party leaders vote in 1914 in support of their nation's war, and having witnessed the SPD coming to power in 1918 under a leader, Friedrich Ebert, who announced that he hated revolution 'like the plague', she could not have fallen into the theoretical trap of blaming the working classes for the politics of their leaders.

As noted above, the constant purpose of Luxemburg's insistence on the 'active embracing' of what is written in party programmes was that the working class become the subject of its own emancipation. As Oskar Negt writes in explaining the 'principle difference' between Luxemburg and Lenin: whereas 'Lenin studied the structure of revolutionary processes from the standpoint of organization', Luxemburg did so from the standpoint 'of spontaneity and the initiative of the masses' – that is to say, her analysis of social relations and class struggles were 'never idealistically directed upwards toward the ideas, programmes, organizational directives, central committees; rather she opened the analytical concepts of the critique of political economy downwards [*nach unten*] toward the actual experiences of the masses, of individuals' (Negt, 1974, pp.159, 161). Only through such a 'downward' opening can the analytical concepts of historical materialism cease to be abstract, be filled with meaningful content, and become, as Engels (1981, p.475) put it, 'corrected mirror-images' [*korriegierte Spiegelbilder*] of historical reality.

The first step in a 'downward' opening of the categories consists of taking seriously what Lukács dismissed as the mere everyday 'empirical consciousness' of the real living individuals who make up the working class. If, as Marx (1978b, p.154) noted, 'consciousness' (*das Bewusstsein*) is the 'conscious being' (*das bewusste Sein*) of individuals, and if that 'being' is 'their real life-activity', then the forms of working-class subjectivity cannot be grasped by means of a deterministic derivation from the forms of social objectivity,[14] but only in relation to the 'real life-activity', the concrete experience, of the working class. That experience includes not only the reduction of living labour to a mere factor of production in the capitalist labour-process (on which Lukács exclusively focused) and the immediately antagonistic relation between wage-labourers and their capitalist employers (which, at the very least, Lukács should also have considered). Equally importantly, that experience includes: the constant attacks on workers' resilient,

---

[14] On this, see also the concluding section of Helmut Reichelt's contribution to this volume.

but nevertheless vulnerable bodies by the capitalist labour process,[15] the economic fragility of working class-life; the often traumatic economic challenges of working-class family life; the need for some kind of recreational escape from work and poverty; and workers' political ideas that are derived not only from the aforementioned factors, but also from their own experience with party leaders who claim to speak in their name and in their best interests. Though party leaders and intellectuals are easily frustrated when workers do not act politically as they are 'supposed to', they have generally been rather blind to workers' frustration with their self-proclaimed leaders. Workers' political experience, even in 'worker' parties, has consisted primarily of being the objects, the passive recipients of party politics. This, of course, does little to enable workers to become the subjects of their own emancipation. Worse, it very often has the effect of provoking workers' disgust with politics altogether. The only possible way for Marxist theoreticians to begin to avoid these problems is to follow Luxemburg's 'downward' opening of historical-materialist theory and categories, to let the categories gain content and be corrected by the concrete experience of workers. Only in this way can, as Marx (1976) put it in his third thesis on Feuerbach, the educators also be educated. Only by beginning with worker experience, whatever it may be, can a meaningful and efficacious socialist politics be developed. Even if Lukács had been right about the reified empirical consciousness of the working class, then that would have to be the starting point of socialist politics rather than a substitution of the party as the agent of worker emancipation.

The greatest indication, however, that Lukács was not right about working-class subjectivity and the greatest support for Luxemburg's insistence that the working class itself be the focus of party politics came in the crucial period of 1929-1932 when Hitler's SA was creating a Nazi public sphere. There is sufficient historical evidence of worker willingness to confront the Nazis on the streets. Had the two self-proclaimed worker parties followed that lead and supported a systematic counter-offensive, it certainly would have disrupted, possibly diverted, perhaps even halted the Nazi march to power. The leaders of both the Socialist and Communist parties, however, were fully occupied with betraying the working class by insisting that their own was the truly proletarian party while the other only sought to dupe workers. The hierarchical separation of both parties from the class they claimed to represent contributed in no small way to Hitler's success. In the election of November, 1932, which eventually brought Hitler to power, the combined vote for the SPD (20.7 per cent) and KPD (16.9 per cent) exceeded that

[15] In the chapters of *Kapital* vol. I on the production of absolute and relative surplus value Marx also chronicles how the capitalist design of technology and definition of jobs entails systematic and crippling attacks on the bodies and minds of workers. Later critics of Marx often view such brutal working conditions as byproducts of the bygone era of early industrialism. But in her book, *The Electronic Sweatshop*, Barbara Garson shows, as she puts it in the subtitle, 'How Computers are Turning the Office of the Future into the Factory of the Past' – with different but equally debilitating attacks on workers' bodies. Then as now, this is why Lukács's claim that society in its immediacy is the same for all is completely unfounded.

cast for the NSDAP (33.1 per cent). The contrast between the potential of a united working-class movement against Nazism and the reality in which the SPD and KPD spent more time fighting against each other than against the Nazis is a desperate and tragically unheeded call for the kind of politics that Luxemburg advocated and that still remains to be elaborated from the insights she provided.

One of the most important elaborations consistent with Luxemburg's insights is the work of Oskar Negt and Alexander Kluge on a workers' public-sphere.[16] Linking their project to hers, Negt (1974, p.190) writes: 'The foundation of Luxemburg's historical materialism is neither an imaginary class substance, for example, the proletariat as historical subject [e.g. Lukács], nor an organization [e.g. Lenin], rather it was the working class itself, more specifically: a proletarian public-sphere'. Seeking to counter the inability of so much Marxist theory to articulate anything meaningful about worker experience, Negt and Kluge sketch an outline of an organizational form that does not block, numb, or dictate worker experience, but that allows it expression, thereby enhancing it and pointing toward the self-emancipation of the working class.

A workers' public-sphere, Negt and Kluge insist, is not simply a proletarian counterpart of, identical in form to, the bourgeois public-sphere; and by differentiating between the two, they not only explicate the characteristics of a properly working-class public-sphere, but also show the adverse affects that follow from the adoption of bourgeois forms for the workers' public-sphere. The two moments of the bourgeois public-sphere are, on the one hand, 'certain *institutions*, arrangements, activities (e.g. the use of public power, press, public opinion, the public, publicity work, streets and plazas)', and on the other,

> a general social *horizon of experience* in which is summarized all that is really or supposedly relevant for all members of the society. In the first case the public-sphere is a matter of a few professions (for example, politicians, editors, functionaries); in the latter it is something that concerns everyone and only realizes itself in the heads of people, [it is a] dimension of their consciousness (Negt and Kluge, 1972, pp.17-18).

The function of the bourgeois public-sphere is to produce a horizon of experience that does not point beyond, but legitimizes, the existing social order based on private property. This is by no means a democratic process controlled from below; rather, the framing of socially relevant experience is determined by bourgeois institutions and by the professionals that administer them.

The bourgeois public-sphere is concerned with individuals only in their capacity as 'citizens', which guarantees them certain political and legal rights and freedoms. Though citizens are guaranteed the right to *pursue* 'life, liberty, and estate' (which Locke summarized under the 'general Name, *Property*' and which the US Declaration of Independence euphemistically rendered as life, liberty, and happiness), they are guaranteed neither life, nor liberty, nor property, nor

---

[16] Because of changes in the composition of the work force, I shall use the term 'worker's' instead of 'proletarian' public-sphere – but the key factor remains the same, the wage-labour relationship.

happiness. Resting on a political/legal foundation, the bourgeois public-sphere considers 'the economy' a public matter insofar as the 'free enterprise' of individuals must be legally protected. Of public concern is only the formal and equal *right* of citizens to own private property, but the concrete questions of how much and what kind are another matter. An individual's work, or even whether an individual has work, is considered a matter of 'private' enterprise, outside the bourgeois public-sphere and outside or, better, beneath the bourgeois concept of freedom. Thus the discrepancy between those few individuals who own an immense amount of 'private property' in the form of the means of production, and the many who have none but their own labour-power (which may or may not suffice to find work), is not of public concern. As a result, both the determining factor of workers' experience (the private control of the means of production by the few that transforms the many into 'naked labour-power') and the socially necessary fact of work as the means through which individual needs are satisfied and society is reproduced fall outside the bourgeois public sphere. Work is not a private matter, nor are workers' organizations 'special interests' as they have successfully been branded by the bourgeois public sphere in the U.S. – which is being ever more closely followed in the United Kingdom, Germany and elsewhere in Europe.

For this reason, a workers' public sphere must expose the capitalist inversion that makes an individual's work a private matter, while corporations (in the U.S. at least) are legally protected 'individuals' with all the constitutional rights of individuals. It must expose the inverse relation between the devaluation of work in the 'private' capitalist production process and the social value of work. A workers' public-sphere must, in short, organize the experience excluded from the bourgeois public-sphere as the basis of a politics aimed at ending the exploitative relation of 'private enterprise'. As the organizational form of the opening of historical materialist categories *nach unten*, a proletarian public-sphere must be built up and out from the workplace, organized around the immediate experience of workers in the capitalist production process and around their immediate needs. As Negt and Kluge (1972, p.163) put it, 'the interest of the producing class must be the driving force' of a workers' public-sphere which itself must be able 'to relate the particular interests of the different branches of production to the social whole'. And in a very Luxemburgian formulation, they conclude that the building of this worker public-sphere must be seen as an ongoing process, as 'the form of the unfolding of proletarian interest itself' (ibid.).

Since Luxemburg's time the challenges confronting the development of a worker public-sphere have monumentally increased. Negt and Kluge emphasize the dangers of a separation of the political goals of a party organization from the economic needs of the working class, 'from the production context of living labour'. The separation of party from class, of political from economic struggle reproduces in a worker public-sphere the forms of the bourgeois public-sphere, especially in that the determination of the relevant factors of experience is made by the party professionals. Instead of being 'the organizer of the working class as the greatest force of production, whose goal is to produce the life relations and social forms themselves' (ibid., p.416), the party separated from the concrete experience of the working classes succumbs to a self-absorbed 'bunker mentality' (ibid., p.65) that subordinates workers' interests to the party's interests and thereby narrows the horizon of worker experience. This has of course been true both of social-democratic and Leninist parties.

Referring to the period from roughly 1900-1930, Negt and Kluge (1972, p.163) called this separation of the political from the economic struggles and the consequent emergence of party bunker mentalities a 'disturbed development'. The problem, however, is that the conditions of the 'disturbed development' are not early twentieth-century exceptions; rather the emergence of competing worker political and economic organizations, and the organizational tendency toward oligarchy and self-perpetuation instead of the active embracing of the party program, are the more or less normal adverse conditions within which a workers' public-sphere must be developed. And a further hindrance is what Negt and Kluge (1972, p.163) called 'the obstructive and destructive influences of the bourgeois public-sphere' whose ability, especially through its control of old and new communication media, to obstruct and divert and deform (or ignore) critical political discourse and thereby to frame and deform experience in a legitimizing manner has never been greater.

The development of a working-class public-sphere under such adverse conditions is the constant challenge of socialist politics in capitalist society. Momentarily underestimating the effects of a quarter-century of party politics driven by the 'bunker mentality', Luxemburg vainly pinned her immediate hopes on the appearance of a 'revolutionary period' in which both the capitalist economy and the legitimizing organs of the bourgeois public-sphere would be in crisis and which would effect the 'spontaneous' dissolution of the separation of working-class political and economic organizations. In her impatience and revolutionary expectations she was, as Nettl argued, very much a product of her time. But her understanding that 'Socialism must be made by the masses' that 'the chains of capital must be broken where they are forged', and that 'the masses' can only 'learn how to use power by exercising power', points directly, not at theories of organization which is the privilege of intellectuals, but at struggle which is the daily experience of workers, even if the struggle is not daily overt.[17] This is not to

[17] In *The Class Struggle in the Ancient Greek World* (1981), de Ste. Croix, defines 'class' as 'essentially a relationship' that is 'the collective social expression of the fact of exploitation, the way in which exploitation is embodied in a social structure' (p.43). Accordingly, he defines class struggle as 'the fundamental relationship between classes (and their respective individual members), involving essentially exploitation, or resistance to it. It does not necessarily involve collective action by a class as such, and it may or may not include activity on a political plane' (p.44). One thing, however, is certain: 'the process of "class struggle"...is not something spasmodic or occasional or intermittent but a permanent feature of human society' (p.49). Therefore, 'to adopt the very common conception of class struggle which refuses to regard it as such unless it includes *class consciousness* and *active political conflict*...is to water it down to the point where it virtually disappears in many situations'. He concludes consequently, '[b]ring back *exploitation as the hallmark of class*, and at once class struggle is in the forefront, as it should be' (p.57). Mészáros (1989, p.451) makes the same point in his *The Power of Ideology*.

say that no thought should be given to organization, nor that intellectuals have no role in socialist politics. It is simply to say that the *workers'* class struggle is primary and that the appropriate forms of organization must be developed in and through the workers' struggle, and not outside of it, even if supposedly in their name. It is the working class itself, the workers' public-sphere, that is the measure of the appropriateness of theoretical formulations and organizational forms.[18] And if today the obstacles to the construction of a workers' public-sphere may be greater than ever, it is still the challenge; and the alternatives are still as clear as when Luxemburg formulated them.

Had Luxemburg lived to confront Lukács and other purveyors of reification, she surely would have realized how easily disappointed revolutionary expectations can turn into misplaced theories of the 'backwardness' of proletarian subjectivity – and from there all too easily into the dogma that the party, as the bearer of proletarian class consciousness, 'is always right'. The realization of the difficulty of the challenge, the realization that the struggle will be much more complex and intricate, and above all, much longer than it once seemed, does require the renunciation of politics based on revolutionary expectations. It does not, however, require renunciation of the socialist goal; and to retain that goal requires patience, commitment, and courage.

For this reason, Luxemburg's political and intellectual courage is now more timely than ever. It was in the wake of both the failure of the socialist and communist parties to prevent fascism and Stalin's wielding of theory as an executioner's sword that Horkheimer (1974, p.150) understandably attempted to prevent its cooptation by injecting a degree of modesty into its claims: 'I can say what is false, but I cannot define what is right'. As I have argued above, theory can always use a good dose of modesty, but it does not need an overdose – as we are experiencing today in 'post-modernity' when the unwillingness to go beyond saying what is wrong has become epidemic. It is not difficult to say what is wrong, nor to draw the obvious conclusion that what is wrong should be righted. It is not necessary to claim absolute truth in order to claim that there are alternatives – and ones worth fighting for as our world becomes more barbaric daily. What is required, now more than ever, is to take a stand on what is more right and just and, in Sojourner Truth's words, to 'speak truth to power' – and to have the courage to keep doing so, however hopeless it seems. Now, as in her own time, Luxemburg's uncompromising proclamation that socialism is the only alternative to barbarism is both prophetic and pressing.

The many tragic dimensions in Rosa Luxemburg's life and surrounding her work, as well as the lingering value of both, lie in her untimely timeliness. Given what needs to be done, her insights into the party-class relation, the nature of political education, political tactics and political commitment, even if in partially outmoded terminology and in need of elaboration in response to the great changes in the last century, still remain timely in a world that is more capitalist than ever. Therein lie both their value and their tragedy – their lack of realization is one

[18] See Negt (1974, p.190) and Negt and Kluge (1972, p.660).

reason why we still face the same choice that she did. The lingering tragedy of Rosa Luxemburg is that despite the urgent timeliness of her work, her time has still not yet come.

References

Adorno, T. (2003) *Ästhetische Theorie*, in *Gesammelte Werke*, Vol. 7, Suhrkamp, Frankfurt.

Anderson, P. (1976), *Considerations on Western Marxism*, New Left Books, London.

Bonefeld, W. and S. Tischler (eds.) (2002), *Leninism, Anti-Leninist Marxism and the Question of Revolution Today*, Ashgate, Burlington VT.

De Ste. Croix, G.E.M. (1981), *The Class Struggle in the Ancient Greek World*, Cornell University Press, New York.

Engels, F. (1981), 'Karl Marx, "Zur Kritik der Politischen Ökonomie"', MEW, Vol. 13, Dietz, Berlin.

Garson, B. (1988), *The Electronic Sweatshop*, Simon and Schuster, New York.

Groh, D. (1973), *Negative Integration und revolutionärer Attentismus*, Ullstein, Frankfurt.

Horkheimer, M. (1974), 'Zur Kritik der gegenwärtigen Gesellschaft', in *Gesellschaft im Übergang*, Athenäum-Fischer, Frankfurt.

Jacoby, R. (1981), *Dialectic of Defeat, Contours of Western-Marxism*, Cambridge University Press, Cambridge.

Lenin, W. (1988), *What is to be Done?*, International Publishers, New York.

Liebman, M. (1975), *Leninism under Lenin*, Merlin Press, London.

Lukács, G. (1985), *History and Class-Consciousness*, trans. R. Linvingstone, MIT Press, Cambridge Ma.

Lukács, G. (2000), *A Defence of History and Class Consciusness. Tailism and Dialectic*, trans. E. Leslie, intro. J. Rees with a postface by S. Zizek, Verso, London.

Luxemburg, R. (1974), *Gesammelte Werke*, 5 volumes, Dietz, Berlin.

Marcuse, H. (1962), *Vernunft und Revolution*, Luchterhand, Darmstadt.

Marx, K. (1964), *Die Gründung der I. Internationale*, Dietz, Berlin.

Marx, K. (1976), *Theses on Feuerbach*, in *Collected Works*, Vol. 5, International Publisher, New York.

Marx, K. (1978a), 'Preface to the Critique of Hegel's Philosophy of Right', in R. Tucker (ed.), *Marx-Engels Reader*, Norton, New York.

Marx, K. (1978b), *The German Ideology*, in R. Tucker (ed.), *Marx-Engels Reader*, Norton, New York.

Merleau-Ponty, M. (1973), *Adventures of the Dialectic*, trans. J. Bien, Northwestern University Press, Evanston.

Mészáros, I. (2002), *Socialism or Barbarism*, Monthly Review, New York.

Mészáros, I. (1995), *Beyond Capital*, Monthly Review Press, New York.

Mészáros, I. (1989), *The Power of Ideology*, New York University Press, New York.

Michels, R. (1968), *Political Parties: A Sociological Study of the Oligarchic Tendencies of Modern Democracy*, trans. E. and C. Paul, intro. S. M. Lipset, Free Press, New York.

Negt, O. (1974), 'Rosa Luxemburg: Zur materialistischen Dialektik von Spontaneität und Organisation', in C. Pozzoli (ed.), *Rosa Luxemburg oder Die Bestimmung des Sozialismus*, Suhrkamp, Frankfurt.

Negt, O. and A. Kluge (1972), *Öffentlichkeit und Erfahrung. Zur Organisationanalyse von bürgerlicher und proletarischer Öffentlichkeit*, Suhrkamp, Frankfurt; Engl. edition published as *Public Sphere and Experience. Toward an Analysis of Bourgeois and Proletarian Public Sphere*, University of Minnesota Press, Minneapolis, 1993.

Nettl, J.P. (1969), *Rosa Luxemburg*, Oxford University Press, Oxford.
Nettl, J.P. (1965), 'The German Social Democratic Party 1890-1914 as a Political Model', *Past and Present*, No. 30, pp.65-95.
Ritter, G. (1963), *Die Arbeiterbewegung im Wilhelminischen Reich*, Colloquium, Berlin.
Schorske, C. (1955), *German Social Democracy 1905-1917*, Harper and Row, New York.

Chapter 7

Time of Reification and Time of Insubordination. Some Notes

Sergio Tischler[1]

Introduction

The essay focuses on the conception of time and its subject is the *time of the state form* and the time of insubordination. The state form is itself a moment of the capitalist constitution of time. The rupture of this time-form is of fundamental importance in the anti-capitalist struggle for social autonomy.

The essay argues that class struggle produces, in antagonism to capital's conception of time, its own temporality – a time of human dignity and therewith a time of individual human needs. Revolutionary conceptions that leave this important dimension aside expose themselves to a reifying impoverishment. Revolutionary practice has to guard itself against the danger of such impoverishment, especially the fetish of revolution as progress and the myth that temporality is subsumed (*aufgehoben*) in the *state form*.

Walter Benjamin's work is here of central importance. He demolished the frozen dialectic of revolutionary conceptions that derived the means and ends of struggle from those same reified forms that they officially opposed. His endeavour run counter to the orthodox conception of human dignity where dignity is secured, guaranteed, decreed and established by the state form. The essay is inspired by Benjamin's theorizing, and his insights are discussed in the final section.

I consciously omitted tedious punctual references to the authors discussed in this essay. It is intended as a theoretical intervention, a sort of guide to reflection, that, by way of condensed, synthetic insights, interprets the conceptual *fund* of the anti-capitalist struggles for social autonomy.

I

Capitalism is characterized, amongst other things, by the production of a temporality that is uniform and continuous. The time of the clock ticks to the movement of this temporality like some kind of time-machine or, better, as a

[1] I am grateful to John Holloway for his comments and observations.

machine that feeds on the substance of life by transforming the multiplicity of human activity into quantities deprived of all quality. The cyclical time of rural societies and the extraterrestrial time of religions vanish in the sovereignty of this abstract time. In other words, the process that Max Weber called the 'disenchantment of the world' (that is, its secularization quâ rationalization) expresses itself in the form of objective rationality, a rationality that belongs to objects. The objectification of time as abstract time is the time of reification. Its penetration into every conceivable area of social life is the foundation of the disappointment with the project of the Enlightenment where myth is restored in the form of objective (instrumental) rationality and progress (see Horkheimer and Adorno, 1972). The crisis of socialism and of the idea of a radical subject of revolution has its roots in the same phenomena.

II

The *value form* of social existence characterises a type of domination that subordinates history to the object, to capital. Inside this form, time exists as an apparently independent objectivity that creates its own norms and its own beliefs and uncertainties, rendering human beings mere personifications of their own life-practice. The appearance of an independent existence renders this objectivity metaphysical, an illusory – though real – characteristic of capitalist social relations.

The *value form* is a form of human existence: the time that defines it is an unending repetition of the negation of human dignity – it negates human time by transforming quality into quantity. This negation is however not independent of human social practice. Rather, it is a time of struggle over the reduction of human creativity into profit, that is, the subordination of human beings to the needs of the continuous growth of abstract wealth.

History, seen as a plurality of experiences and collective memories, entails a diversity of times. In the *value form* this richness of human history has the 'right' to exist only in the form of a degeneration, a kind of carnival or spectacle (see Debord, 1995; Vanegeim, 1994); that is to say, the richness of human experience is only allowed to exist on the condition that it submits to the instrumental rationality of the object, that is, to the general, homogeneous time of capital. However, the time of reification cannot exist in and of itself. Its mere existence requires what it denies in its form, that is, the spontaneity of 'doing'. Time of reification is thus always precarious. The insubordination of the plurality and diversity of human doing to the homogeneity of the value form renders the value-form a 'living' contradiction. The time of insubordination subsists *in* and *against* the *value form*.

The *value form* exists through struggle, and its temporality consists of both, domination and resistance: it is the affirmation of what exists as the product of a continuous and abstract-objective time; and it is the challenge of the potentiality of collective time of the self-determining subject.

III

The notion of abstract temporality is not of a metaphysical nature, but of a historical and material kind (a fact that does not exclude the question of its subjective form, but rather contains it as a moment of practice). The autonomy of time materialized in the world of objects is one of the most important points in Marx's analysis of the double character of labour, especially of the category of abstract labour as a specific form of existence of human 'doing' in capitalist society.[2]

Although there are other forms of organization of human life – 'residuary' or 'emerging', in the words of Williams (1997) – abstract labour is the form of existence of labour in capitalist society. In chapters XIV and XV of *Capital* (manufacture and modern industry), Marx offers a detailed analysis of this issue. There is no need here to study his analysis in depth, save only in order to illustrate the contradictory character of labour (and of doing) in capitalist society. On the one hand, Marx argues that the source of the process of labour is the worker herself, her physical and mental capacity to transform nature into useful objects and to transform herself in this process (the dialectical nature of the process of labour and the foundation of human history). Nevertheless, the worker is subordinated to capital. Thus, human creativity can be realised only within the framework of a form of power that is alien to it. 'Doing' appears thus personified in the object, in the 'done'. This 'done' is formalised in the law of private property, a formalization that is based on the separation of labour from the means of production. Private property is legalised expropriation. The rule of law formalises and thus guarantees the circulation of capital. Law thus is the legal expression of the separation of the worker from the objective conditions of labour – a historical requisite of the capitalist form of social organization.

Marx analysed the rise of modern private property as the process of expropriation of the direct producer from her means of production and of the creation of a new kind of worker, one that embodied the contradiction between formal freedom and real oppression: the worker is rendered free from servile bonds and also free from the means of production. In other words, the worker becomes free to sell her capacity to work as a commodity, as labour power. The accumulation of capital is the continuity of this process of separation. It rests on, reproduces and expands this separation as if it were a natural law, rather than a temporality of capital's constituted existence. Separation is the constitutive logic of capital's temporality.[3] The laws of accumulation are no more than the – always already contradictory – reproduction of this form of separation.

The subordination of labour to capital is not a natural process of power organization, as if it were an extra-human law of nature. In contrast to other forms of domination, such as serfdom and slavery, the capitalist form of domination is

---

[2] On the notion of 'doing' as opposed to 'power', see John Holloway (2002).

[3] On primitive accumulation as the constitutive genesis of the forms of capital, see Werner Bonefeld (2002).

impersonal. The dominated are formally free. Capital does not appropriate a person, the worker; it appropriates the labour power that the worker sells for a specific period of time (the working day). This form of domination and exploitation thus appears as legal (formal) freedom. The violence of capitalism's original beginning appears in the civilised form of legal regulation. This 'civilizing' and legitimising attribute of social relations as relations of generalised exchange, where quality is reduced to quantity, is inconceivable without abstract labour.

Abstract labour is not of a strictly economic nature, as if it were merely something that belongs to the sphere of the production and the circulation of commodities. It is the organizing principle of the capitalist mode of production in all its distinct forms of existence (cultural, political). In other words, it entails totality (an issue we shall be discussing later).

In *Capital* Marx analyses the form of capitalist production as the incarnation and organization of abstract labour. The passing from manufacture to the modern factory, from the skilled worker operating specialised instruments to the machine: abstract labour achieves historical reality in these process and transitions, and indeed renders them effective. Equally, the technological changes brought about by the industrial revolution amount to an objectification of this type of labour. These changes manifested the radical separation between the mechanical activity realised by workers and the command over their productive activity, a command given by machine-time. This subordination of the worker to the dictate of machine-time is fundamental – it involves the rationalization of time. Time becomes a productive form, constantly reducing human creative time into abstract time, of human productive power into an extension of abstract clockwork.

The rationalization of production through the introduction of the machine amounted to a radical change in the social existence of the worker. This change resulted from a long struggle by capital to separate workers from their creative subjectivity, subordinating their subjectivity to the instrumental rationality of a productive cogwheel. The alienation of creative subjectivity in the form of the machine reduces the activity of doing, of creative activity, to a *one-dimensional* practice.[4]

The logic of separation relegates the worker to an 'appendix of the machine' (Marx), reducing her creative capacity to monotonous, repetitive movements. This mutilation of labour is the price of capitalist rationalization. The *real subsumption* of labour to capital is thus realised through the separation of the worker from her creative being. The subordination of human creativity to the logic of an objectified production process expropriates the worker's creativity, skill, and experience. The

[4] What Marcuse (1985) defines as a characteristic feature of postwar capitalism, is a manifestation of the principle of abstract labour.

worker becomes a personification of the machine, that is to say, human doing is subordinated to the logic of the object (capital).[5]

Capital substitutes instrumental rationality and velocity for creativity, quantity for quality. This substitution is neither contingent nor a force of nature. It is a necessary substitution and as such characterises the capitalist form of social existence. Its necessity is contained in the subordination of use value to exchange value, of living labour to dead labour. Capitalist rationality means the consumption of living labour by dead labour; it is the predominance of the 'done' over the 'doing' (see Holloway, 2002). In other words, it is the predominance of the object over the subject.

Capitalist society is characterised not only by an immense production and circulation of commodities, but also and above all, by the domination of dead labour over living labour. This domination entails a specific constitution of time. Social time is determined by dead time and that is, capitalist accumulation is dynamic only in and through the stasis of abstract time as the measure of wealth. That is to say, its dynamic is the constituted temporality of the expanded accumulation of capital for the sake of accumulation. Instrumental rationality and functionality tend to replace creativity, and thus appear objectively valid. However, this appearance abstracts from its social content, a content that is merely 'carried along' as an object of functional planning. From the standpoint of functionality and instrumental rationality, human creativity is a scandal because its potential for dysfunctionality inserts uncertainty into the 'well-oiled' machinery of accumulation. Instrumental rationality and functional planning render creativity a resource, negating its purpose. There cannot be creativity on the basis of a separation between mental labour and physical labour, between mechanical, repetitive activity and the organization of this activity. The technicians of instrumental rationality participate in the rationalization of an abstract temporality that tends to annihilate creativity, for in this temporality use value is subordinated to value, human difference and dignity is subordinated to things, and thus denied.

Sensuous human social practice whose creativity cannot be calculated on the pyramids of accumulated abstract wealth, appears thus as insubordination. It implies the struggle against the logic of separation, a logic upon which the capitalist calculability of abstract time rests. In this sense, abstract labour is the negation of the subject – better: *it contains it* but in the *form of its negation.*

The concept of class struggle is based on this dialectic of labour (see Rooke, 2002). The category of class does not denote a social group that is formally defined according to a certain abstract principles. Rather, it entails the social practice of negation: it negates the subordination of the subject to the object, i.e. the commodity form of the existence of labour, wage labour. Class is constituted in and through this process of negation. Following Holloway's (2002) argument, it is not *being* but *doing* that negates the indignity of human creativity in the form of a

---

[5] Marx's distinction between formal subsumption and real subsumption is important because it represents a qualitative change in the form of subordination. In formal subordination the separation of the subject from the object has not yet been fully realized.

labouring commodity.[6] The struggle of the working class is a struggle against the reduction of its labour power to a commodity.[7]

The social totality of abstract labour is a false totality (see Lukács, 1971). It is a totality of reification where the value-form, the relations between the things themselves, appears as the objective form of social integration, as if it were a person apart. In capitalism, the social context of human existence makes itself effective behind the backs of the individualised individual. Rather then Man having mastery over his social conditions, social conditions have mastery over Man. Human dignity subsists in the mode of being denied, that is, it exists against itself in the form of value. The totality of capitalist social relations is thus a negative totality: it negates the dignity of the human subject by objectifying the person in the thing and by subjectifying the thing in the person.

IV

Abstract labour entails the alienation of the subject from her doing, her physical and mental activity. It is alienated labour.

I already discussed that the social form of abstract labour is not limited to the sphere of production. Nor can the principle of abstract labour be reduced to instrumental economic reason. Rather, it is a principle of social life as a whole. It constitutes, shapes and circulates through all the fibres of the social body. Foucault's notion of power focuses this well. For Foucault (1975), power constitutes the bodies and the 'soul' in the form of disciplinary practices and discourses. Power is not located in a specific place or sphere, it circulates through the whole of society; furthermore, he argues that power is not something that can be owned, but a sum of devices used from strategic positions. The constitution of power is impersonal and yet exists within and through persons.

The notion of impersonal power criticises not only the idea of power as a thing that is used by a subject as an instrument but, also, the idea that the state apparatus is the locus of such power. On the contrary, power, according to this understanding, is located in the whole of society, insofar as it is embedded in the practices and discourses, that is, in the institutions of everyday life. Embedded, but not in an evident manner. It is hidden in the various specialized practices that claim to represent a knowledge separate from power; yet, this knowledge is linked to power, it is a knowledge-power, part of an immense disciplinary mechanism of the bodies and the soul, a 'political economy' of the body.

Foucault conception of power has been criticised as circular and enclosing, for one cannot exit this imprisoning situation; there are no practices and discourses beyond the realm of power, and there is no, as it were, free-speech situation in conditions defined by the absence of power. Foucault's conception of power entails

---

[6] See also John Holloway's contribution to this volume.

[7] E.P. Thompson's (1977) work on the creation of the working class in England remains one of the most important texts against reductionist and anti-dialectical definitions of class.

three important aspects: a) power resides to a considerable degree in the hidden (not evident) social practices and discourses of everyday life – that is, it exists in and through the civilised normality of bourgeois society; b) it allows a comprehension of power beyond particular and fragmentary practices, which are usually rationalised in the division of academic knowledge according to specific academic disciplines. Foucault overcomes this fragmentation, and at the same time shows that this fragmentation is typical of the rationalization-process of capitalist social relations; c) the rationalization of power into separate domains is a doubly forceful mechanism of power because it entails the concealment of power as an impersonal objectivity.

These three aspects are no doubt very important. Nevertheless, it seems to me that Foucault's important conception of power hangs in the air inasmuch as he does not offer a theory of its social constitution. His conception might therefore be understood better by redefining it through the lenses of abstract labour. In other words, power needs to be conceptualised from within the material form of capitalist society. This will reveal power as a form of impersonal domination that subsists through every aspect of the homogenizing and rationalizing temporality of capitalist social relations, and that obtains in every aspect of capital's reduction of human quality, of human life, to a resourceful quantity, to cash and product.

What Foucault masterfully points out is the diversified nature, the various ways in which the separation of subject from object objectifies itself in everyday life in a rational manner in forms of science and technology, and forms of classification and systematization. The genesis of the process is always hidden in its assumed form of objective rationality. Every aspect of society is permeated by it and thus subordinated to *general time* as an abstract objectivity. This general time is the power of capital that exists through *division* – general time is a kind of (real) abstraction that is embedded in the alienated form of human doing in capitalist society. Thus, rationalization is a power device because it is the grammar of the abstract temporality that defines the law of motion of capitalist society.

Abstract labour and abstract temporality are categories that allow us to comprehend the imprisoning forms of modern power. The rationalization of the forms of life and power is rendered effective in and through the submission of social life to *general* (abstract) *time*. This real abstraction operates at every level of social existence. The laws of capitalist accumulation do not rest on some sort of economic logic. Rather, they proceed through a multiplicity of devices and forms of power that inform and are in-formed by general labour and general time. Thus, the forms of capitalist society, from the mundane to the typical forms of power are moments of a totality that is defined by that form of abstraction. The *state form* is contained within it.

V

We already saw that the accumulation of capital entails a homogeneous temporality. In this temporality the use value of time is that of an abstract measure whose dynamic rests on the reduction of creative human activity into product and cash. The separation of the state from the economic is constituted by this temporality. The struggle over this separation is an important moment of the formation of capitalism (see Thompson, 1971). The *state form* entails a specific temporality that is at the same time total. Discussions about 'micro-power' do not capture the intensity of this temporality. In contrast, Max Weber's conception of the modern state still offers important insights.

Weber (1979) sees *instrumental rationality* as the typical organizational principle of the production process, and he argues that this principle cannot be generalised without the state. The state's bureaucratic apparatus is responsible for the organization of domination that the mode of instrumental rationality entails. However, the 'iron cage' of bureaucracy is in itself insufficient to secure modern domination. According to Weber, bureaucratic domination needs to be compensated by another type of domination. This type is directly related to political parties and the parliament (see Weber, 1991). In his view, state action combines these two modes of domination, and the modern state exercises domination through their combined effort. On the one hand, power is exercised through rational administration. However, legitimation of domination through rational-legal means is by itself not sufficient. Instrumental rationality is thus only an aspect in the formulation of strategies of power. On the other hand, the political parties and the parliament rationalise the irrationality of the masses. While these are also embodiments of the rationalization of domination, they do however provide additional means of legitimation. The treatment of every member of society according to established rules, procedures and laws, that is, according to criteria of formal equality, is the modern form of legitimation – impersonal, objective, and impassionate. Its operation thus requires the additional legitimating resources of passion and conflict. This resource provided by the political parties and parliamentary debate. The rationalization of irrational mass society through parliament and political parties achieves legitimation through the political game of 'due process', including the liberal-democratic 'due-process' of representation, and competition between parties.

Regardless whether one agrees or disagrees with Weber's view, he does provide important insights into the workings of the modern state. The modern state is seen as the location of the various forms of domination qua rationalization. The state is based on the separation and specialization of politics as a distinct and apparently autonomous sphere. This apparent autonomy legitimises the state as a supposedly neutral space. The state is characterised, in Weber's celebrated definition, as the 'monopoly holder of the legitimate use of violence'. This also entails the 'depoliticization' of social and economic relations, and that is, their organization on the basis of law and order. The labour contract between two formally equal partners, between capital and labour, is thus guaranteed by the state as the political master of the law. The separation between the economic and the political is thus part of the real abstraction that operates in the totality of capitalist social relations. Unlike the much praised spontaneous order of the market, the state is invested with the task of integrating society not only on the basis of law but, also through the provision of legitimising, loyalty-creating means, symbols, and spectacles. The state is thus charged with providing a sense of 'organic' being, purpose, and interest, securing the abstract and homogeneous temporality of capital by investing it with 'sense'. On the one hand, then, the state invests the homogenous time of capital with symbolical meanings; on the other, it recomposes lineal time in the form of an historical narrative, creating a *Weltanschauung* based on the regressive equality of historical myth, ancestral community and archaic bonds.

What Weber theorises as rationalization effected through political parties and the parliamentary systems of representation is partly the restoration of this *myth*, upon which domination depends for its perpetuation. Gramsci offered in fact a similar assessment from a different perspective. He, too, focuses on the modern state, and he discussed the issue of legitimacy and state power in terms of his well-known relationship of coercion and consensus.

The argument so far can be summarised as follows: a) the *state form* is part of the real abstraction of capitalist social relations; b) the state is the embodiment of capitalism's constitutive logic of separation; c) the state is not just 'a field' of conflict; it is a *form* of class antagonism, an antagonism that is embedded in the *value form*; d) the separation of the state from the economic is consistent with the value form as a form of instrumental rational action (using Weberian terminology); e) this separation also entails the illusory compensation for homogenous general time through means of 'national' values, myth, ancestral notions of community and the like. By invoking this temporality of the community, the state appears to reconcile the present with the past, restoring 'universal human time'. This restoration takes the form of rituals and spectacles: cyclical elections, political conflicts between different parties of the same kind, national celebrations and ceremonies, flag-waving, patriotic declarations, etc. It is as if time as a fetish were concentrated in the *state form*. On the one hand, then, we find bureaucratic, instrumental rationality. On the other, there is the state as the figure of reconciliation of 'national' time, formulating the common destiny of the nation. That is to say, the *state form* entails the reification of time. Whatever one might make of the contemporary discussion of the state under conditions of globalization, the *state form* always already entails the reification of time and its representation.

VI

The state, however, does not just represent time as reification. It is the coercive master of reification, fragmenting opposition (the time of insubordination) and transforming alternative practices of social time into the hegemony of abstract social time. As the political master of time as reification, it opposes, fragments, contains and undermines the struggle for time as a human need. Against the 'doing' it represents the hegemony of the 'done'. Against the 'doing', it represents the temporality of the value form, through means of coercion and myth. The subsumption of labour to capital, of subject to object, entails the *state form* as the concentrated coercive force of abstract social time.

The struggle over the political economy of time is one of the most important sites of the struggle for human emancipation, if not the most important. Marx's analysis of the value form discusses two antagonistic forms of temporality. He contrasts the temporality of abstract labour with the temporality of the worker. His analysis of the struggle over the length of the working day suggests it comprises a battlefield for and over time. His analysis is of great theoretical and practical importance.[8] On one hand, there is the capitalist organization of labour, the productive consumption of labour power; on the other, the resistance of workers to this consumption. It is in this dialectic that *class* comes to the fore as struggle, far removed from sociological, formal and static definitions. Class, one could argue, embodies an antagonism that, in the case of the exploited and oppressed, is a kind of negative, subversive temporality.

Walter Benjamin's 'Theses on the Philosophy of History' (1968) can be read as a critique of the idea of revolution as some sort of radicalization of bourgeois notions of progress. Benjamin's offers a critique of linear conceptions of time; and it this conception that such revolutionary ideas espouse. Following Benjamin, the idea of revolution as progress affirms lineal and homogeneous (abstract) time, the temporality of capital, as the organizing principle of the means and ends of revolution. Indeed, in practice it amounts to the renunciation of revolution. Instead of human emancipation from the dictate of homogenous, abstract time where human dignity obtains in the mode of being denied, as a human resource and personification of abstract social laws, revolution is conceived as the emancipation of instrumental rationality from existing bourgeois prejudices. Following Benjamin, this idea of revolution does not redeem humanity; instead, it prolongs, under the banner of progress and revolution, human indignity. Benjamin thus argues that revolution has to break free from the myth of progress and that it therefore has to espouse a different temporality. This is the temporality of the struggle of the oppressed, a temporality that is negated in the form of the continuous present. The idea of the future as the prolongation of the present has therefore to be rejected as an idea that conceives of the future as a mirror image of the present. The notion of progress entails this prolongation of the present. The idea of history as the forward march of the present into the future is, of course, an important modern myth. And this myth is an ideological form of the reification of time in capitalist society. In other words, the revolutionary struggle for human emancipation, for human dignity, has to produce a real alternative to capitalist time. The time of the democratic self-determination of the realm of necessity through the realm of freedom is different from the conception of time which holds that time is money.[9] Revolution is, in this sense, the practical negation of this lineal and abstract time, it is the creation of a different temporality, a 'messianic' (Benjamin) temporality.

This messianic temporality is the time of Man as the subject that restores to itself the lost unity (redemption) of society. Restoration does not denote an archaic myth. Rather it summons the social autonomy of Man over his conditions. Messianic time redeems the past in the present. This redemption of the past breaks

[8] See the important analysis of Adrian Wilding (1995).

[9] On this see also Werner Bonefeld's contribution to this volume.

its abstract temporality, and therewith overcomes the myth of progress. In this sense, revolution is pregnant with the past: it redeems the history of suffering, defeats, and struggles of the oppressed.

Lineal time is the time of separation. It separates the past from the present and recognises the past only as past. It forces us to think about the present only, allows no reconciliation with past injustices of domination and exploitation. It allows no memory. Lineal time is the time of domination. The present is what it *is* and nothing else. In other words, the idea of the past as a past invokes a social identity without memory of the past. Lineal time denies Man's existence as an historical being.

The past is of course irreversible. The dead are dead. However, Benjamin's notion of revolution as redemption does not focus on individuals. Rather, it focuses on the struggles, the resistances, and the utopias and desires, the experiences and memories of all past generations, as our struggles, etc. Redemption entails historical knowledge and solidarity; its conception of time is collective. The Zapatistas, for example, elaborated the depths of collective time, discovering in the continuity of struggles and resistances the collective time of insubordination of which they are an active part. They thus recover the continuity of a time that the Mexican State had tried to fragment, to codify as dead, past time, frozen in a past, and through this expropriation of memory, is placed into the service, through myth and spectacle, of power itself. The Zapatistas recovered the struggles associated with Morelos, Zapata, and many others, from their administered present, gave them presence, and by doing so experienced their struggle as a messianic force. The same occurs in revolutions. It is *general time*, i.e. the time of capital and the state, which negates the temporalities of past struggles. General time fragments historical experience and knowledge, cuts the present off from the past, and so separates history as a history of struggle from the present. By freezing past struggles in time, bestowing them with the title of 'past', history is rationalised as a resourceful tool that can be mobilised to secure the relations of domination in the present. In short, the legitimation of domination through the creation of myth and the containment of the oppressed through the expropriation of historical memory, knowledge, and experience, belong together.

Benjamin's conception of messianic time entails, then, not only the redemption of the past in the subversion of the present. It entails more than just an understanding that the present is *filled* with struggles and negated temporalities of a potentially disruptive nature. The notion of messianic time involves, also, a radical critique of the categories of abstract temporality, including the category 'state'. Thus, he conceives of revolution as a radical transformation of time, from the political economy of abstract time to human time, a time of individual needs. For as long as revolution is derived from the categories of general-linear time, revolution is conceived as a fetish, as part of the mystic canon of the ideology of progress. Revolution, thus, implies the criticism and dissolution of these categories, of capital and its state. Hence, thinking against the current is embedded in the time of insubordination, the struggle for human dignity.

The Zapatistas say that they do not want to seize power, that they might be defeated but that they are sure that they shall win. They shall win because as long as there is history, there shall be someone to take up their example; not as a heroic, individual act, but as the irreducible temporality of resistances and struggles.

A concept of revolution that is reduced to a theory of the organization of the state as the privileged *locus* of revolutionary action is dominated by the myth of progress and abstract temporality. It is precisely this that radical change has to think and act against.

The time of radical change is not merely the continuation of the struggles of the oppressed, it is the construction of an alternative subjectivity, a subjectivity that must break with the domination of objective and abstract time to realise a collectivity consisting of individuals – the 'communist individual' (Marcuse, 2000).[10]

I am not arguing here for a leap into the dark. My argument simply amounts to this: changing the world through the critique of what exists, including all forms of power that make this existence possible.

Thus, conceived in critical terms, class is the movement against the negation of the subject in capital, a movement that allows for 'flashes of lightning', the possibility of 'messianic time'. Everyday life is saturated by this potentiality to defy the figures of capital and instrumental reason, as are the jails through which the subject is constructed, according to Foucault.

'Messianic time' is the opposite of *general time*; it is a form of collective existence that arises from the insubordination of the subject against the reified relations of capital.

References

Benjamin, W. (1968), 'Theses on the Philosophy of History', in *Illuminations*, trans. H. Zorn, ed. and introd. Hannah Arendt, Harcourt, Brace & World, New York.

Bonefeld, W. (2002), 'Capital, Labour and Primitive Accumulation: On Class and Constitution', in A. C. Dinerstein and M. Neary (eds.) *The Labour Debate. An Investigation into the Theory and Reality of Capitalist Work*, Ashgate, Aldershot.

Debord, G. (1995), *The Society of the Spectacle*, Zone Books, New York.

Foucault, M. (1975), *Discipline and Punishment*, Penguin, London.

Holloway, J. (2002), *Change the World Without Taking Power. The Meaning of Revolution Today*, Pluto Press, London.

Horkheimer, M. and T. Adorno (1972), *Dialectic of Enlightenment*, Herder and Herder, New York.

Lukács, G. (1971), *History and Class Consciousness*, trans. R. Livingstone, MIT Press, Cambridge Mass.

Marcuse, H. (1968), *One Dimensional Man*, Sphere, London.

Marcuse, H. (2000), *Reason and Revolution*, Routledge, London.

Marx, K. (1965), *Capital*, Vol. I, Progress Publishers, Moscow.

Rooke, M. (2002), 'The Dialectic of Labour and Human Emancipation', in W. Bonefeld and S. Tischler (eds.), *What is to be Done? Leninism, Anti-Leninist Marxism and the Question of Revolution Today*, Ashgate, Aldershot.

[10] On this, see also Debord (2002) and Vaneigem (1994).

Thompson, E.P. (1991), *The Making of the English Working Class*, Penguin Books, London.
Thompson, E.P. (1971), 'The Moral Economy of the English Crowd in the Eighteenth Century', *Past & Present*, no. 50, pp. 76-136.
Vaneigem, R. (1994), *The Revolution of Everyday Life*, Rebel Press – Left Bank Books, London.
Weber, M. (1979), *Economy and Society*, trans. E. Firschoff et al, edited by G. Roth and C. Wittich, University of California Press, Berkeley.
Weber, M. (1991), 'Parlamento y gobierno en una Alemania reorganizada. Una crítica de la burocracia y de los partidos', in *Estudios Políticos*, Editorial Alianza, Madrid.
Wilding, A. (1995), 'The Complicity of Posthistory', in W. Bonefeld, R. Gunn, J. Holloway and K. Psychopedis (eds.) *Open Marxism. Emancipating Marx*, Vol. 3, Pluto Press, London, 1995.
Williams, R. (1997), *Marxism and Literature*, Oxford University Press, London and New York.

Translated from Spanish by Anna-Maeve Holloway

Part III
Human Dignity: Anti-Capitalism and Perverted Forms of Resistance

Chapter 8

Nationalism and Anti-Semitism in Anti-Globalization Perspective

Werner Bonefeld[1]

I

Global capital is choking itself on the pyramids of accumulated abstract wealth. Yet, when looking at social conditions, when listening to the ever more urgent demand for greater labour flexibility, it seems as if the global crisis is really just a consequence of a scarcity of capital. This is indeed the conclusion one would have to reach when one looks at Africa's misery, when one sees the thousands and thousands of children living in poverty, not just in Africa, not just in Latin America and Asia, not just in those areas of the world deemed inessential by global capital but also in the centres of globalization, in Europe and the USA. Yet, the dramatic increase in poverty and misery across the globe is not caused by conditions of economic scarcity. There is too much capital, too many commodities that can not be sold for profit, too many workers are 'overexploited', on the one hand, and, on the other, too many workers are not even exploitable. Over the last two decades, profits have risen and so too has unemployment. Labour productivity has increased dramatically and poverty has increased, wages have stagnated, and conditions deteriorated.

Against this background, Oskar Negt (2001) is surely right when he charges many left critics of globalization for their failure to offer any views on how socially necessary labour can be organized to liberate millions and millions of people, not only in the 'developing' societies but in the centres of wealth too, from conditions of misery and poverty. Critics urge the creation of new forms of political regulation at the national and international level to contain capital's 'neo-liberal' self-destructive force in favour of the common good. In opposition to global institutions

---

[1] I am grateful to Ana Dinerstein, John Holloway, Greg Schwarz, and Susanne Soederberg for their helpful comments and advice. The usual disclaimers apply. An earlier version was presented to the international conference *The Work of Karl Marx and the Challenges of the 21st Century*, Institute of Philosophy, Havana, May 2003, and appeared in Spanish as 'La antiglobalización significa autodeterminación', in *Herramienta*, no. 23, 2003, and in English as 'Anti-globalization versus Anti-Capitalism', in P. Chandra, A Gosh and R. Kumar (eds.) *The Politics of Imperialism and Counterstrategies*, Aakar Books, Delhi, 2004. The present chapter is a revised and expanded version of these earlier versions.

like the WTO, which are seen to affirm neo-liberal values and institutionalize an unfair system of trade, critics urge the renewal of democratic controls of capital to regulate trade more fairly and limit the power of global finance and global financial institutions that keep so-called developing countries in debt and force them further into debt. Others call for the de-linking of 'developing' countries from the world market to secure national economic development. Globalization is seen here as a form of American imperialism and global institutions, like the IMF, are seen as agencies of US imperial power. National self-determination is seen as a socialist opposition to imperialist globalization, and the struggle against 'neo-liberal' globalization through forms of 'progressive nationalism' (Radice, 2000) affirms the national state an effective instrument of national economic organization. Without doubt the national state is such an effective instrument (see, Holloway, 1996)! What, however, is anti-capitalistic in anti-capitalism when it seeks to regulate capital on a national basis without touching the relations of exploitation, when it poses the national state as the sovereign power that places controls on capital to secure the common national good? What is the common national good? The function and role of the state is to achieve homogeneity of national conditions. In its liberal conception, this means the equality of all before the law. In its Leninist conception, it means the equality of labour. In its nationalist version it means the equality of a homogenous people, a *Volk*. In its essence, the nationalist conception of equality in terms of *Volk* entails the projection of a classless 'national community' whose existence is threatened by the 'external enemy within'.

The anti-globalization movement of the political Left, at least in Europe, grew out of resistance against the new anti-immigration populist right led by, for example, Le Pen in France and Haider in Austria.[2] The populist right poses national identity and communality as a responds to the perceived threats of globalization. The common feeling of these nationalist backlash forces was well focused by Mahathir Mohamad, the former Prime Minister of Malaysia. His assessment of Malaysia's financial collapse in 1997 is symptomatic: 'I say openly, these people are racists. They are not happy to see us prosper. They say we grow too fast, they plan to make us poor. We are not making enemies with other people but others are making enemies with us'.[3] Leaving aside the discrimination of particularly Malaysian citizens of Chinese background, what is meant by 'we' and who are the 'racist they'? Mahathir Mohamad's denunciation of capitalism as 'Jewish capitalism' and his espousal of Malaysian economic development does indeed appear, as the *Financial Times* (October 23 2003) suggested, to have taken its cue from *The International Jew*, a book commissioned by Henry Ford in the 1920s. Similarly, Buchanan's (2002) Aryan dream of a white fortress America that he sees to be in crisis because of the nefarious effects of 'critical theory' for which holds 'those trouble making Communist Jews' responsible. The nationalist idea of a hard working one-national people and the denunciation of money and reason as uprooting powers finds in the projected figure of the Jew its perfect evocation. It

[2] On globalization and the neo-fascist right in Europe, see Grigat (2003) and Wallerstein (2003).

[3] Quoted in 'Malaysia Acts on Market Fall', *Financial Times*, September 4 1997.

conceals the social antagonism, distracts from relations of exploitation, displaces social discontent onto an abstract enemy figure, and through this ideological mystification, offers popular discontent with capitalism an outlet that is directly useful for capitalist reproduction.

In its structure, the conception of 'speculators' as the external enemy within bent on destroying relations of the national harmony of interests, belongs to modern anti-Semitism. It summons the idea of finance and speculators as merchants of greed and, counterposed to this, espouses the idea of a national community. In the nationalist conception of equality, the 'folk is "subject to blood", it arises from the "soil", it furnishes the homeland with indestructible force and permanence, it is united by characteristics of "race", the preservation of whose purity is the condition of the folk's "health"' (Marcuse, 1988, p.23). The attempt to neutralize discontent with conditions through the collective approval of resentment and the displacement of the antagonism between capital and labour onto an external enemy is intrinsically racist. The depiction of the 'external enemy within' as an abstract, evil power presupposes an equally abstract power, namely, the national state as the gatekeeper of the one-national 'homeland'. Nationalism offers a barbaric response to globalization.

The contemporary conditions of poverty, misery and hopelessness are not just an appearance of the contradictions of capitalist social reproduction on a global scale – that too.[4] They are also sharp reminders of a conception of progress that entailed barbarism from its inception.[5] Critics argue, rightly, that if unchecked, globalization will lead to barbarism. However, barbarism has already been. In relation to an earlier resolution to global crisis, Adorno's (1990) insight demands serious consideration: Auschwitz, he argued, not only confirmed the violence of the bourgeois relations of abstract equality and abstract identity. It also confirmed the bourgeois exchange relations of pure identity as death. It is, however, the case that the horror of Auschwitz persists as a potentially barbaric form of crisis-resolution for as long as those social relations exist that made Auschwitz possible (Adorno, 1969, p.85). Racism is truly terrible. However, 'it is the absolute normal result of the deep and growing inequality within the world system and cannot be addressed by moral exhortation' (Wallerstein, 2003, p.77). Its objective is not to 'exclude people, much less to exterminate them. The objective of racism is to keep people within the system, but as inferiors (*Untermenschen*) who can be exploited economically and used as political scapegoats' (ibid., p.78). However, anti-Semitism is pregnant with horrifying dangers, which contain racism's objective and go beyond them.

Racism and anti-Semitism are different-in-unity. All forms of racism project the Other as a disintegrating power, allegedly undermining the integration of the one-national boat. Racism projects the power of the Other as an inferior or 'sub-human'

[4] On this see, amongst others, Bales (2000), Bonefeld (2004), Chossudovsky (1997), Dalla Costa and Dalla Costa (1995), Kyle and Koslowski (2001), Negt (2001), Seabrock (2001), van den Anker (2004).

[5] On this, see the exchange between de Angelis, Bonefeld and Zaremka in *The Commoner* – 'Debate on Primitive Accumulation' (www.commoner.org.uk).

(*Untermenschen*) power. This power is in contrast to anti-Semitism, perceived as a rooted power. That is, the projected Other is seen to have national roots (Germans of Turkish background are 'guest workers' from Turkey) and should accept their position of inferiority as 'sub-humans' within 'nations' without question. Racism regulates the Other through institutional racism, forced return to 'their homelands', segregation, racial profiling, slander, arson, and murder, and projects the Other as a potential or real slave. Racism transposes feudal relations of social hierarchy, position and privilege on to bourgeois society modernizing, as it were, the relations between master and slave as relations of an 'organic' society where everybody knows their place in the social hierarchy, and where the racialized Other provides the excuse for a damaged life and as such a scapegoat, becomes the object of resentment. It thus sustains the abstract exchange relations of capital through the racist differentiation of the dependent masses, and that is, the institutional regulation of a racialized underclass.

Anti-Semitism, in contrast, projects the Other as rootless. For the anti-Semite, the Jew comes from no-where. Lyotard (1993, p.159; see also Zizek, 2002, pp.109-10) summarizes this projection well. 'The Jews are not a nation. They do not speak a language of their own. They have no roots in a *nature*...They claim to have their roots in a book'. The anti-Semite does not project the Jew as sub-human. Instead, theirs is the power of an immensely powerful, intangible, international conspiracy (cf. Postone, 1986). Their power cannot be defined concretely; it is an abstract, invisible power. 'Anti-Semitism is the rumour about Jews' (Adorno, 1951, p.141). The Jew is seen as the one who stands behind phenomena. Racism's acceptance of the Other as a real or potential slave contrasts with anti-Semitism's projection of the 'rootless and invisible' power of the Jew as evil personified. This Other can thus not be regulated, neither politically nor economically. It has to be, as the anti-Semites have it, destroyed, that is, exterminated.

Wallerstein's (2003, p.78) argument that Hitler's *Endlösung* missed the point of racism – 'one was to be racist just up the point of an *Endlösung*, but not further' – is partially correct. He does however not account for the anti-Semitic definition of the Other as an abstract invisible Other. This Other is not a potential or real slave – instead, this Other is seen as the enemy of the social interests of the one-national friends. This enemy is invisible and abstract and because of this, is feared as an immensely powerful force that can not be 'held down'. The enemy that anti-Semitism projects is an invisible enemy and the invisible cannot be enslaved. It has to be made visible through dehumanization and then treated as if it were really invisible – the projected foe of the relations of national harmony is forced to disappear, to vanish, into smoke. Wallerstein's argument implies this when he argues, correctly, that the 'concept of the citizen inevitably excludes every bit as much as it includes' (ibid., p.85). The concept hides the barbarism of its inception, which it carries within itself as violence civilized (Benjamin, 1965). The politicization of the relations between the included and the excluded brings the hidden violence to the fore, breaks the bounds of its civilized coercive form, and unmask the violence of its inception in its barbaric actualization. Further, the concept also pretends concreteness that reveals itself on closer inspection as abstractness: the equal citizen endowed with abstract rights whatever the inequality in the equality of property. It thus does not recognise concrete individuals but only abstract individuals. In short, it hides the class antagonism and focuses, instead, the social individual as an individualized, atomic market agent endowed with standardized rights – the rights of private property. It views this individualization that is characteristic of class society, as an absolute. Sustaining this absolute against antagonistic tensions posits racism as a means of displacing the class struggle, transforming its historical presupposition in barbarism into a potentially horrifying result of its reproduction.

The nerve-centre of barbarism is a fetish critique of the world market society of capital. It projects a class-divided society as a national community, subsuming, through arson and murder, class relations into the abstract identity of national sameness – the national 'we'. National wealth and autonomy is seen to be undermined by external forces, which are held responsible for the ill-effects of economic development. Thus 'national disharmony' is merely imported from the outside. The nationalist critique of global capital, then, favours the strong and capable state that restores the cohesion, integrity, and wealth creating potentials of 'its' national economy against external threats. Such an endeavour requires the identification and persecution of the 'external' enemy within. This machination is inherently racist and can easily tip over into anti-Semitism. Racism stands for a barbaric conception of 'equality'.

II

In the Preface to his *Philosophy of Right*, Hegel argued that those who render abstractions effective in social life are engaged in the destruction of social reality. Auschwitz stands for such an imposition of abstraction. There is of course a difference between the anti-Semitism that culminated in Auschwitz and the anti-Semitism of the post-1945 world. However, whether anti-Semitism persists because or despite of Auschwitz is, ultimately, an idle question. The notions 'despite' and 'because' presuppose that the power of anti-Semitic thought was somewhat put to rest at Auschwitz. It thus gives credence to Auschwitz as a factory of death that is assumed to have destroyed anti-Semitism. Furthermore, and connected, anti-Semitism is viewed as a phenomenon of the past, that merely casts its shadow on the present but has itself no real existence. In this way, overt expressions of anti-Semitism are deemed ugly merely as pathological aberrations of an otherwise civilized world.

Human values such as honesty, sincerity, tolerance, and dignity have no price and can not be quantified, neither sold nor bought. These values connote individual human distinctiveness, difference, sense and significance, that is, Man (*Mensch*) in possession of himself as a subject. Yet, we are used to think in terms of abstractions, such as capital, the market, the state, the nation, etc. These, following Sohn-Rhetel's (1970) terminology, are really existing abstractions (*Realabstraktionen*). The purpose of Marx's critique of fetishism was to demystify their ostensibly objective force and to show that their apparent independence is a objective (*gegenständliche*) delusion. The subject constitutes its own social world and vanishes in the form of its constituted inversion: capital.[6] He argued that their objective force has a real existence as forms of social relations, that is, as forms constituted by and reproduced through human social practice. Their objective delusion is fostered by the capitalist exchange relations themselves. They suggest that rationally acting subjects meet on the market to realize their rational interests, whereas in fact they act as executives of abstract social laws which they themselves have generated historically and reproduce through their rational behaviour and over which they have no control (cf. Reichelt, 2002, p.143). The critique of political economy is fundamentally a critique of fetishism where social relations appear as self-constituted and self-regulating relations between things, as abstractions.

Dignity has not price. It can however be destroyed when critical-practical judgement is suspended through the identification of really existing humans as mere personifications of abstractions or as derivatives of hypothazised social structures. There is only one human standard which, though unchangeable and indivisible, can be lost – through the imposition of abstract identity (cf. Adorno, 1990). Thinking in terms of abstractions is all pervasive. This is especially relevant in relation to Israel. The state of Israel is rightly condemned for its policy towards the Palestinians. The incarceration of human beings in camps and suicide bombers have become the expressions of a world that recognizes the Other as a mere enemy beyond humanness and thus as a foe upon whose liquidation the promised nationhood of a secure people is said to rest. The condemnation of the politics of the state of Israel all too easily takes anti-Semitic forms when really existing individuals are identified with the abstract form of their nationalized existence, that is, as mere embodiments of presupposed abstract properties. The derivation of the social individual from its disenchanted forms of existence, abstracts from antagonistic social relations and presupposes the individual as a mere agent of presumed ethnic or national characteristics.

The mounting scale and sheer extent of the anti-Semitic tidal wave especially in the Middle East has blurred any distinction between the critique of the state of Israel and concrete human beings in their social relations, that is, their class-divided mode of existence. The anti-imperialist left tends to dismiss rampant Islamist anti-Semitism as a mere epiphenomenon of justified anger at Israel and US imperialism. It condemns the denial of nationhood of the Palestinians and condemns the national existence of Israel as a bridgehead of US imperialist interests in the Middle East (see, for example, Amin, 2004; Gautney, 2003; Petras, 2004). Anti-imperialist resistance presupposes the concept of national liberation as a revolutionary task. Such liberation substitutes the socialist idea of general human emancipation with the idea of the liberation of the form of the state from the social individual. National liberation and the emancipation of the 'communist individual' (cf. Marcuse, 2000) belong to different worlds.

---

[6] On this, see also Helmut Reichelt's contribution to this volume.

The identification of a people in terms of assumed national characteristics or as personifications of abstract properties tends to rebound politically. 'If "differance" has become the hallmark of theoretical anti-reason, "the Other" has become the hallmark of practical anti-reason' (Rose, 1993, p.5). There should be no attempt to '"understand" Arab anti-Semitism...as a "natural" reaction to the sad plight of the Palestinians'. It has to be resisted 'unconditionally' (Zizek, 2002, p.129). Similarly, there should be no attempt to 'understand' the measures of the state of Israel 'as a "natural" reaction against the background of the Holocaust' (ibid.). Such 'understanding' accepts the barbarism of extermination as a legitimizing force of state action. There can be no such legitimation.

> The Israeli-Palestinian conflict is, in the most radical sense of the term, a *false* conflict, a lure, an ideological displacement of the 'true' antagonism. Yes, the Arab 'fundamentalists' are 'Islamo-fascists' – in a repetition of the paradigmatic Fascist gesture, they want 'capitalism without capitalism' (ibid., p.131).

Yes, the state of Israel legitimizes itself as the 'exception' to the liberal principle of a secularized state, 'advocating a state based on ethnic-religious identity – and this in a country with the highest percentage of atheists in the world' (ibid.). Equally, to 'understand' Islamic anti-Semitism as a 'justified' expression of anger against imperialism is to claim, by implication, that 'anti-Semitism articulates resistance to capitalism in a displaced mode' (ibid., p.130). Displaced forms of resistance do not resist capitalism. Instead, they amount to an 'ideological mystification' (ibid.). Marx defined ideology as the objective appearance of human social relations as relations between things and his critique of ideology intended to demystify the world of things on a human basis.[7] Displaced modes of resistance do not question the objective appearance of things – they merely pervert the critique of ideology into propaganda for a differently configured world of things.

Islamic fundamentalism can itself be seen as a reaction against the 'heavy artillery' of global capital to create a world after its own image. Against this, Islamic fundamentalism espouses the quest for authenticity, seeking to preserve through the purification of imagined ancestral conditions and traditions existing social structures. The fight against 'westoxication', as Khomeini called the ideas of liberalism, democracy and socialism, indicates that Islamist anti-Semitism is unlikely to be assuaged by an Israeli-Palestinian settlement. It is more likely to be inflamed. At base, it is the depiction of Israel as an imperialist bridgehead of 'Jewish' capitalist counterinsurgency that fuels the hatred of Israel as a 'Jewish' state. What one may ask is a Jewish state? The attribute does not refer to concrete human beings, be it Ariel Sharon or Karl Marx, Albert Einstein or Emma Goldman, Vladimir Ilich Lenin or Leon Trotsky. Instead it summons those same projected abstract, reason-defying, imagined 'qualities' upon which anti-Semitism rests – this deadly displacement from the focus on class antagonism to totalitarian conceptions of the national friend and national foe. Within this relationship, reason is suspended

[7] On this, see Bonefeld (2001) and the contributions by Helmut Reichelt and Hans-Georg Backhaus to this volume.

and instead of a critique of its irrational constitution, critical thought is led to the equally irrational belief that the enemy of my enemy is my friend. However justified the critique of Israeli nationalism, and however justified the critique of American neo-imperialism, there should be neither understanding nor sympathy with fundamentalist 'resistance'. The one does not justify the other; both are abhorrent and indifferent to human life.[8] Thus, and as Kosmas Psychopedis argues, the question of revolution is not whether one is in favour of This course of action or against That outrage, or *vice versa*, but to negate the social preconditions that constitute the possibility and actuality of This and That.

Similarly, the idea of 'subaltern nationalism' as 'progressive' (Hardt and Negri, 2000, p.105ff) has to be rejected. What they celebrate as the 'modernizing' effect of nationalist movements contrasts sharply with the unleashing of rival nationalisms, religions and ethnicities, all of which have gone to war to sustain and assert their kind of 'difference' (See Petras, 2003, p.15). Hardt and Negri do of course not subscribe to traditional conceptions of national liberation. They argue for the post-modern: 'the anti-modern thrust that defines fundamentalisms might be better understood...not as a *pre*modern but as a *post*modern project' (ibid., p.149). Their post-modern take on 'subaltern nationalisms' suggests that they are not class-ridden, but rather dominated communities that defend their identity and assert their purity of purpose in opposition to the disintegrating powers of Empire. For the national bourgeoisie of such countries, the easiest political option is of course to suppress internal revolt by blaming the continuation of imperialist forms of domination of their countries while masking their own complicity and class-interest in this domination (cf. Hoogvelt, 1997, p.49). Whether resistance to such suppression is indeed post-modern, is a matter of political conviction. It is a well known fact that in the world of philosophical convictions, unfavourable conditions need not to be changed. All that is required is to interpret them more favourably. In contrast to the politics of conviction, a critical theory of society has to distinguish between the critique of ideology and propaganda.

III

The Marxist left on the whole agrees with Marx's judgement that the coercive character of bourgeois society is concentrated in the form of the state, and that the purpose of this political form is to guarantee the reproduction of the capital-labour class antagonism. If one takes this view seriously one would have to investigate the relations of antagonism and their organized social interests. Instead, then, of imposing the abstraction Jew on Israeli society, one would have to analyse the class-structure of Israeli society and, rather than condemning those who resist rotten policies, one would have to recognize their 'critical-practical activity' in and against inhuman conditions. Thus solidarity with the *refusniks* is called for and the courage of their conviction has to be recognized. What then is a Jew? It is anti-

[8] On this, see also Kosmas Psychopedis in this volume.

Semitism that produces the Jew (cf. Satre, 1976) and it is this same rumour about the Jews that underlies the conception of the state of Israel as a state that is not form-determined by the social relations of production, but by this rumour itself: Jewishness. Israel's policy towards the Palestinians has nothing to do with 'Jewishness'. That the state of Israel understands itself as a Jewish state and its 'security' policy as a compensation for the Holocaust is neither here nor there. Every state legitimizes itself by summoning the past, injuring the dead by mythologizing their suffering for the purpose of state-power and violence over and against populations.[9] Perry Anderson (2001) is therefore right when he argues that the potential of violence against the Other is nationalism's trade mark. Bourgeois society, that is, the world market society of capital, does not find identity in itself. It finds it only negatively in the projected foe, be it the competitor on the world market, the racialized Other, or, as in the case of bourgeois anti-capitalist capitalism, in the abstract category 'Jew'.

Anderson's correct characterization of nationalism is however blinkered by his anti-imperialist stance. After Auschwitz, anti-Semitism hides behind Anti-Zionism. The rumour about Jews appears to have found national expression in the state of Israel. Juri Iwanow's anti-imperialist call for 'class struggle of the oppressed masses against their Jewish capitalist oppressors' offers interesting insights. He argued that

> modern Zionism is the ideology and the far-reaching organizational system and political practice of the rich Jewish bourgeoisie, in association with the monopolistic circles in the USA and other imperialist powers...The Zionist corporation is at the same time one of the most extended capital-associations, a self-proclaimed agency for the concerns of world Jewry, an international centre of conspiracy, and a well organized centre for the purpose of deception and propaganda. Its essential aim...is the safeguarding of capitalist profits and wealth, its power and parasitic prosperity (quoted in IFS, 2000, p.43).

And today's condemnations? The language is seemingly more cautious and moderate. Yet, the projections remain the same. 'Entrenched in business, government and media, American Zionism has since the sixties acquired a firm grip on the levers of public opinion and official policy towards Israel, that has weakened only on the rarest of occasions' (Anderson, 2001, p.15). The Jews, then, have not only conquered Palestine but they have also taken control of America, and as Petras (2004, p. 210) sees it, the current effort of 'US empire building' is shaped by 'Zionist empire builders'. For Anderson, Israel is a Jewish state, its nationalist triumphs are Jewish triumphs, and its economy is a Jewish economy – a rentier economy, that is, its wealth is not earned through productive labour.

Anderson's characterization belongs to the tradition of anti-imperialist thought that gave ideological backing to the national liberation movements of the last Century. Originally, as Immanuel Wallerstein (1995, p.156) argues, the orthodox Left was hostile to the concept of national liberation and 'quite suspicious of all talk about the rights of peoples, which they associated with middle-class nationalist

[9] On this, see also Sergio Tischler's contribution to this volume.

movements'. It was only at the Baku congress in 1920 that the emphasis on class struggle 'was quietly shelved in favour of the tactical priority of anti-imperialism, a theme around which the 3rd International hoped to build a political alliance between largely European Communist parties and at least those of the national liberation movement...that were more radical' (ibid.). After Baku, anti-imperialist struggles were 'given the label of "revolutionary" activity' (ibid., p.211). Since the Russian Revolution, then, the orthodox Left has not denounced nationalism per se, but argued instead that nationalism in all of its various manifestations is not necessarily an obstacles to building socialist consciousness, and that nationalism can be used to combat capitalist world domination. The seminal text that informed this conversion from class struggle for general human emancipation to anti-imperialist struggle for national liberation is Stalin's *Marxism and the National Question*, written in 1913. Defining a nation as a 'historically evolved, stable community of language, territory, economic life, and psychological make-up manifested in a community of culture', he declared with remarkable foresight of things to come in the name of national security, that 'it is sufficient for a single one of these characteristics to be absent and the nation ceases to be a nation' (Stalin, nd., p.8). Inclusion into the national berth depends, then, on exclusion to maintain national characteristics. It is through the politics of exclusion that the included are given both a sense of their 'national destiny' and a scapegoat that is held responsible for the ills of the nation. The Great Purges, as Leon Trotsky commented as early as 1937, espoused anti-Semitic demagogy to such an extent against the Marxists of internationalist persuasion that it almost amounted to a science (quoted in Poliakov, 1992, p.47). In the Soviet version of class struggle as anti-imperialist national liberation, anti-Semitism dressed up as anti-Zionism was rampant. The Jew appeared here in many disguises – liberal, freemason, Social-Democrat, Trotskyite, fascist or Zionist – but he embodies everything that is defined as capitalist, imperialist, Western and above all non-Russian (see ibid.).

In Marx's *Jewish Question* and the writings of the Frankfurt School, the category 'Jew' stands for a social metaphor. In contrast, however, to Anderson's affirmative categorization, it was a critical category that challenged 'categorization'. That is, the meaning and significance of the 'Jewish Question' was approached through the lens of the critique of the fetishism of bourgeois relations of production. Expanding on Marx's critical question, 'why does this content [human social relations] assume that form [the form of capital]' (cf. Marx, 1962, p.95), the Jewish question as a critical category asks why does the bourgeois critique of capitalism assume the form of anti-Semitism? In contrast, the affirmative use of the category 'Jew' rationalizes anti-Semitism as a manifestation of the hatred of capitalism, and through its rationalization, is complicit in the 'rumour about Jews'.[10] The critique of anti-Semitism amounts thus to a critique of those forms of

[10] See, for example, Ulrike Meinhof's view that 'Auschwitz meant that six million Jews were killed, and thrown on the waste-heap of Europe, for what they were: money Jews. Finance capital and the banks, the hard core of the system of imperialism and capitalism, had turned the hatred of men against money and exploitation, and against the Jews...Anti-Semitism is really a hatred of capitalism' (quoted in Watson, 1976, p.23).

anti-capitalism that do not oppose, but rather derive their rational from constituted capitalist forms (see Marx, 1964). The argument of this paper does not suggest that anti-Semitism is the only way in which the world market society of capital expresses itself negatively, nor does it suggest that the argument of those anti-globalization activists who espouse the national state and the development of national industrial capital, tap into the rhetoric of globalization as a Jewish conspiracy – far from it. This is a minority view among critics of globalization, a view both terrible and horrific in its consequences. What it does however suggest is that anti-globalization indifference to its own 'project' – 'another world is possible' – will find that this other world will be defined by socialism's alternative, that is, barbarism. This, then, means that the only way to fight barbarism is to express the anti-capitalist stance in direct way. This, however, also means that the only way to fight resurgent anti-Semitism 'is not to preach liberal tolerance...but to express the underlying anticapitalist motive in a direct, non-displaced way' (Zizek, 2002, p.130). Such tolerance gives in to the intolerable and thus disarms itself. Anti-Semitism is the objective ideology of barbarism (Enderwitz, 1991). It channels discontent with conditions into forms of an anti-capitalist capitalism where the dream of a better world dissolves into blind resentment against the projected Other as the 'external enemy within'.

The remainder of the essay focuses on that form of anti-Semitism that found its raison d'être in Auschwitz. Such an examination sheds light on the contemporary connection between globalization and nationalist forms of anti-globalization. It argues that anti-Semitism is directly related with 'modernity's' attempt at reconciling its constituting contradiction, that is, the class antagonism between capital and labour. Max Horkheimer's (1988, p.9) dictum that whoever wants to talk about fascism but not about capitalism should shut up, puts this contention into sharp focus and raises, against the background of the militarization of foreign and domestic policy, its contemporary significance.[11] The conclusion returns to the wider discussion on anti-globalization and offers some suggestions.

IV

In what follows I have freely borrowed from Horkheimer and Adorno (1989) and Postone (1986). In their *Dialectic of the Enlightenment*, Max Horkheimer and Theodor Adorno emphasize that Enlightenment's 'reason' obtains fundamentally as 'instrumental reason' or 'instrumental rationality'. The determination of 'reason' as reason being denied in the form of 'instrumental reason' entails that instrumental reason is reason's false friend and that, as such a friend, it negates reason's promise to destroy all relations where humanity exists as a mere factor of production, a

[11] Leaving aside its propagandist aspect, the following quotation from the early 1970s expresses the dangers of this militarization well: '[t]he fascism of today no longer entails the conquest of the Ministry of the Interior by groups of the extreme-right, but the conquest of France by the Ministry of the Interior' (*Gauche prolétarienne*, quoted in Brückner and Krovoza, 1972, p.7).

human resource. Horkheimer and Adorno build on discussion of anti-Semitism as a form of hatred that identifies Jews as the representatives of the sphere of capital circulation, especially in its most elementary form of M...M', and argue that anti-Semitism projects Jews as personifications of hated forms of capitalism, leading to the murderous demand that the liberation from capital amounts to the liberation from Jews. Moishe Postone deepens this insight arguing that anti-Semitism amounts to a fetish critique of capital and thus to a critique on the basis of capital. Anti-Semitism is a constituted form of the capital fetish: it amounts to a perverted, bourgeois form of anti-capitalism that is directly useful for capitalism.

Anti-Semitism does not 'need' Jews. The category 'Jew' has powers attributed to it, which can not be defined concretely. It is an abstraction that excludes nobody. Anyone can be considered a Jew. The concept 'Jew' knows no individuality, can not be a man or a woman, and can not be seen as a worker or beggar; the word 'Jew' relates to a non-person, an abstraction. 'The Jew is one whom other men consider a Jew' (Sartre, 1976, p.69). For anti-Semitism to rage, the existence of 'Jews' is neither incidental nor required. 'Anti-Semitism tends to occur only as part of an interchangeable program', the basis of which is the 'universal reduction of all specific energy to the one, same abstract form of labor, from the battlefield to the studio' (Horkheimer and Adorno, 1989, p.207). Thus, anti-Semitism belongs to a social world in which sense and significance are sacrificed in favour of compliance with the norms and rules of a political and economic reality that poses sameness, ritualized repetition, and object-less subjectivity as Man's only permitted mode of existence. Difference, and therewith the elevation of human dignity to a purpose of social existence, beyond the ritualized mentality of empty and idle thought stands rejected. The mere existence of difference, a difference that signals happiness beyond a life of rationalized production and its expansion into every area of social life fosters the blind resentment and anger that anti-Semitism focuses and exploits but does not itself produce (cf. ibid., pp.207-8).

Anti-Semitism differentiates between 'society' and 'national community'. 'Society' is identified as 'Jewish'; whereas community is modelled as a counter-world to society. Community is seen to be constituted by nature and 'nature' is seen to be at risk because of 'evil' abstract social forces. The attributes given by the anti-Semite to Jews include mobility, intangibility, rootlessness and conspiracy against the – mythical and mythologized – values of an 'ancestral', that is, original community. The presumed 'well-being' of this community is seen to be at the mercy of evil powers: intellectual thought, abstract rules and laws, and the disintegrating forces of communism and finance capital. Both, communism and finance capital are seen as uprooting powers and as entities of reason, and both are seen as the property of the 'rootless' intelligence of 'Jews', an intelligence based on reason and critical judgement. Reason stands rejected because of its infectious desire to leave behind relations of domination and exploitation. Reason is the weapon of critique. It challenges conditions where Man is degraded to a mere economic resource that stands to attention clicking his heels to do what ever is required. For the anti-Semite independence of thought and the ability to think freely without fear, is abhorrent. It detests the idea that '*Man is the highest being for Man*' [*Mensch*] (Marx, 1975, p.182). Instead, it seeks deliverance through the furious affirmation of its own madness. The anti-Semites' portrayal of the Jew as evil personified is in fact their own self-portrait. 'Madness is the substitute for the dream that humanity could organize its world humanely, a dream that a man-made world is stubbornly rejecting' (Adorno, 1986, p.124). Just as the economic idea of Man as a mere human factor of production, the nationalist idea of the nation connects with the idea of Man as a mere agent of its own degradation.

Anti-Semitism has always been based on an urge that its instigators held against the Social Democrats: the urge for equality. Social Democracy sees equality as emanating from the project of the Enlightenment. It urges equality to achieve a just and fair society. This demand focuses on the sphere of distribution where equality of opportunity is seen as a good that compensates for the absence of humanity at the point of production. Anti-Semitism urges a different sort of equality – an equality that derives from membership in a national community. This equality is defined by the mythical 'property' of land and soil based on the bond of blood. Blood and soil are configured as the mythical bond of a national community. The fetish of blood and soil is itself rooted in the capital fetish where the concrete in the form of use value obtains only in and through the abstract in the form of exchange value. Anti-Semitism construes blood, soil, and also machinery as concrete counter-principles of the abstract. The abstract is personified in the category Jew (cf. Postone, 1986). The anti-Semitic revolt, then, against the abstract amounts to a conformist rebellion in favour of the extension of capitalist factory discipline to society at large. For the apologists of market liberalism, the reference to the invisible hand operates like an explanatory refuge. It explains everything with reference to the Invisible. 'Starvation is God's way of punishing those who have too little faith in capitalism' (Rockefeller Sr., quoted in Marable, 1991, p.149). For the anti-Semites, however, the power of the invisible can be explained – the Jew is its personification and biologized existence. It transforms discontent with conditions into a conformist rebellion against the projected personification of capitalism.

The nationalist conception of equality defines 'society' as the Other – a parasite whose objective is deemed to oppress, undermine and pervert the 'natural community' through the 'disintegrating' force of the abstract and intangible values of – bourgeois – civilization. The category 'Jew' is seen to personify abstract thought and abstract equality, including its incarnation, money. The *Volksgenosse*, then, is seen as somebody who resists 'Jewish' abstract values and instead upholds some sort of natural equality. Their 'equality' as Jews obtains as a construct, to which all those belong who deviate from the conception of the *Volksgenosse*, that is, mythical concrete matter. The myth of the Jew is confronted with the myth of the original possession of soil, elevating nationalism's 'regressive egality' (Adorno, 1951, p.56) to a liberating action. The *Volkgenosse* sees himself as a son of nature and thus as a natural being. He sees his natural destiny in the liberation of the national community from allegedly rootless, abstract values, demanding their naturalization so that everything is returned to 'nature'. In short, the *Volksgenosse* portrays himself as rooted in blood and ancestral tradition to defend his own faith in the immorality of madness through the collective approval of anger. This anger is directed towards civilization's supposed victory over nature, a victory that is seen as condemning the *Volksgenosse* to sweat, toil and physical effort, whereas the Other is seen to live a life as banker and speculator. This the *Volksgenosse* aspires for himself with murder becoming the climax of his aspiration. The *Volksgenosse* speculates in death and banks the extracted gold teeth.

For the *Volksgenossen*, the Jews 'are the scapegoats not only for individual manoeuvres and machinations but in a broader sense, inasmuch as the economic injustice of the whole class is attributed to them' (Horkheimer and Adorno, 1989, p.174). Pogroms are not only conceived as a liberating action but, also, as a moral obligation: anti-Semitism calls for a 'just' revenge on the part of the 'victimized' national community against the powers of 'rootless' society. 'Community' is seen to be both victimized and 'strong'. Strength is derived from the biological conception of the national community: blood constituted possession and tradition. This biologization of community finds legitimation for murder in the biologization of the 'action': biology is conceived as a destiny. From this follows the demand to overturn and break society's hold on community in order for the latter to assume its authenticity and purity – better: to render it effective through the deed.

Reason that escorted the primitive accumulation of capital with the promise of human dignity appears transformed into the idle occupation of killing for the sake of killing. Kant's notion that reason was to lead mankind to maturity formulated reason's claim to think beyond itself in order to find deliverance in significance and meaning, in humanity. This is reason's revolutionary imperative. However, the established form of reason has a darker side. It subsists, as Marx argued, in the irrational form of relations between things. This is the form of rational irrationality that instrumental rationality focuses – a joyless rationality interested only in calculability be it in terms of an all-pervasive market rationality or production processes where any capture of additional atoms of labour time is the basis of success. Instrumental rationality does not know human values. Everything and everybody is just a tool, an utility, in the forward march of accumulation for accumulation's sake. For instrumental rationality, human values are a scandal for they inhibit the full utilization of technical efficacy and humanity is merely conceived as an irritating factor of production, a living resource that has to be integrated into the well-oiled systems of economic production and political machines. Reason's claim to lead the exodus to a better world and the resourceful rationality of instrumental reason are two halves of the same walnut: Revolution and its containment in the name of revolution itself. 'The thought of happiness without power is unbearable because it would then be true happiness' (ibid., p.172). Instrumental reason is reason denied. It allows merely technological revolutions and is interested only in the corrosion of character – Men with no qualities, humans of standardized and yet flexible issue, always prepared to be called upon to function as resourceful tools for profitable calculations, whatever the 'product'. All that instrumental rationality wishes for itself is how best to achieve the optimum result, how best to increase efficiency be it in terms of produced cars or gassed corpses. It is interested only in quantifiable results regardless of content. The efficient organization and the cold, dispassionate execution of the deed – 'the cruelty of silence in the house of the hangman' (cf. Adorno, 1986) – is mirrored by its disregard for individuality: corpses all look the same when counting the results and they are equal to each other; and nothing distinguishes a number from a number except the difference in quantity – the measure of success. The mere existence of happiness is a provocation. Judgement is suspended. Everybody is numbered and assessed for use. 'The morbid aspect of anti-Semitism is not projective behaviour as such, but the absence from it of reflection' (Horkheimer and Adorno, 1989, p.189).

Anti-Semitism's stigmatization of reason and money as evil not only mythologizes reason and money as forces that come, like their projected personification, the Jew, from no-where. It also produces the legend that those with a 'home', 'tradition', 'roots' and 'soil' are mere objects of evil, abstract forces of darkness. The insight that 'the constitution of the world occurs behind the backs of the individuals, yet it is their work' (Marcuse, 1988, p.151) is turned against itself: nationalists agree that the world makes itself manifest behind the backs of what they consider as the People. Yet, they deny that it is their work. Instead, it is a world of evil global forces conspiring to undermine relations of national harmony. The evil force is personified in the category 'Jew'. In the struggle between 'good' and 'evil' reconciliation appears neither possible nor desirable. Evil needs to be eradicated in order for the 'good' to be set free. The attack on 'reason' rests on the employment of reason's other self: instrumental rationality, confirming, rather than denying, the circumstance that Nazism was less an aberration in the forward march of instrumental reason than the transformation of the forward march itself into delusion. The attack on reason set 'loose all irrational powers – a movement that ends with the total functionalization of the mind' (ibid., p.23). Auschwitz, then, confirms the 'stubbornness' of the principle of 'abstraction' not only through extermination for extermination's sake but also, and because of it, through 'abstractification'. The biologization of the abstract as 'Jew' denied not only humanity, as the 'Jew' stands expelled from the biologized community of the concrete. The abstract is also *made* abstract: all that can be used is used like teeth, hair, skin; labour-power; and, finally, the abstract is made abstract and thus invisible. The invisible hand of the market, identified as the abstract-biological power of the 'Jew', is transformed into smoked-filled air.

V

National Socialism projected itself as an anti-capitalist movement. Yet, National Socialism also embraced industrial capital and new technology. Indeed, according to Götz Aly and Susanne Heym (1988), the preparation of the Final Solution in occupied Poland was based less on anti-Semitism as an ideology, but, in fact, followed the instrumental reasoning of Neo-Malthusian resource management. Their argument is that, for the Nazis, the economic viability of occupied Poland depended on the reduction of the population per capita in order to secure that capital exported to Poland could be applied efficiently.

What is the relationship between Nazism's anti-capitalist ideological projection and the rational calculation of economic resources that proposes mass murder as a 'solution' to capitalist profitability? Nazi anti-Semitism is different from the anti-Semitism of the old Christian world. This does not mean that it did not exploit

Christian anti-Semitism. Christian anti-Semitism constructed the 'Jew' as an abstract social power: The 'Jew' stands accused as the assassin of Jesus and is thus persecuted as the son of a murderer. In modern anti-Semitism, the Jew was chosen because of the 'religious horror the latter has always inspired' (Sartre, 1976, p.68). In the Christian world, the projected category of the 'Jew' was also a social-economic construct by virtue of being forced to fill the vital economic function of trafficking in money. Thus, the economic curse that this social role entailed, reinforced the religious curse.

Modern anti-Semitism uses and exploits these historical constructions and transforms them: The Jew stands accused and is persecuted for following unproductive activities. His image is that of an intellectual and banker. 'Bankers and intellectuals, money and mind, the exponents of circulation, form the impossible ideal of those who have been maimed by domination, an image used by domination to perpetuate itself' (Horkheimer and Adorno, 1989, p.172). The biologically defined possession of land and tradition is counterposed to the possession of universal, abstract phenomena. The terms '*abstract, rationalist, intellectual*...take a pejorative sense; it could not be otherwise, since the anti-Semite lays claim to a concrete and irrational possession of the values of the nation' (Sartre, 1976, p.109). The abstract values themselves are biologized, the abstract is identified as 'Jew'. Both, thus, the 'concrete' and the 'abstract' are biologized: one through the possession of land (the concrete as rooted in nature, blood and tradition) and the other through the possession of 'poison' (the abstract as the rootless power of intelligence and money). The myth of national unity is counterposed to the myth of the Jew. Jewry is seen to stand behind the urban world of crime, prostitution, and vulgar, materialist culture. Tradition is counterposed to reasoning, intelligence, and self-reflection; and the nationalist conception of community, economy and labour is counterposed to the abstract forces of international finance and communism (cf. Postone, 1986). The *Volksgenossen* are thus equal in blindness. 'Anti-Semitic behaviour is generated in situations where blinded men robbed of their subjectivity are set loose as subjects' (Horkheimer and Adorno, 1989, p.171). They were set loose as subjects of instrumental reason and are thus robbed of their subjectivity as social individuals to whom reason has and reveals meaning and significance. While reason subsists in and through the critique of social relations, the *Volksgenosse* has only faith in the efficiently unleashed terror of instrumental rationality. The collection of gold-teeth from those murdered, the collection of hair from those to be killed, and the overseeing of the slave labour of those allowed to walk on their knees for no more than another day, only requires effective organization.

Anti-Semitism articulates a senseless, barbaric rejection of capitalism that makes anti-capitalism useful for capitalism. 'The rulers are only safe as long as the people they rule turn their longed-for goals into hated forms of evil' (ibid., p.199). The Jews seem ready made for the projection of horror.

> No matter what the Jews as such may be like, their image, as that of the defeated people, has the features to which totalitarian domination must be completely hostile: happiness without power, wages without work, a home without frontiers, religion without myth.

> These characteristics are hated by the rulers because the ruled secretly long to possess them (ibid.).

Anti-Semitism invited the ruled to stabilize domination by urging them to dehumanize, maim and kill, suppressing the very possibility and idea of happiness through their participation in the rationally organized slaughter, robbing the projected – capitalist – Others of all possession, including their life. Fascism, then, 'is also totalitarian in that it seeks to make the rebellion of suppressed nature against domination directly useful to domination. This machinery needs the Jews' (ibid., p.185). This insight poses the issue of Nazism's anti-capitalist capitalism, that is, its espousal of capitalist enterprise and its tirades against 'Jewish capitalism'. The fetish critique of capitalism as 'Jewish capitalism' argues that capitalism is in fact nothing more than an unproductive money-making system – a rentier economy that lives off and in doing so, undermines the presumed national community of creative, industrious individuals, subordinating them to the rootless forces of global money (cf. Postone, 1986), or as Mahathir Mohamad had it, 'they are not happy to see us prosper'.

Marx's critique of fetishism supplied an uncompromising critique of this dualist conception by making clear that the two, use value and exchange value, industrial capital and money capital, do not exist independent from each other but are in fact each other's mode of existence. The critique of capital has to be a critique of economic categories, and that is, a critique of the fetishism of the value form, which entails the exploitation of labour and the form of money as its presupposition. Without such a critique, it is all too easy to succumb to the objective delusion that the commodity form presents. On the one hand, there is the separation of reality into concrete matter and abstract destructive force, leading to the fetish-like endorsement of the concrete, of creative enterprise and of industry supplying material products that satisfy wants. On the other hand, there is the abstract sphere occupied by money, specifically speculation and global finance capital. The celebration of the concrete goes hand-in-hand with the rejection of the mobility, universality and intangibility of finance capital that is charged with knowing neither national identity nor national 'responsibility'. This view endorses thus a dualist world view where the concrete activity of an industrious people is confronted by abstract systemic forces.[12] The Vampire-like figure of capital sucking labour in the quest for surplus value, portrayed by Marx in *Capital*, is thus displaced: the Vampire becomes money. Industrial enterprise, rather than being conceived in terms of an enterprise of exploitation, is projected as the 'national laboratory' of concrete, creative labour. It is projected as a national community where national labour is employed in the much praised one-national boat. The viability of this labour is seen to be threatened by money. Money is conceived as the root of all evil and the cause of all perversion. Enterprise and industry are fetishized as concrete community, as concrete nature. National industrial endeavour is thus portrayed as a 'victim' of the evil forces of abstract values, of money. In

[12] For a critique of such dualist conceptions, see Helmut Reichelt's contribution to this volume.

sum, modern anti-Semitism is the barbaric ideology of what Marx (1966, p.438) described in his analysis of the role of credit as the 'abolition of the capitalist mode of production within the capitalist mode of production itself'.[13] National Socialism focuses the resolution of this negative abolition on the national state as the 'harmonies' last refuge' (Marx, 1973, p.886) that restores, in the face of global economic turmoil, the alleged 'communal interests' of the *Volk* through terror.

For the anti-Semites, the world appears to be divided between finance capital and concrete nature. The concrete is conceived as immediate, direct, matter for use, and rooted in industry and productive activity. Money, on the other hand, is not only conceived as the root of all evil, it is also judged as rootless and of existing not only independently from industrial capital but, also, over and against the industrial endeavour of the nation: all enterprise is seen to be perverted in the name of money's continued destructive quest for self-expansion. In this way, money and financial capital are identified with capitalism while industry is perceived as constituting the concrete and creative enterprise of a national community. Between capitalism as monetary accumulation and national community as industrial enterprise, it is money that calls the shots. In this view, industry and enterprise are 'made' capitalist by money: money penetrates all expressions of industry and thus perverts and disintegrates community in the name of finance capital's abstract values. This destructive force puts claim on and so perverts: the individual as entrepreneur; the creative in terms of a paternalist direction of use-value production; the rooted in terms of *Volk*; the community in terms of a natural community. Instead of community's natural order of hierarchy and position, money's allegedly artificial and rootless force is judged to make the world go round by uprooting the natural order of the *Volksgenossen*. In this way, then, it is possible for the *Volksgenossen* not only to embrace capitalism but, also, to declare that the exploitation of labour creates freedom: *Arbeit macht frei*. 'They declared that work was not degrading, so as to control the others more rationally. They claimed to be creative workers, but in reality they were still the grasping overlords of former times' (Horkheimer and Adorno, 1989, p.173). By separating what fundamentally belongs together, that is 'industrial' exploitation and money, the differentiation between money on the one hand, and industry and enterprise, on the other, amounts to a fetish critique of capital that, by attacking the projected personification of capital, seeks its unfettered expansion through means of terror.

With the biologization of creative activity, the unfettered operation of the exploitation of labour in the name of mythologized concrete values is rendered attainable by the elimination of the cajoling and perverting forces of the abstract – the 'Jew' who stands condemned as the incarnation of capitalism. In this way, the ideology of blood and soil, on the one hand, and machinery and unfettered industrial expansion, on the other, are projected as images of a healthy nation that stands ready to purge itself from the perceived perversion of industry by the abstract, universal, rootless, mobile, intangible, international 'vampire' of 'Jewish capitalism'. The celebration of the *Volksgenosse* as the personification of the

[13] For an assessment of this negative abolition, see Bonefeld (1996).

concrete, of blood, soil, tradition and industry, allows the killing of Jews without fear. Yet, it manifests 'the stubbornness of the life to which one has to conform, and to resign oneself' (ibid., p.171): the idle occupation of killing is efficiently discharged. As *Volksgenossen* they have all committed the same deed and have thus become truly equal to each other: their occupation only confirmed what they already knew, namely that they had lost their individuality as subjects.

Everything is thus changed into pure nature. The abstract was not only personalized and biologized, it was also 'abstractified'. Auschwitz was a factory

> to destroy the personification of the abstract. Its organization was that of a fiendish industrial process, the aim of which was to 'liberate' the concrete from the abstract. The first step was to dehumanize, that is, to strip away the 'mask' of humanity, of qualitative specificity, and reveal the Jews for what 'they really are' – shadows, ciphers, numbered abstraction.

Then followed the process to

> eradicate that abstractness, to transform it into smoke, trying in the process to wrest away the last remnants of the concrete material 'use-values': clothes, gold, hair, soap (Postone, 1986, pp.313-14).

Conclusion

Adam Smith was certain in his own mind that capitalism creates the wealth of nations and noted that

> the proprietor of stock is properly a citizen of the world, and is not necessarily attached to any particular country. He would be apt to abandon the country in which he was exposed to a vexatious inquisition, in order to be assessed to a burdensome tax, and would remove his stock to some other country where he could either carry on his business, or enjoy his fortune more at his ease (Smith, 1981, pp.848-49).

David Ricardo concurred, adding that 'if a capital is not allowed to get the greatest net revenue that the use of machinery will afford here, it will be carried abroad' leading to 'serious discouragement to the demand for labour' (Ricardo, 1995, p.39). According to Hegel, the accumulation of wealth renders those who depend on the sale of their labour power for their social reproduction, insecure in deteriorating conditions. He concluded that despite the accumulation of wealth, bourgeois society will find it most difficult to keep the dependent masses pacified, and he saw the form of the state as the means of reconciling the social antagonism, containing the dependent masses. Ricardo formulated the necessity of capitalist social relations to produce 'redundant population'. Karl Marx developed this insight and showed that the idea of 'equal righs' is in principle a bourgeois right. 'The power which each individual exercises over the activity of others or over social wealth exists in him as the owner of *exchange value*, of *money*. The individual carries his social power, as well as his bond with society, in his pocket' (Marx, 1973, pp.156-57). Against the bourgeois form of formal equality, he argued that communism rests on the equality of individual human needs. Theodor Adorno and Max Horkheimer argued that anti-Semitism is a fetishistic, barbaric critique of capitalism that makes the hatred of capitalism functional for capitalism. Rosa Luxemburg argued that the fight against barbarism is a fight for socialism.

The history of capitalism shows that the so-called golden age of the capitalism of the 1950s was an exception, if indeed it was golden at all. It did not come about as a result of either cosmopolitan reason or commitments to redistributive justice. As Gambino (2003) has shown, Fascism and Nazism were not in their origins the losing versions of Fordism, but were forced to become such thanks to the class struggles of the 1930s in the United States. This struggle is the practical question of our time.

What is the contemporary meaning of this question? 'The renunciation of internationalism in the name of resurgent nationalism' is the biggest danger (Clarke, 2001, p.91). 'Anti-globalization' gives in to reactionary forces if its critique of globalization is a critique for the national state. The history of protectionism, national self-sufficiency and 'national money' has always been a world market history (Bonefeld, 2000). Nationalist conceptions of anti-capitalism invert the subject of emancipation into the object of the political sovereign, the national state. Their focus is the strong and capable state that depoliticizes social relations and that thereby monopolizes the political as the 'concentrated and organized force of society' (Marx, 1983, p.703). This, then, is the form of the state, whose purpose is the 'perpetuation of the labourer' – the 'sine qua non of the existence of capital' (ibid., p.536).

What is the opposite term to the unfettered global accumulation of capital? Is it really the national state that, with transformed regulative powers, forces capital to guarantee the common – national – good? Or is the opposite term the renewal of democratic control at the transnational or cosmopolitan level? Whatever, the idea of saving capitalism through institutional reform has to be exposed to reveal its meaning and that is, that money must manage and organize the exploitation of labour. This content is entailed in its form. The ethical appeal of the demand for liberal-democratic reform at the national and global level, resides in its critical comparison between the less than perfect reality of capitalist relations and the pleasant norms of abstract equality and formal freedom. Such critical comparison fails to see that these norms are adequate to their content, the bad reality of a capitalist mode of production. Marx's critique of 'the foolishness of socialists...who want depict socialism as the realization of the ideals of *bourgeois* society' (Marx, 1973, p.248) was unambiguous:

> What divides these gentlemen from the bourgeois apologist is, on the one side, their sensitivity to the contradictions included in the system; on the other, the utopian inability to grasp the necessary difference between the real and the ideal form of bourgeois society, which is the cause of their desire to undertake the superfluous business of realizing the ideal expression again, which is in fact only the inverted projection [*Lichtbild*] of this reality (Marx, 1973, pp. 248-49).

In short, the much desired benevolent regulation of capital presupposes inhuman conditions and these find a political expression in the form of the state which Marx summarised as: 'the concentration of bourgeois society'. In short, discontent with – neo-liberal – politicians amounts to, paraphrasing Marx, a critique of character-masks, deflecting from the social constitution of their existence and because of this, it affirms the state as if it were an 'independent being which possesses its own *intellectual, ethical and libertarian bases* (Marx, 1968, p.28). It thus amounts to a mere rebellion for a virtuous state – a state, that is, which secures the 'communal interests' of bourgeois society. Regardless of its historically changing forms (Agnoli, 1997, Clarke, 1992), the function of the capitalist state has always been to secure the 'communal interests' of a capitalistically organized form of social reproduction: capital accumulation.

The critique of globalization fails if it is merely a critique of speculative capital and that is, a critique for productive accumulation. It was the crisis of productive accumulation that sustained the divorce of monetary accumulation from productive accumulation (Bonefeld and Holloway, 1996). Further, globalization is not responsible for the ever more precarious conditions of work, poverty, and debt, and the ever more destructive force of speculation. Rather, and as Cohen (1997, p.15) has argued, it is the restructuring of work that makes globalization possible and gives globalization a bad name. This then means that 'anti-globalization' has to be a critique of the capitalistically constituted relations of production. The critique of, for example, the WTO is not enough. Trade, whether deemed fair or unfair, presupposes capitalist relations of exploitation. Without a critique of capitalist social relations, the critique of speculation conceals the relations of exploitation and is complicit, whether intentionally or not, in the denunciation of finance as parasitic.

The theoretical and practical orientation on the utopia of the society of the free and equal is the only realistic departure from the inhumanity that the world market society of capital posits (cf. Agnoli, 2000). In short, those who seriously want freedom and equality as social individuals but do not wish to destabilize capitalism and instead wish to regulate 'abstractions', be it capital or the market, through the state contradict themselves. The attempt to regulate abstractions affirms their constituted existence and thus renders them effective. The struggle for socialism is a struggle against abstractions – and 'abstractifications' – and that is, a struggle for the equality of individual human needs. It is, then, 'precisely necessary to avoid ever again to counterpose "society" as an abstraction, to the individual' (Marx, 1959, p.93).

Anti-capitalism has, thus, to mean the complete democratization of all social forces, making them accountable to individual human needs in and through the democratic organization of socially necessary labour time by the freely associated producers themselves. The democratization of human social relations opens the right perspective for the struggle for a world where the free development of each is the condition for the free development of all, where the social individual realizes itself as the subject of its own social world. '*Every* emancipation is a *restoration* of the human world and of human relationships to *man* [*Menschen*] *himself*' (Marx, 1964, p.370).

The democratic organization of economic relations of necessity and the reduction of labour time belong together as each other's presupposition. How much labour time was needed in 2005 to produce the same amount of commodities that was produced in 1995? Twenty per cent? Forty per cent or fifty per cent? Whatever the percentage might be, what is certain is that labour time has not decreased. It has increased. What is certain too is that the distribution of wealth is as unequal as never before. And how does bourgeois society cope with the expansion of 'redundant populations', on the one hand, and, on the other, the overaccumulation of capital? The contradiction between the forces and relations of production does seeks resolution: destruction of productive forces, scrapping of labour through war and generalized poverty and misery, the racist demand for national equality, and all this against the background of an unprecedented accumulation of wealth and ever more destructive attempts to valorise atoms of time through greater labour flexibility, regardless of the deterioration in the conditions of human life and the destruction of the environment.

The reduction of working time is the central means of human emancipation. It is the social basis of human social self-determination. The realism of anti-globalization conceptions of cosmopolitan democratic renewals lacks social contents and is, in fact, much more removed from social reality than the concept of humanity that embraces Kant's categorical imperative: act in such a way that you recognize humanity in your person and in all other persons always as a purpose, never as a means. Democracy, if taken seriously, entails this conception of humanity in action. Such democratic recognition stands in sharp contrast to a conception of time that holds that time is money. Time as the measure of wealth and time as human social self-determination belong to different worlds.

In conclusion, anti-capitalism has to demand the democratic organization of socially necessary labour time by the associated producers themselves. This, then, is the splendid category of full employment in and through the emancipation of labour that Marx conceived as the democratic organization of necessity through the realm of freedom. Democracy means human self-determination, that is, human sovereignty and thus human dignity. Anti-capitalist indifference to the project of human emancipation does not pose an alternative to capitalism. It succumbs to abstractions, deprives itself of the weapon of reason, espouses ideological mystifications, displaces resistance against capitalism onto potentially shameful modes of resistance, and thus leaves the door open to socialism's alternative, that is, barbarism.

The demand for national liberation from global capital is regressive – it posits the unfreedom of the individual as the freedom of the national state to hold the global down. Rather then human dignity, the aim is thus to dignify the state as the abstract universal of a territorialized people. The state, then, is not only endorsed an instrument of anti-globalization but, also, as a means of neutralizing all forms of non-displaced anti-capitalism. Nationalist modes of political regulation are the form of appearance of the terror that the world market society of capital entails. In short, nationalist displacements of anti-capitalist struggles replicate what they denounce. They replicate 'the democratic state of emergency' (cf. Zizek, 2002, p. 154) that, under the guise of the war on terror, divides the world into 'them' and 'us' and in doing so, sets out to neutralize anti-capitalist struggles for the democratic organization of socially necessary labour time by the associated producers themselves. In short, 'the continued existence of National Socialism *within* democracy [is] potentially more threatening than the continued existence of fascist tendencies *against* democracy' (Adorno, 1986, p.115).

The twentieth century was a lousy century. It was filled with dogmas that one after another have cost us time and suffering. It would, however, be wrong to see it in this one-sided way. It was also, as Löwy (2003) reminds us, a century of hope in the alternative entelechy of solidarity and human emancipation – from Mexico (1914) to Petrograde (1917) and Kronstadt (1921), from Berlin (1918), Budapest (1919) and Barcelona (1936) to Berlin (1953) and Budapest (1956), from Paris (1968), Gdansk (1980) Chiapas (1994) to the Argentinean *piqueteros* (2001).[14] These, and many more, have been the intense moments of the struggle for human social autonomy, constituting points of departure towards the society of the free and equal. In conclusion, the struggle for human social autonomy is a struggle for the democratic self-organization of society by the associated producers themselves.

References

Adorno, T. (1951), *Minima Moralia. Reflexionen aus dem beschädigten Leben*, Suhrkamp, Frankfurt.

Adorno, T. (1969), *Stichworte. Kritische Modelle 2*, Suhrkamp, Frankfurt.

Adorno, T. (1986), 'What does Coming to Terms with the Past Mean?', in G. Harman (ed.) *Bitburg in Moral and Political Perspective*, Indiana University Press, Bloomington.

Adorno, T. (1990), *Negative Dialectics*, trans. E. B. Ashton, Routledge, London.

Agnoli, J. (1997), *Faschismus ohne Revision*, Ça ira, Freiburg.

Agnoli, J. (2000), 'The Market, the State and the End of History', in W. Bonefeld and K. Psychopedis (eds.) *The Politics of Change. Globalization, Ideology and Critque*, Palgrave, London.

Aly, G. and S. Heym (1988), 'The Economics of the Final Solution', *Simon Wiesenthal Centre Annual*, no. 5, pp.3-48.

Amin, S. (2004), 'The US Imperialism and the Middle East', in P. Chandra et al (eds.).

Anderson, P. (2001), 'Scurrying Towards Bethlehem', *New Left Review*, 2nd series, no. 10, pp.5-30.

Bales, K. (2000), *Disposable People: New Slavery in the Global Economy*, University of California Press, San Francisco.

Benjamin, W. (1965) *Zur Kritik der Gewalt und andere Aufsätze*, Suhrkamp, Frankfurt.

Bonefeld, W. (1996), 'Money, Equality and Exploitation', in W. Bonefeld and J. Holloway (eds.).

Bonefeld, W. (2000), 'The Spectre of Globalization. On the Form and Content of the World Market', in W. Bonefeld and K. Psychopedis (eds), *The Politics of Change. Globalization, Ideology and Critique*, Palgrave, London.

Bonefeld, W. (2001), 'Social Form, Critique and Human Dignity, *Zeitschrift für kritische Theorie*, no. 13, pp. 97-113.

Bonefeld, W. (2004), Against War and the Preconditions of War, *Disclosure*, no. 13, pp.107-19.

---

[14] For a conceptualization of the means and ends of human emancipation, see the collection of essays published in Bonefeld and Tischler (2002).

Bonefeld, W. and J. Holloway (eds.) (1996), *Global Capital, National State and the Politics of Money*, Palgrave, London.

Bonefeld, W. and S. Tischler (eds.) (2002), *What is to be Done? Leninism, Anti-Leninist Marxism and the Question of Revolution Today*, Ashgate, Aldershot.

Brückner, P. and A. Krovoza (1972), *Staatsfeinde: Innerstaatliche Feinderklärung in der BRD*, Rotbuch, Berlin.

Buchanan, P. (2002), *The Death of the West*, Dunne, New York.

Chandra, P., A. Ghosh and R. Kumar (eds.) (2004) *The Politics of Imperialism and Counterstrategies*, Aakar Books, Dehli.

Clarke, S. (1992), 'The Global Accumulation of Capital and the Periodisation of the Capitalist State Form', in W. Bonefeld, R. Gunn and K. Psychopedis (eds.) *Open Marxism. Dialectics and History*, Vol. I, Pluto Press, London.

Clarke, S. (2001), 'Class Struggle and the Global Overaccumulation of Capital', in R. Albritton, M. Itoh, R. Westra and Z. Zuege (eds.) *Phases of Capitalist Development. Booms, Crises and Globalization*, Palgrave, London.

Cohen, D. (1997), *Fehldiagnose Globalisierung*, Campus, Frankfurt.

Chossudovsky, M. (1997), *The Globalization of Poverty*, Zed Books, London.

Dalla Costa, M. and G. Dalla Costa (eds.) *Paying the Price*, Zed Books, London.

Enderwitz, U. (1991), *Anti-Semitismus und Volksstaat. Zur Pathologie kapitalistischer Krisenbewältigung*, Ça ira, Freiburg.

Gambino, F. (2003), 'A Critique of the Fordism of the Regulation School', in W. Bonefeld (ed.) *Revolutionary Writing*, Autonomedia, New York.

Gautney, H. (2003), 'The Globalization of Violence in the 21st Century: Israel, Palestine, and the War on Terror', in S. Aronowitz and H. Gautney (eds.) *Implicating Empire*, Basic Books, New York.

Grigat, S. (ed.) (2003), *Transformation des Postnazismus*, Ça ira, Freiburg.

Hardt, M. and A. Negri (2000), *Empire*, Harvard University Press, Cambridge, Mass.

Holloway, J. (1996), 'Global Capital and the National State' in W. Bonefeld and J. Holloway (eds.).

Hoogvelt, A. (1997), *Globalization and the Post-Colonial World*, Palgrave, London.

Horkheimer, M. (1988), 'Die Juden in Europa', in *Schriften 1936-1941*, Vol. 4, Fischer, Frankfurt.

Horkheimer, M. and T. Adorno (1989), *Dialectic of Enlightenment*, Verso, London.

IFS (2000), Initiative Sozialistisches Forum, *Furchtbare Antisemiten, ehrbare Antizionisten*, Ça ira, Freiburg.

Kyle, D. and R. Koslowski (eds.) (2001), *Global Human Smuggling*, The John Hopkins University Press, Baltimore.

Löwy, M. (2003), 'Dialectica de civilizacion: barbarie y modernidad en el siglo XX', *Herramienta*, no. 22, pp. 141-50.

Lyotard, J.F. (1993), *Political Writings*, trans. B. Readings with K. P. Geiman, University College London Press, London.

Marable, M. (1991), *Race Reform and Rebellion*, 2nd ed., University Press of Missisippi, Jackson.

Marcuse, H. (1988), *Negations. Essays in Critical Theory*, trans. J. J. Shapiro, Free Association Press, London.

Marcuse, J. (2000), *Reason and Revolution*, Routledge, London.

Marx, K. (1959), *Economic and Philosophical Manuscripts of 1844*, Lawrence & Wishart, London.

Marx, K. (1962), *Das Kapital*, vol. 1, MEW, Vol. 23, Dietz, Berlin.

Marx, K. (1964), *Zur Judenfrage*, MEW, Vol. 1, Dietz, Berlin.

Marx, K. (1968), *Kritik des Gothaer Programms*, MEW, Vol. 19, Dietz, Berlin.

Marx, K. (1966), *Capital*, vol. III, Lawrence & Wishart, London.
Marx, K. (1973), *Grundrisse*, Penguin, London.
Marx, K. (1975), 'Contribution to the Critique of Hegel's Philosophy of Law. Introduction', in *Collected Works*, Vol. 3, Lawrence & Wishart, London.
Negt, O. (2001), *Arbeit und menschliche Würde*, Steidl, Göttingen.
Petras, J. (2003), *The New Development Politics*, Ashgate, Aldershot.
Petras, J. (2004), 'Empire Building and Rule: U.S. and Latin America', in P. Chandra, et al. (eds.).
Poliakov, L. (1992), *Vom Antizionismus zum Anti-Semitismus*, Ça ira, Freiburg.
Postone, M. (1986), 'Anti-Semitism and National Socialism', in A. Rabinbach and J. Zipes (eds.) *Germans and Jews since the Holocaust. The Changing Situation in West Germany*, Holmes & Meier, New York.
Radice, H. (2000), 'Responses to Globalization: A Critique of Progressive Nationalism', *New Political Economy*, vol. 5, no. 1, pp.5-19.
Reichelt, H. (2002), 'Die Marxsche Kritik ökonomischen Kategorien. Überlegungen zum Problem der Geltung in der dialektischen Darstellungsmethode im "Kapital"', in I. Fetscher and A. Schmidt (eds.) *Emanzipation als Versöhnung. Zu Adornos Kritik der "Warentausch"-Gesellschaft und Perspektiven der Transformation*, Verlag Neue Kritik, Frankfurt.
Ricardo, D. (1995), *On the Principles of Political Economy and Taxation*, Cambridge UP, Cambridge.
Rose, G. (1993), *Judaism & Modernity*, Blackwell, Oxford.
Sartre, J-P. (1976), *Anti-Semite and Jew*, trans. G. J. Becker, Schocken Books, New York.
Seabrook, J. (2001), *Children of Other Worlds: Exploitation in the Global Market*, Pluto Press, London.
Sohn-Rhethel, A. (1970), *Geistige und körperliche Arbeit*, Suhrkamp, Frankfurt.
Smith, A. (1981), *The Wealth of Nations*, Vol. II, Liberty Fund, Indianapolis.
Stalin, J. (nd), *Marxism and the National and Colonial Question*, International Publishers, New York.
Van den Anker C. (ed.) (2004), *The Political Economy of Slavery*, Palgrave, London.
Wallerstein, I. (1995), *After Liberalism*, The New Press, New York.
Wallerstein, I. (2003), *The Decline of American Power*, The New Press, New York.
Watson, G. (1976), 'Race and the Socialists', *Encounter*, November, pp.15-23.
Zizek, S. (2002), *Welcome to the Desert of the Real*, Verso, London.

Chapter 9

Stop Making Capitalism

John Holloway

I

In Mary Shelley's famous story, Dr. Frankenstein creates a Creature, and the Creature then acquires an independent existence, a durable existence in which he no longer depends on the creative activity of Dr. Frankenstein. In another story, a story by Jorge Luis Borges, 'Las Ruinas Circulares', a man creates another man, but he does it not in a laboratory but by dreaming. The man created has all the appearance of being a normal man with an independent, durable existence, but in fact he is kept alive only by the constant creative activity, the dreaming, of the first man. His existence is not an illusion, but his duration is: his existence depends, from one moment to another, on the creative activity of the dreamer.

The story of Frankenstein is often taken as a metaphor for capitalism. We have created a society which is beyond our control and which threatens to destroy us: the only way we can survive is by destroying that society. But perhaps we should think rather in terms of the story by Borges: we have created a society which appears to be totally beyond our control, but which in reality depends upon our act of constant re-creation. The problem is not to destroy that society, but to stop creating it. Capitalism exists today not because we created it two hundred years ago or a hundred years ago, but because we created it today. If we do not create it tomorrow, it will not exist.

Each day we create a world of horrors, of misery and violence and injustice. We take an active part in constructing the domination that oppresses us, the obscenity that horrifies us. We create surplus value, we respect money, we accept and impose unreasoned authority, we live by the clock, we close our eyes to the starving. We make capitalism. And now we must stop making it.

What does it mean to think of revolution not as destroying capitalism, but as ceasing to create capitalism?

Changing the question does not solve the problem of revolution, it does not mean that now we know how to do it, but perhaps it can lead us to a re-thinking of the categories of revolutionary thought. Perhaps it opens a different grammar, a different logic of revolutionary thought, a different way of thinking about revolutionary politics. Perhaps it opens a new hope. That is what I want to explore.

II

The idea that revolution means destroying capitalism rests on a concept of duration, that is, on the idea that capitalism now is and will continue to be until we destroy it. The problem is that, by assuming the duration of capitalism, revolutionaries undermine the basis of their own call for revolution.

Any system of domination depends on duration, on the assumption that, just because something exists in one moment, it will continue to exist in the next. The master assumes that because he ruled yesterday, he will continue to rule tomorrow. The slave dreams of a different tomorrow, but often locates it beyond death, in heaven. She assumes in that case that there is nothing she can *do* to change the situation. The power of doing is subordinated to that which is.

This subordination of doing to being is a subordination of subject to object. Duration, then, is a characteristic of a society in which subject is subordinated to object, a society in which active subjectivity is assumed to be incapable of changing objective reality. Objective reality, or society-as-it-is stands over against us: subject is separated from, and subordinated to, object. And verbs (the active form of speaking) are separated from and subordinated to nouns (which deny movement).

Under capitalism the separation of subject and object, and therefore duration, acquires a peculiar rigidity. This is rooted in the material separation of subject and object in the process of production. The commodity which we produce stands over against us as something external, as an object which denies all relation with the work of the subject who produced it. It acquires an existence apparently completely separate from the work that constituted it. This separation between subject and object, doing and done, verb and noun is fundamental to the way that we subjects relate to each other under capitalism, so fundamental that it comes to permeate every aspect of social existence. In every aspect of our lives there is a separation of subject from object, doing from being, a subordination of subject to object, doing to being. Duration rules. This is expressed clearly in clock time, in which one minute is exactly the same as the next and the next and the next, and the only revolution conceivable is the one that goes round and round.

To think of changing society, we must recover the centrality of human doing, we must rescue the buried subject. In other words, we must criticize – understanding by criticism, genetic criticism, criticism *ad hominem*, the attempt to understand phenomena in terms of the doing that produces them. Marx's labour theory of value is such a criticism: at its core, the labour theory of value says 'The commodity denies our doing, but we made it'. With that, the subject (our doing) is restored to the centre of the picture. The object claims to be independent of the subject, but in fact it depends on the subject. Being depends on doing. This is what opens up the possibility that we can change the world.

All criticism (understood in this sense) is an attack on duration. Once subjectivity is restored to the centre of society, duration is broken. It can no longer be assumed that one minute is the same as the next. It can no longer be assumed that tomorrow will be like today, because we may make it different. Criticism opens up a world of astonishment. When Marx says at the beginning of *Capital* that the commodity stands outside us, alien to us, but its secret is that we made it (labour theory of value), then our reaction is one both of horror and of hope. We are astonished that we should spend our lives making objects that deny our existence, that are alien to us and dominate us, but at the same time we see hope, because those objects depend totally upon us for their existence: our doing is at the centre of everything, our doing is the hidden sun around which everything revolves.

The object, which dominates the subject, depends on the subject which creates it. Capital, which dominates us, depends on our work which creates it. The master who dominates the slave depends on the slave. There is a relation of domination and dependence, in which the movement of domination is a constant flight from the dependence, a constant struggle by the master to escape from his dependence upon the slave – an impossible struggle, of course, because, if he succeeded, he would cease to be master. But in this relation of domination and dependence it is not so much the moment of domination (the traditional arena of left discourse) as the moment of dependence that interests us, because that is where hope is to be found.

All social phenomena, then, exist because they have been made by people: money or the state are just as much human products as the motor-car. But more than that: all social phenomena exist only because they have been made and are constantly being re-made. A car exists as a car only because we constantly re-create it by using it as a car; a state exists as a state only because we constantly re-create it by accepting its authority and its forms. Money exists only because we constantly reproduce it in our relations with others. If we stopped reproducing money in our social relations, the paper and the coins would continue to exist, but it would no longer be money. These phenomena are not like Frankenstein's Creature but like the creature produced by Borges's dreamer. They depend for their existence upon us, from one minute to the next.

The existence of capitalism is no illusion. What is an illusion is the separation of its existence from its constitution, in other words its duration.

Duration, of course, is not just imaginary: it is generated in the real social separation of subject and object in the process of work, so that it is only through a complete transformation of the social organization of work (doing) that duration can be destroyed. But the attack on duration is central to the attack on the capitalist organization of work.

To attack duration is to demystify it, to show it to be an illusion. To demystify is to pierce the unreality of an enchanted world and to show that the world really revolves around human doing. However, it feels like just the opposite. We have always lived in the 'enchanted, perverted, topsy-turvy world' of capitalism, the world of objects, of duration, of clock-time. Consequently, the world into which criticism introduces us feels like a dream-world, a Wonderland world, a world of impossible intensity, a world in which everything is infinitely fragile because it depends on its constant re-creation.

In this wonderland-world, in this communist-moving, nouns are dissolved into verbs, into doings. Nouns fetishize the product of doing, they tear the results of doing away from that doing and enshrine them in a durable existence which denies that they are dependent on being constantly re-created. Marx criticized value to show that its core was human activity, work, but his critical method of recuperating the centrality of human doing can be extended to all nouns (but, in the duration-world in which we live, with its duration-talking, it is difficult to write without using nouns – so that critical thought really requires creating a new talking, what Vaneigem calls the poetry of revolution.)

Communism, then, is not the culmination of history, but the breaking of the continuum of history (Benjamin), the dissolution of the continuity of nouns into the absolute fragility of human doing. A self-determining society is a society in which it is explicit that only that exists which in that moment is being done, a world of verbs. The notion of the culmination of history implies a positive movement, a movement of accumulation of struggle, a movement of extension. Breaking the continuum of history implies a negative movement, not an accumulation of struggles but the generation of new intensities incompatible with the dead identifications of capitalism. Perhaps we should think of totality, that concept which criticizes the fragmented nature of bourgeois thought, not as a movement of extension but more as a movement towards the totalizing of social existence into the intensity of each particular moment: the pursuit of an absolutely intense *Jetzt-Zeit*, or *Nunc Stans* (Now-Time) in which time stops and capitalism explodes, or perhaps implodes. Communism would be a self-determining society, that is, a society without duration, without nouns: a terrifying, exhilarating thought.

III

What we want is a moment of terrible social intensity that shatters the continuum of history, a moment so intense that clock time is broken for ever. Such moments occur: revolutions are like that. Everything stops, social relations are turned upside down as people go out on the streets and everything is concentrated in the act of saying NO.

But we cannot wait for the Great Revolutionary Moment. We cannot go on producing capitalism, we must break the continuum of history now. Individually and collectively, we must turn to capital and say 'Go on, now go, walk out the door, just turn around now, cos you're not welcome any more. We will survive'. Go away, capital! *¡Que se vayan todos!* All the politicians and all the capitalists. You're not welcome any more. We will survive.

To say goodbye to capital is to break a relationship, to start afresh, to create a *tabula rasa*, to make the world anew. Breaking the continuum of history is like breaking the continuum of an oppressive relationship in daily life. While we are in the relationship, it seems impossible, inconceivable that we should ever break out of it, but it is not. Capital is beating us, killing thousands of us each day, but *¡ya basta!* Those who want to build a party and take state power would take us to marriage counsellors and the divorce courts before breaking the relationship. But no, we cannot wait. There is no intermediate step. Bye-bye, *ciao*, as simple as that.

Is it really so simple? No. Of course not. But perhaps it is not as impossible as we usually think.

Capital exists because we make it. It depends absolutely on us. This is all-important: if there is no work, there is no capital. We create capital, and it is only by assuming our own responsibility that we can understand our strength. Only if we understand that we make capital with all its horrors can we understand that we have the power to stop making it. State-oriented (and hegemony-centred, and discourse-centred) approaches lose sight of this crucial axis of dependence: they turn our eyes away from the Achilles' Heel of capitalism, its crucial point of vulnerability.

If capital depends upon us, then *refusal* is the key to our strength. If capital exists because we make it, then we must refuse to make it.

A sustained global mass strike would destroy capital completely, but the conditions do not exist for that at the moment. It is hard to see how everybody in the world could be persuaded to refuse to work for capital at the same time.

For the moment at least, the only way of thinking of revolution is in terms of a number of rents, tears, holes, fissures that go spreading through the social fabric. There are already millions of such holes, spaces in which people, individually or collectively, say 'NO, here capital does not rule, here we shall not structure our lives according to the dictates of capital'. These holes are refusals, disobediences, insubordinations. In some cases (the EZLN in Chiapas, the MST in Brazil, the uprising in Bolivia, the *piqueteros* and *asambleas barriales* in Argentina, and so on), these insubordinations, these holes in the fabric of capital are already very big. The only way in which we can think of revolution is in terms of the extension and multiplication of these disobediences, of these fissures in capitalist command. There are those who argue that these disobediences, these fissures in world capitalism, acquire real significance only when they are institutionalized in the form of disobedient or revolutionary states, and that the whole movement of disobedience must be channelled towards that end. But there is no reason why disobediences should be institutionalized in state form and very many reasons why they should not.

These refusals are refusals of indignity, affirmations of dignity. Indignity is being commanded by others, being told what to do, as though one did not have the maturity to decide for oneself, in conjunction with others. Dignity then is the refusal of indignity, the refusal of alien command, the affirmation of oneself as part of the drive to social self-determination. There are two moments here: refusal and affirmation, No and Yes, a Yes present in the No. Stop making capitalism and do something else instead.

Refusal itself is not difficult. Most of us find it easy not to go to work under the command of others. Refusal is the crucial pivot in any attempt to change the world. But it is not enough, for two reasons. Firstly, refusal to work in present society confronts us immediately with the problem of starvation. If we do not sell our labour power, how do we obtain the means necessary to survive? In the richer countries, it is often possible to survive on state benefits, and this is what many of those in revolt against work do. But state benefits are very limited and in any case do not exist in most countries. Refusal to work under capitalist command is difficult to maintain unless it is accompanied by the development of some sort of alternative doing.

Secondly, and just as important as the need to avoid starvation, is dignity, the drive towards the social self-determination of our doing. This is the drive to do something that we judge to be necessary, desirable or enjoyable. This is the struggle of doing against work, of the content against its capitalist form. Even in modern capitalism, where the subordination of doing to capital in the form of work is a very real subordination (or subsumption), there is always a residuum of dignity, of the insubordination of content to form. To be human is to struggle for the insubordination of doing to work, for the emancipation of doing from work. The worst architect always struggles against being converted into the best bee. That is the meaning of dignity.

The struggle of doing against work, that is, the struggle for the emancipation of doing, is an everyday practice. It is common for people to work (or do) in-and-against capital, trying to do well what they do in spite of the capitalist form of organization, fighting for use value against value. Obviously there are also many jobs in which it is very difficult to see any space for a revolt of doing against work. In such cases, perhaps the struggle of-and-for dignity can be understood only as a struggle of total negation (sabotage and other forms of refusal of work).

But there are clearly many examples which go beyond that, of people occupying factories or schools or clinics and trying to organize them on a different basis, creating community bakeries or workshops or gardens, establishing radio stations of resistance, and so on. All these projects and revolts are limited, inadequate and contradictory (as they must be in a capitalist context), but it is difficult to see how we can create an emancipated doing other than in this interstitial form, through a process of weaving the different forms of the struggle of doing against work, knitting together the different doings in-and-against-and-beyond capital.

The emancipation of doing means the self-determination of doing. This implies some sort of council organization, some form in which people come together to determine what to do and how to do it. The council (or soviet) tradition has a long history in the communist movement and recurs in different forms in all rebellions. Its central point is the insistence in the collective self-determination of doing. This means the rejection of leadership from outside, the acceptance that people here and now, with all their problems and weaknesses and neuroses, with all the habit inculcated by centuries of domination, should determine their own activity.

In these many experiments (whether or not they are imposed by the necessity to survive), the central theme is not survival but the emancipation of doing, the creation of a doing shaped not by profit but that which the doers consider desirable.

Any revolution that is not centred in the emancipation of doing is condemned to failure (because it is not a revolution). The emancipation of doing leads us into a different time, a different grammar, a different intensity of life. The emancipation of doing is the movement of anti-fetishization, the recovery of creativity. Only in this way can the fissures become poles of attraction instead of ghettos, and only if they are poles of attraction can they expand and multiply. The revolutions in Russia and Cuba were initially poles of attraction for many who dreamed of another type of life: the fact that there was no real emancipation of doing in these societies meant that they gradually ceased to exert that attraction (although support and solidarity continue in the case of Cuba). And the same is true of many alternative projects today: if the only result of these projects is that the participants are poor, isolated and bored, then the projects will not be poles of attraction. If rebellions are not attractive, they will not spread. In other words, ceasing to make capitalism has to be thought of as a realistic project, but if the realism is not a magic realism, it ceases to be realistic.

The struggle of doing against work is a struggle to create a different human richness: a richness shaped by social desires and not by capitalist appropriation, a richness that is not appropriated by capital. Now people produce an enormous richness each day, but nearly all of it is appropriated by capital, so that the only way in which we can have access to that richness is by bending low, bowing to the command of capital. It is easy to refuse to work for capital, but how can we survive without subordinating ourselves to capital?

Any attempt to gain access to the richness of human doing comes up against the value form 'property'. But property is not a thing but a verb, a daily repeated process of appropriating the product of our doing. The process of appropriating (which is constantly being extended to new areas of doing) is supported by violence, but it depends greatly on the fetishization of the process, on the transformation of the verb 'to appropriate' into the noun 'property'. The resistance to the process of appropriation is part of the same process of constructing another doing, a doing which defetishizes at the same time as it creates another sociality.

IV

Stop making capitalism: refuse. But this involves a second moment: do something else instead. This something else is a prefiguration, the embryo of a society yet to be born. To what extent can this embryo grow in the womb of existing society? There are many problems, unavoidable problems, and there is no model solution to apply. But one thing is clear: that we must stop making capitalism now, that we must stop creating the misery, oppression and violence that surround us. *¡Ya basta! ¡Que se vayan todos!* The slogans of recent years make it clear that very many people have had enough of capitalism.

Of course, there are many problems. After we say 'go on, now go, walk out the door', there are still many forces that suck us back into the relationship. Yet the axis of our thought must be not continuity but discontinuity, break, rupture. We must stop making capitalism now. The problem of theorists is that perhaps we spend our time untying (or even tying) Gordian knots when what we need is to start from the energy of Argentina in December of 2001, of Bolivia in October of 2003, of Mexico in 1994. Not domination, rupture is the centre of our thought.

Rupture does not mean that capitalism vanishes. The fissures do not mean that capitalism disappears. But rather than think of revolution as an event that will happen in the future (who knows when) and be relatively quick, it seems better to think of it as a process that is already under way and may take some time, precisely because revolution cannot be separated from the creating of an alternative world.

We see where we want to go. It shimmers in the morning mists like an island on the other side of the sea. But we cannot get there by putting stepping stones and jumping from one step to another to another, building the party, winning control of the state, implementing social reform. That will not work, because the island we see shimmering in the mists is not in the sea but in the sky, and the only way to get there is to fly. It seems impossible until we realize that we are flying already.

Index